THE WONDER BOOK

OF

PLANT LIFE

BY

J. HENRI FABRE

TRANSLATED BY
BERNARD MIALL

Vivisphere edition 2001

ISBN 1-58776-003-7
ISBN-13: 978-1-58776-003-7
Library of Congress Catalogue Number 2001093661

Printed in the United States of America

Vivisphere Publishing
is a division of
NetPub Corporation,
675 Dutchess Turnpike
Poughkeepsie, New York 12603

VIVISPHERE
PUBLISHING

THE WONDER BOOK

OF

PLANT LIFE

CONTENTS

PART I

PART II

ILLUSTRATIONS

FIGURES IN TEXT

vii

FULL-PAGE PLATES

PART I

CHAPTER I

CORAL AND THE TREE

*The Hydra—Its structure—Its multiplication by budding—Coral—Polyps,
simple and compound—Multiplication of polyps—Longevity of polyp
communities—Variety of structure—Coral Islands—Geographical im-·
portance of Corals—The Corals of past geological periods—The
fundamental organization of the Vegetable.*

THE plant is the sister of the animal : like the animal,
it lives, feeds and reproduces itself. If we wish to
understand the plant we shall often find it a very good
plan to consult the animal ; and again, if we wish to
understand the animal organism, we shall often ascertain
what we wish to know by inquiring into the nature of
the plant. I shall therefore begin by telling you something
of certain peculiar animal organisms whose manner of
living will enable us to understand the fundamental
structure of the plant, and will give us the most valuable
insight into vegetable life.

Amidst those tiny, circular green leaves, commonly
known as duckweed, which float, in close contact, on the
surface of stagnant waters, forming a brightly-coloured
carpet, we shall find, in our dykes and ponds, a curious
little creature known to the naturalists as the Hydra.
This fragile organism, which consists of a sort of green
jelly, measures at most some three-quarters of an inch in
length. Picture to yourself a small elongated sac, one
end of which adheres to some aquatic plant, while the
other end puts forth eight flexible arms, or tentacles,
which have the power of moving in all directions : there

3

you have the Hydra.   The eight arms, or tentacles rather, are arranged in a circle round an orifice communicating with the inside of the sac :   that is, with the cavity in

which the digestion of food takes place.   This orifice has two functions, which, in an animal of a more ordinary kind, would seem to be absolutely incompatible : it swallows the prey seized by the tentacles and rejects the undigested residue.   In order to obtain its food the Hydra outspreads its arms in the water and remains motionless.   If some animalcule happens to pass that way the arm nearest to it immediately seizes upon it, and carries it to the Hydra's mouth.

FIG. 1.—The Hydra.

Let us place a well-grown specimen of Hydra in a glass of water containing duckweed.   After the lapse of several weeks, or it may be months, according to the time of year, we shall see two, three, four or more tiny warts growing on the lower part of the creature's trunk.   These warts increase in size, and are finally crowned with eight tiny nipples, which protrude more and more every day ; finally opening as a bud opens to form a flower.— Can you guess the true character of these curious animal flowers ? They are young Hydras, with their digestive sac and their eight arms : young Hydras, growing upon the mother, just as twigs grow upon a bough.   We call the little warts from which they are born buds, because they produce animals resembling the parent organism, just as the boughs of a tree give birth to shoots or twigs.

The Hydra—which is in reality an animal, since it has the power of moving from place to place, of travelling whither it chooses, and is sensitive to pain, hunting, seizing and devouring its prey—the Hydra in one respect behaves like a vegetable : it buds, giving birth to tiny Hydras just as the stem of a plant sends forth branches.

But these little Hydras, still quite young, incapable of trapping their own food, and earning their own livelihood, are forced for some time to rely on the maternal organism for nourishment. Accordingly, then, the digestive sac of the parent Hydra communicates with the cavities of the young Hydras ; the stomachs of the nurslings open into the stomach of the parent. It is the parent Hydra alone that lies in wait for her prey, and eats and digests it ; but the liquid nutriment, ready for absorption, finds its way from the mother's digestive sac into the stomachs of her nurslings, through narrow connecting passages, so that the young Hydras are often full-fed although they have eaten nothing. But at last a day comes when the narrow communicating passage leading from stomach to stomach closes up ; a constriction appears at the point of junction of the parent and offspring, and the young Hydras, like so many ripe fruits, break away in order to live an independent life elsewhere, and in their

FIG. 2.—Coral.

turn to produce, by budding, yet another generation.

Now glance at the above illustration. Would you not take it for some species of shrub covered with flowers ?

As a matter of fact it is not a plant at all ; it is a piece
of coral. You must be familiar with the pretty red beads
which are often made up into necklaces. You have been
told that this is coral. So indeed it is ; but before it was
made into beads by a skilled workman, the coral was
shaped like a small bush or shrub, of a brilliant red, with
twigs, branches and boughs. But the little shrub contains no woody substance ; it is of stone, as hard as
marble, although this does not prevent it from covering
itself, under water, with beautiful little flowers. Now,

these so-called flowers, that grow
on the stony branches of the
coral, are really animals, the
coral being their common home,
their dwelling-place and support.
They are known as polyps.
Their organization is similar to
that of the Hydra.

Each polyp is a hollow globule
of gelatinous matter, a little sac
whose mouth is bordered by

FIG. 3 —Coral Polyp.

eight leaf-shaped appendages, fringed at the edges ; eight
tentacles, opening like the petals of a flower. Apart from
the shape, which is rather different, you will recognize in
the Coral " Insect " the general structure of the Hydra.
It is still a digestive sac fixed at the base and crowned by
eight arms, especially adapted to seize and hold the
polyp's prey. As we find it beneath the surface of the
sea, the coral is covered with an unsubstantial husk
or shell, riddled by a host of cellular cavities, in each
of which a polyp is lodged. Beneath this living rind
is the stony support, whose colour is a brilliant red.

Although each polyp has its own cell and is endowed
with a separate existence, the polyps of the same branch
of coral are no strangers to one another. Thanks to the

inter-communication of their digestive sacs, all profit by
what one of them digests. With their fringed arms outspread like the points of a rosette, the polyps, like the
Hydra, grasp at such nutritive particles as the ocean
currents may bring to them. Chance does not favour
them all in an equal degree ; one may make an abundant
catch, while another does not once draw in the net of
its tentacles. Yet, at the end of the day, all have been
equally well fed ; those polyps whose stomachs have
been busily digesting their catch have provided the rest
with their allotted ration.

How has it been established, this rigid and reciprocal
communism of the stomach—a communism which the
human mind, even in its wildest aberrations, would assuredly never have conceived ? How is it organized, this
strange refectory, in which the individual who has a full
larder feeds his neighbour who has no food ? This is
how it is done : Every twig of coral is begun by a single
polyp, which, hatched from an egg, and at first wandering
through the waters, finally anchors itself to some rock
beneath the surface, there to found a colony. This
polyp, once it has settled down, buds, as the Hydra
buds, or a plant. It buds, and a new polyp grows from
the side of the first. The communication between the
digestive cavity of the second polyp and that of
the original " insect " is at first indispensable, so that the
food seized and digested by the latter may nourish the
young polyp, as yet incapable of supplying its own needs.
This communication is effected precisely as in the Hydra,
with the difference that it is not intended, eventually,
to be interrupted. The coral polyps, having reached
maturity, do not take their departure, to establish themselves elsewhere ; they continue to live as members of
a family, mutually and indissolubly united. And now
the first polyp, which developed from a bud, is followed

by a second, a third, a fourth, etc. The first generation
of offspring gives birth, in turn, to a second generation,
and this to a third ; and so on, no definite limit being set
to their powers of reproduction ; and thus successive
generations are piled upon one another by dint of repeated
buddings, whose numbers are day by day increased.
As for the common domicile, the coral, it results from the
exudations of all its inhabitants, for these exude stone
as the snail excretes the materials of its shell. Each
new-born polyp provides its share of calcareous matter,
and the stony structure increases, branching in all directions. Such is the process of formation observed in
coral and a host of analogous submarine structures,
known as polyparies or polypidoms : that is, the stony
growths inhabited by polyps. According to this definition
coral is itself a polypary.

It follows from its mode of formation that no definite
term can be set to the life of a polypary ; that it ought
not to perish save by accident. The polyps themselves
doubtless die when old, as all animals die ; but before
they die they leave in the polypary numbers of offspring,
which, in turn, leave even greater numbers ; and as this
multiplication goes on continually there is no reason why
the polypary should cease to be. Far from perishing,
unless some accident does occur, the polypary, constantly restored, and incessantly increased, by successive
generations, ought to live, still full of vigour, to any age
you please. The Bee and the polyp die ; the swarm
and the polypary remain ; the individual perishes, but
the society of which it forms a unit endures. In the
Red Sea there are polyparies of such dimensions that if
we estimate their age by their rate of growth, we must
conclude that their antiquity is prodigious. They are
still in the prime of life, although they cannot be less
than three or four thousand years old ; they date from

the time when the Pyramids were building, and were contemporaries of the Pharaohs. Time has no meaning for these agglomerations of polyps ; the individual dies, but the community endures, through the centuries, always young, always at work.

There are many species of polyp, and the structures which they build display a great variety of forms. As a general thing the polyparies—that is, the corals and madrepores—are of a pure white, the natural colour of the carbonate of lime of which they consist ; more rarely they are red, like the coral used for personal adornment, or they may display still other colours. Nothing could be more graceful than the shape of these structures. Some are like little trees of stone, that put forth branches as graceful as those of an actual tree ; some display parallel tubes, grouped together, like organ-pipes, or clusters of cells like those of a honey-comb. At other times the polypary may develop a round head, like that of a cauliflower, or a mushroom, whose surface, bristling with plates arranged in mathematical formation, displays a multitude of stars, or a network of geometrical accuracy, or a labyrinthine pattern of furrows and ridges ; or yet again, it may be outspread in a wide, stony leaf, as thin as a sheet of paper and perforated as profusely as a piece of lace. On all these structures are thousands of blossoming animalculi, that is, polyps, with their tentacles outspread like exquisitely fragile rosettes, which, at the slightest alarm, are suddenly retracted.

These frail workers enjoy every advantage that might enable them to build up structures which prove their ability and energy to be far superior to our own. For them, duration, numbers and materials possess no limits. In the warm seas of the tropics, on every favourable spot, wherever their colonies are to be found, dwelling side by side, they heap storey upon storey, polypary upon

FIG. 4.—Various forms of Polypary.

polypary, until the surface of the sea sets a term to the scaffolding needful in their building operations. However, their structures, being checked in their upward development, are continued in the horizontal plane ; the crest of the polypary becomes a reef ; the reef, attaining the surface of the sea, becomes a small island, and the ocean surrounds yet one more tract of dry land.

A coral island is thus the upper surface of an agglomeration of polyparies, whose foundations are rooted in some submarine shoal. At first it is merely a barren surface, but sooner or later the ocean currents and the winds bear thither seeds, or plants, so that its dazzling white area is eventually shaded by vegetation. As a rule a few insects or lizards, arriving on drifting tree-trunks, are its first inhabitants ; then the sea-birds build their nests there, while birds of inland species that have lost their way come thither to seek rest and shelter. Lastly, when the soil has become fertile, man appears and builds his palm-leaf hut.

Coral islands rise but a short distance above the level of the sea. As a general rule they consist of a belt of dry land, circular or elliptical, enclosing a shallow lagoon which communicates with the sea. Their appearance is as remarkable for its strangeness as for its beauty. Imagine a girdle of land covered with coco-nut palms, whose sombre green foliage stands out boldly against the limpid blue of the sky. Surrounded by this tree-covered girdle is a salt-water lake, in which the polyps are still building, accompanied by various species of shell-fish ; while outside the girdle is a wide beach of the purest white, consisting entirely of broken coral, and surrounded by a circular belt of reefs, on which the ocean, always turbulent, breaks in a flurry of whirling foam. In their savage onslaught the waves threaten at every moment to engulf the island, but the island, low, fragile, and exposed though it be, is enabled to resist by the polyps, that bear their part in the conflict, day and night, always at work, repairing the damaged structure, surrounded, particle by particle, by a rampart of reefs, constantly demolished and as constantly rebuilt. With their soft, gelatinous bodies these fragile creatures hold their own against the raging ocean ; with their patient architecture they overcome the terrible power of the waves which granite barriers would have been powerless to subdue.

Now take a glance at the chart of the world, if you wish to obtain some idea of the extent of dry land which is due to the work of the polyp ; and above all, reflect upon that multitude of archipelagos, consisting of shoals and small islands, which stretch across the Pacific Ocean from America to Asia. Well ! many of these archipelagos are of madreporic origin ; and those whose origin is other than this are at least surrounded by a barrier reef of coral. The Maldive Archipelago alone, situated in the Indian Ocean, comprises no less than 12,000 reefs, rocks or islands of madreporic structure. One coral reef off the eastern coast of New Holland covers an area of 33,000 square miles. A fifth of the whole world— Oceania—is thus for the most part the work of polyps. Even though the whole human race were to devote itself to this stupendous task for a hundred thousand years it would never succeed in completing the work performed by the gelatinous animalcule of the polypary. The part played by these builders of worlds was no smaller in those bygone geological periods whence our continents eventually emerged. Certain geological strata, certain ranges of mountains, consist of long-dead polyparies ; in certain parts of France one treads all day upon ancient beds of coral ; while many of our cities are built of a stone whose smallest fragment contains broken relics of madreporic origin.

This preliminary history of the Hydra and the Coral Polyp leads us directly to our proper subject : to the plant, in respect of which I was anxious first of all to explain to you something of its fundamental organization. This organization, which will presently explain a host of facts which would otherwise be inexplicable, may be summed up as follows : A plant or vegetable may be compared with a polypary covered with its polyps ; it is not a simple but a collective being, an association of individuals, all related, all closely united, rendering one another mutual service, and working for the prosperity of the whole ; like the coral, it is a sort of living hive, all of whose inmates live a <u>life in common</u>.

CHAPTER II

THE INDIVIDUAL LIFE OF THE VEGETABLE

Buds—The Individual—The Tree is a collective being—Proofs derived from the Vine and the Weeping Willow—The bud is the individual or unit of the vegetable world—Data derived from the size of trees and from grafting—Dupont de Nemour's definition.

LET us take a twig of Lilac, or of any other shrub; in the angle between each leaf and the supporting twig, an angle known as the *axil of the leaf,* you will see a small rounded body covered with brown scales. This is a bud, or sprout, or as the gardeners sometimes call it, an eye. It is destined to become a second twig, growing out of the first, just as those other buds, a wart-like growth occurring on the body of the Hydra or the polyp, become other Hydras, other polyps, growing out of the original organism. Well!—this bud, and therefore the shoot which would have resulted from it, is, to the tree, as a whole, what a polyp is to a mass of coral considered as a whole. It is a member of the family, an inhabitant of a community, an individual unit of a vegetable society. But as long as it is a bud it is a new-born citizen, or rather one in process of formation, fragile as yet and incapable of work. It will play no part in the general activity of the tree until the next spring, when it will become a twig. Until then it is merely a nursling, fed at the expense of the community ; it has nothing to do but to grow stronger and larger, like the child in its swaddling-bands and the fledgling in its nest.

14

The whole work of the tree falls to the lot of the leaf-bearing twigs or shoots : to the leaf-bearing twigs of the current year. These twigs are the foster-parents of the community ; through the medium of the roots they draw refreshment from the soil ; with the help of the leaves they draw it from the air ; and by mingling, associating and combining the raw material obtained from these two sources, they prepare that sticky liquid, the sap, of which everything in the vegetable world is made. By the

FIG. 5.—Twig with Buds.

following year these new shoots, which are to-day so industrious, will, so to speak, be pensioned off, and will enter upon a period of rest ; and to-day's buds, which will then have developed into shoots, will be busily performing the common task, until other buds come to replace them in turn. The tree, accordingly, consists of a series of annual generations, following one another in due succession. They may be numbered by keeping track of the various ramifications of the tree, from the centre of the trunk to the latest shoot. The present generation is represented by the leaf-bearing shoots. It is in this generation that the activity of the plant resides. The buds represent the generation which will make its appearance in the immediate future. It is for their sake especially that the tree is now in travail. Lastly, the trunk, the branches and their sub-divisions, down to the leaf-bearing shoots, represent the various generations of the past. These bygone generations are no longer active ; sometimes even they are dead. They constitute, so to speak, the vegetable polypary ; that is, they serve as a support for future generations.

We have a superabundance of data which prove that a vegetable is not a simple, but a collective being, an association of individuals, living in common, and that the comparison of a tree with a polypary covered with its polyps, far from being a mere form of words, is really a precise expression of the truth. I shall now try to explain to you how this comes about.

According to its etymology the word individual denotes that which cannot be divided. There is, of course, no question here of the simple and forcible division of matter such as science or physics understands it, which consists of dividing a whole into smaller or larger portions, without regard to that delicate problem, the maintenance of life, since from this point of view all things are indefinitely divisible. By individual we mean any creature that forms a living unity, and cannot be divided without losing its life. A dog, a cat, a bullock, or other familiar domestic animal, is an individual, an indivisible entity which will perish if divided. Who would be so foolish as to operate on his cat with a hatchet, in order to divide it into two equal parts, in the hope that the two portions would continue to live, and would form two separate animals, each thereafter living its own life ? Such an action would be insane, and contrary from all that we have learned from everyday experience and the innate convictions that have their roots in our very consciousness of our own existence. The individual is indivisible ; the indivisible is individual.

But we can without misgiving turn our axe against a tree without fear of imperilling its life ; more, we may be persuaded that by such a procedure we can multiply the tree to any extent we may desire. To divide the animal is, in the vast majority of cases, to destroy it ; to divide the vegetable is to multiply it.

The vine-grower, if he wishes to plant his vines on the hillside but newly brought into cultivation, will cut, from a vine, with his billhook, as many branches as he wishes to obtain vines. With one end planted in the ground, these cuttings take root, and in a few years' time become so many vine-stocks, bearing grapes and giving off vigorous shoots that in their turn will serve to plant other vineyards. Considerable tracts of land, whole districts indeed, may thus be covered with vineyards whose vines are cuttings directly or indirectly derived from a single original vine-stock. For all we know, a few vine-stocks, a few cuttings, imported into Gaul twenty-four centuries ago by the Phocæans who founded Marseilles, may have given us a great part of our present vineyards, thanks to a series of amputations, the work of the pruning-knife in times long past, as a result of which every vine-stock gave rise to fresh plants. Where, in this case, is the individual and where the indivisible ? It is certainly not the vine, which may be divided indefinitely, living again in each of the runners detached from it and planted. To say that a single vine constitutes an individual is to admit that all the thousands upon thousands of vines that may have been derived, and may still be derived, by the division of a single stock, their common point of departure, must, considered as a whole, be regarded as one sole, individual vegetable.

As the vine can also be propagated from seed, many of our vineyards were created, recently or remotely, by sowing the seed of the grape. Each seed gives birth to a new vine ; but this does not in any way invalidate the fact that vines are more frequently multiplied by the amputations of runners, nor does it affect our deductions as regards the individual vegetable. I will take yet another example. All over Europe gardeners have cultivated the graceful tree which we know as the Weeping Willow, because of its long, pliant branches, which droop disconsolately like the unbound tresses of a woman overwhelmed with grief. The scientists call it the

3

Willow of Babylon, because it was native to the banks of the Euphrates, whence it was imported at the time of the Crusades. This willow is absolutely incapable of producing seed in our climate. It is too early, as yet, to attempt a precise explanation of this inability, for as yet you have not learned how the seeds of plants are formed. At present I will confine myself to telling you that one weeping willow cannot produce fertile seed, capable of germination; the co-operation of two trees, alike in all things, excepting for their flowers, is absolutely essential. Well! —of these two willows, one of which completes the other in the matter of producing seed, we have only one. Of the weeping willows which to-day may be found in profusion in every part of Europe, not one has been raised from the seed; all have been derived, generation after generation, by cuttings, from the tree that some noble Crusader brought home from Babylon and planted beside the moat of his manor-house. Would it not be absurd to regard all the innumerable weeping willows in Europe as one individual vegetable, merely because they are cuttings from the first tree brought hither from the East? Who would entertain such a crazy idea? Each weeping willow now existing is in every sense a separate tree, distinct from all others, living its own life.

The conclusion to be drawn from these two examples and a host of others is obvious: a vine-stock, a willow, a tree or plant of any kind, is not an individual, neither is a branch covered with buds an individual; for it is enough to take a cutting from this branch in order to reproduce the vegetable, provided it is planted in the ground and properly tended. The sole condition of success is that the cutting must bear at least one bud—strictly speaking, the bud itself will suffice for this process of propagation by division; but in this case the new plant, instead of being set in the ground, must, as a rule, be confided to a branch which will feed it with its sap. This transplantation of buds or shoots from one plant to another is known as grafting—we find, then, that a tree may be subdivided into as many new and separate plants as it has branches ; and the branch, in turn, will furnish as many plants as it has buds ; but the bud is no longer divisible ; to divide it is to destroy it. Accordingly, the individual vegetable is the bud.

Many things that would be inexplicable in relation to the organization of a really simple being become perfectly intelligible if we regard the tree as a collective being, whose various individual components, namely, its buds, live in common while retaining a certain amount of independence. When we prune a fruit-tree, removing a number of its branches, this extensive mutilation, which would spell the death of any simple organism, far from being deadly in its effects, is actually beneficial, because those buds that are left profit by the food intended for the buds which have been removed. If, by means of grafting, we add to a tree, buds derived from another tree, the community is not affected by the newcomers, whether members of the family or strangers, the buds unfold, blossom and bear fruit, each one after its own fashion, without acquiring any of its neighbour's habits. Amongst the curious results which may be obtained by means of these artificial associations, based upon the mutual independence of the buds, I might mention a pear-tree, on which, by means of grafting, the whole gamut of cultivated pears was represented. Sweet or sour, dry or juicy, large or small, green or brilliantly coloured, all these pears ripened on the same tree, year after year, always unchanged, faithful to the racial characteristics, not of the tree, their foster-mother, but of the various buds transferred to this common support.

I think my point is sufficiently proved.   I will conclude by this original definition of Dupont de Nemours': " A plant is a family, a republic, a sort of living hive, whose inhabitants are fed in the common refectory upon the common stock of food."

CHAPTER III

THE LONG LIFE OF CERTAIN TREES

Why do trees live so long ?—Chestnut-trees—The Chestnut-tree of the Hundred Horses—Longevity of some Lime-trees—The Oak-tree in the cemetery of Allouville—Ancient Yew-trees—The giant Sequoia of California—The Cypress of Fernando Cortez—The Baobabs of Sengeambia—The Dragon-tree of Orotava.

I₣ it is really a collective being, whose successive generations follow one another in regular sequence, the tree ought to survive for a very long time, and it ought to be subject only to accidental death, if we may use the expression, since the old shoots are followed yearly by fresh buds, thanks to which the vegetable community is always young and able to look forward to a long future life. The individual dies but the community persists, just as it does in the case of the polyparies ; and in speaking of them I mentioned certain polyparies which are flourishing even to-day in the waters of the Red Sea, although their beginnings may go back to the days of the Pyramids. The individual dies but the community persists ; what is true of the polypary is also true of the tree ; and I shall cite, as witness, certain patriarchs of the vegetable world, which rival in antiquity the corals of the Red Sea, and even surpass them. But how are we to tell the age of a tree ? In the case of such trees as grow hereabouts nothing could be simpler. Consider Fig. 6, representing a transversal section of the stem of a young Oak-tree. Between the pith, which is seen at the central point of the section, and the bark, there are six circular strata,

lying one within the other ; six layers of wood, superimposed in concentric circles. These circles can be
distinguished very plainly when the stem is carefully
bisected by means of a very sharp knife. These superimposed strata are known as the *annual lignous layers*,
because one of them is formed each year, as I shall
presently explain. The branches of the tree also
display these annual deposits of woody tissue, the
number varying with their age ; but the main stem
or trunk contains the total number, which equals that
of its years. It therefore suffices to count the annual
rings of wood of which the trunk of a tree is composed,

FIG. 6.

in order to ascertain the age of a
tree that has been felled ; the
number of these rings gives us its
age in years. Thus, the Oak-tree,
a section of which is shown in
Fig. 6, was six years of age. If
the tree is still standing we can
gauge the average thickness of one
layer by examining the section of a
branch, since we can then deduce the age of the tree,
by comparing this thickness with the diameter of the
trunk.

We have many examples of vegetable longevity. We
read of a Chestnut-tree in Sançerre, the circumference of
whose trunk was 13 feet 8 inches. According to the
most moderate estimates it must have been 300 to 400
years old.

There are records of Chestnut-trees very much larger
than this ; in particular one at Neuve-Celle, on the shores
of the Lake of Geneva, and one at Esaü, in the neighbourhood of Montelimart. The first of these trees has a
circumference, just above the root, of 42 feet. We have
creditable evidence that as long ago as the year 1408 it

AN OLD WEEPING WILLOW.

To face p. 22.

sheltered a hermitage. Since then five centuries have been added to its age ; on several occasions it has been struck by lightning ; nevertheless, it is still hale and hearty and puts forth abundant foliage. The chestnut of Esaü is a majestic ruin ; its upper branches are ravaged by the years ; its trunk, some 36 feet in circumference, is cleft by deep crevices, the wrinkles of age. It is hardly possible to tell the age of these two colossi. It might well be a thousand years or more ; yet the two patriarchs still bear fruit and seem still to have long years of life before them.

The largest tree in the world is the Chestnut-tree that grows on the slopes of Etna in Sicily. It is known as The Chestnut-tree of the Hundred Horses, because Joan, Queen of Aragon, having come to see the volcano, was surprised by a sudden storm, and took shelter beneath the tree with the hundred horsemen who formed her escort. Beneath its foliage, a forest in itself, both men and horses found abundant shelter. Thirty men, holding hands, would not quite succeed in surrounding this giant ; the circumference of whose trunk is more than 160 feet. In the matter of bulk the trunk of this mighty tree is something more than a trunk ; it is a tower, a veritable fortress. An opening wide enough to admit two carriages abreast, runs through the base of the tree from side to side, giving access to the cavity of the trunk, which has been turned into a temporary dwelling-house for those who come to gather the chestnuts, for the ancient colossus is still full of youthful sap and rarely fails to yield an abundant crop. It is impossible to estimate the age of this giant tree, for such an enormous trunk has probably resulted from the amalgamation of several adjacent trees, which were originally separate entities. Neustadt, in Wurtemburg, has a Lime-tree, whose branches, overloaded with their burden of years, are supported by a hundred pillars of masonry. One of these branches is nearly 130 feet in length. The tree as a whole, with all its limbs, covers an area 426 feet in circumference. In the year 1229 this tree was already old, for contemporary documents refer to it as " The Great Tree." It is probably 800 to 900 years old.

A century ago, however, the veteran of Neustadt had a rival in France. In 1804 there was, in the grounds of the Château de Chaillé, near Melle, in Deux-Sèvres, a Lime-tree whose circumference was 49 feet. It had six principal branches supported by numerous props. If it is still in existence it must be more than 1,100 years old.

There was once to be seen at Saint-Nicolas, in Lorraine, a table consisting of a single slice of a Walnut-tree, which was more than 25 feet in width and long in proportion. Tradition says that the Emperor Frederick III gave a sumptuous banquet at this table in the year 1472. To judge by the ordinary rate of growth of the Walnut-tree, it is estimated that the tree whose trunk provided this table-top must have been not less than 900 years old.

In the neighbourhood of Balaclava in the Crimea, it is said, there was once an enormous Walnut-tree which yielded an annual crop of 100,000 walnuts. Five families possessed this tree in common. Its age was estimated at 2,000 years.

The cemetery of Allouville in Normandy is over-shadowed by one of the oldest Oak-trees in France. The dust of the departed into which its roots have found their way seems to have given it unusual vigour. Its trunk, on a level with the ground, is 33 feet in circumference. The cell of an anchorite, crowned by a tiny belfry, has been built in the midst of its enormous branches. The lower portion of the trunk, which is partly hollow, has been employed, since 1696, as a chapel, dedicated to our Lady of Peace. The most illustrious personages have

THE PATRIARCH OF THE CEDARS OF LEBANON

J. Boyer.

To face p. 24.

esteemed it an honour to offer up a prayer in this rustic
sanctuary and to meditate awhile in the shade of this
most ancient tree, which has seen so many graves opened
and closed. Judging by its dimensions, this tree is
believed to be some 900 years of age ; so that the acorn
which produced it must have germinated about the year
1000 A.D. To this day the ancient Oak-tree supports its
enormous boughs without an effort, and every spring
sees it clad in a vigorous growth of leaves. Honoured by
men and ravaged by lightning, it faces the centuries
without flinching, confronted, it may be, by a future
equal to its past.

But there are Oak-trees in existence much older than
this. In 1824 a woodcutter in the Ardennes felled a
gigantic Oak-tree in whose trunk were found fragments
of sacrificial urns and ancient medals. According to the
calculations of the most learned botanists this giant can
look back upon the barbarian invasions of Europe, having
lived at least 1,500 to 1,600 years.

Side by side with the great Oak of Allouville we may
mention certain other companions of the dead, for it is
chiefly in those quiet acres, where the sanctity of the
spot protects them from injury at the hands of man,
that trees are able to reach an advanced age. Amongst
others, two Yew-trees in the cemetery of Haie-de-Routot
in the Department of the Eure deserve our notice. In
1832 their sombre foliage overshadowed the whole of the
churchyard and part of the church itself, and they had
suffered no serious damage until that year, when a gust
of wind of extreme violence broke off some of their
branches. Despite this mutilation the two Yew-trees
are still majestic patriarchs. Their trunks, completely
hollow, are in each case over 9 feet in diameter. Their
age is probably some 1,400 years.

But this is less than half the age attained by other

trees of the same species.   A Yew-tree in the graveyard at Fortingal in Scotland was 20 feet in diameter.   Its age was probably 2,500 years.   Another Yew-tree, at Braburn in the county of Kent, was, in 1660, of such enormous girth that it used to be the boast of the whole county.   Its age was then believed to be 2,880 years.

FIG. 7.—The Giant Sequoias of California.

If it is still standing this patriarch of the trees of Europe must be more than 3,000 years old.

The true giants of the vegetable kingdom are certain conifers, by name *Sequoia gigantica*, a species not unlike the Cypress, and not long known to science.   They are found, to the number of eighty or ninety, within a radius of some 1,500 yards on the upper slopes of the Sierra Nevada in California.   Straight and upright as marble columns, they grow to a height of 300 feet and more, towering over the tall trees about them as a Poplar-tree towers above the surrounding hedges. The smaller measure 10 feet in diameter at the base of the trunk; the larger, 30 feet. The Chestnut-tree of Etna is twice the diameter of the latter, but is far from attaining the same height. At the foot of such trees it would look like a tall thicket of brushwood. And we must not forget that the Tree of the Hundred Horses has, it seems, resulted from the amalgamation of a number of adjacent trunks, while the Californian colossi are formed each of a single trunk, standing well alone, and of regular growth. This family of giants has not been respected by the gold-seekers ; a few have fallen beneath the axe and the saw. Merely to climb upon the prostrate trunk of one of these trees a long ladder was needed, as though the woodsman were climbing to the roof of a house. This wonderful trunk was 30 feet in diameter. Its bark was removed in a single piece from a length of 22 feet, and furnished as a living-room, with carpets, a piano and seats for forty persons. A hundred and forty children, in the course of some children's game, managed to find room in the huge sheath of bark.

What was the age of this giant ? In this case there is no uncertainty about the matter. The tree, which was in a wonderful state of preservation, even in the central portion, displayed more than 3,000 concentric layers of wood. It was thus at least 3,000 years old. Three thousand years is quite a respectable age ; it takes us back to the time when Samson released, in the cornfields of the Philistines, foxes, to whose tails incendiary torches were attached.

In Mexico we can go back even farther than this ; we shall find there a tree contemporary with Noah. It is a Cypress, greatly venerated by the natives. It stands in the cemetery of Santa Maria de Tesla, some seven to eight miles from Oaxaca. Cortez, the conqueror of Mexico, is said to have sheltered his little army beneath its boughs. The calculations of the botanists attribute to this tree an age of 4,000 years.

In Senegambia, not far from Cape Verde, there is a curious tree, a sort of gigantic mallow, which, in the matter of age, surpasses even the Mexican Cypress : this is the Baobab or *Adansonia*.   The trunk is hardly more than 12 or 15 feet in height, but its diameter may be as great as 25 to 30 feet.   This powerful foundation is by no means more than is needed to support the crown of foliage, which takes the form of a dome 200 feet in diameter. The leaves are broad and woolly, not unlike those of the Chestnut-tree in shape.   The flowers are like those of the Mallow, but larger ; the fruit, in appearance, is like a Pumpkin, brownish in colour, divided into fifteen sections. The negroes give the Adansonia a name that means " the tree thousands of years old."   Never was a name more justly bestowed ;   for Adanson's investigations show that some of these Senegambian veterans are 6,000 years of age ; we could hardly credit such antiquity were it not that the calculations which proclaim it possess all the direct force of an example in the rule of three.

In 1749 Adanson observed, in the Magdalene Islands, near Cape Verde, certain Baobabs, which had been noted by English travellers 300 years earlier.   These English-men had cut inscriptions on the trunks of the Baobabs, and these inscriptions were found by the French botanist, covered by 300 layers of lignous tissue.

The Baobab, like our European trees, puts on a layer of wood every year.   Now, given the total thickness of the 300 layers of wood, the average thickness of a single layer could be deduced ; and once this was known it was easy, by comparing it with the radius of the trunk, to calculate the age of the tree.   This Adanson did, and the result of this simple calculation was that certain Baobab-

A MAN IS INDEED DWARFED BY THE GIANT "REDWOODS" OF CALIFORNIA.

J. Boyer.

To face p. 28.

trees had been living for 6,000 years.—And are these patriarchs failing—have they at least been damaged by the corroding tooth of time ? By no means ; their bark is green and glossy ; wound it ever so slightly, and an abundant sap flows forth. Theirs is still the vigour of youth ; they have centuries upon centuries of life before them.

The same age, 6,000 years, is attributed to another famous tree : the Dragon-tree of Orotava, a little town in the Canary Isles. Ten men holding hands could not span the giant's trunk, which is crowned by a huge mass of branches bearing long leaves as sharp as swords. In 1819 a terrible gale smote this aerial forest and a third part of the great mass of boughs broke away with a terrible crash. Nevertheless, the mutilated colossus retains its imposing appearance ; immovable on its foundations, it will doubtless add a long tale of centuries to the sixty which it has already seen.

CHAPTER IV

ORGANIC ELEMENTS

Cells—The rate of their formation—Principal forms—Their induration or invasion by lignous matter—Veins—Tracheal tubes—Cellulose—Contents of the elementary organs—Starch—Its extraction from the Potato—Structure of Starch-grains—Their conversion into Glucose.

WHEN he wishes to obtain an exact knowledge of a tract of country that is new to him, the traveller climbs to some point with a lofty outlook, whence he can observe the general lie of the land, the principal contours and boundaries. This comprehensive view will thereafter serve him as a guide in co-ordinating his more detailed observations, and giving to each its proper place.

I am now about to take the reader into a world that is new to him—the world of plants ; so, in order that everything may be classified with method in your mind, so that it may appear to you in a thoroughly intelligible form, I have led you, at the very outset, up one of the lofty peaks of science. Thence we have brought back one fact : one single fact, but a fundamental one, which henceforth will give us the freedom of many a fertile pasture. The plant is a complex being, a society whose individual is the bud. The individuals live their day, fail, and die, death being the inevitable end of all that lives ; but before they die they leave successors, and the communities, perpetually rejuvenated, proceed upon their way through the centuries, or so, at least, do vigorous communities, such as those of the trees, which brave the vicissitudes of the seasons, which are deadly to the weak. This is the explanation of those prodigious examples of longevity, of which I have just been telling you ; it is also the explanation of many other facts which we shall presently consider. For the moment we shall descend from the heights and consider certain details. We shall begin by examining the materials of which every plant is made. Examine with care a scrap of cloth. You will discover, if you did not already know, that cloth is a tissue of interlacing threads, some running in one direction, and others running across them. Now take a pin and unravel the stuff, separating, one by one, the threads that go to make it up. Now the cloth is no longer cloth ; it is a tangle of roughly twisted threads. This process of decomposition may be continued still further. Let us take one individual thread. It is made up of still finer fibres, twisted together. Each of these fibres is a thread of wool, one hair from the fleece of a sheep. We will separate these also, and when this has been done, the process of unravelling comes to an end. The hair cannot be subdivided. Now this fibre of wool is, in a certain sense, the elementary organism of the cloth ; it is this that makes, if often enough repeated, first the thread and then the cloth ; being always the same as regards its substance and approximately the same as regards its dimensions.

The plant also, if unravelled, element by element, may be reduced to the equivalent of the fibre of wool : that is, it may be reduced to something simple, which is not capable of further division ; in short, it may be reduced to its elementary organ, which, if accumulated in sufficient quantities, makes up every part of the plant : leaves, flowers, seeds, fruit, bark and wood, without distinction. This final element is of the same material in all plants and in all their parts ; it always assumes the same form,

and its dimensions are always more or less the same :
now, the elementary organ of the plants is a tiny globule,
so tiny that it would take dozens upon dozens of them to
equal in size an ordinary pin's head. In other words,
you can hardly hope to see it without a microscope.
This globule is hollow. Formed of a delicate membrane
without an orifice, it is like a purse, a bag without an
opening ; it has therefore been given the name of cell.

The cell is in a sense the brick of which the vegetable
structure is built, for, when massed together in sufficient
numbers, in this or that special order, it forms every portion of the plant.   It is difficult to realize the bewildering
rapidity with which the vegetable can manufacture cells,

and build with them. A single leaf of
the Kidney-bean, during its period of
growth, creates at least 2,000 cells in an
hour, and immediately puts them in
their place, grouped in the proper manner.
A Pumpkin will increase in weight at the
rate of two pounds or more daily : two

FIG. 8.—Cells
of the Lily.

pounds of cells, of invisible specks of
matter. The botanist Jungius tells us of a
fungus which, in one single night, increased from the size
of a Hazel-nut to that of a Pumpkin. Comparing the
dimensions of a cell with the bulk acquired by the
fungus, Jungius concluded that the fungus had grown at
the rate of sixty-six millions of cells per minute, or a
total of forty-seven thousand millions during a night.

At the moment of their formation these vegetable
cells are tiny closed sacs, consisting of a transparent
pellicle. At the outset they are spherical or egg-shaped ;
but the space at their disposal is often limited, and,
incommoded by their neighbours, squeezed against one
another, they lose their original form, and their sides
are flattened into facets. The better to fill the space

disputed, angle is accommodated to angle, projecting ridges fit into empty corners, and the inequalities of one cell fit snugly into the inequalities of its neighbours. Sometimes the cell persists in its initial simple form ; nothing is added to its original membrane. This is the

| FIG. 9. | FIG. 10. | FIG. 11. |
| Pith-cells of Elder. | Punctuated Cells. | Striped Cells. |

case with Puff-balls, Toadstools, etc., whose growth is very rapid, but which are short-lived. More frequently, in vegetables whose term of life is longer, the cell acquires an internal lining, a fresh membrane covering the sides of the first envelope. This second membrane is covered

FIG. 12.	FIG. 13.		FIG. 14.
Annular,	Spiral,	and	Striped and
			Reticulated Cells.

by a third, a fourth, always internally, so that the wall of the cell gains in thickness by the addition of fresh strata, while the central cavity diminishes in proportion. Now, these successive envelopes, counting from the second, instead of forming a continuous surface, are cut through, here and there, at certain points, or round irregular surfaces or circular or spiral curves. As these breaches of continuity all precisely correspond, the wall of the cell is more transparent there than elsewhere,

4

since there the outer envelope is not lined by any further membranes ; and this peculiarity results in a great variety of visible forms. Sometimes the cell seems covered with circular specks or short transversal stripes. In the first case it is known as punctuated ; in the second it is known as striped. Sometimes again it is encircled by narrow rings, and is known as an annular cell ; or it contains a corkscrew-like thread, and is known as a spiral cell. Yet again it may be covered by irregular streaks, vaguely resembling the meshes of a net, and in this case it is known as a reticulated cell.

In order to accommodate themselves to the various functions which they will be called upon to fulfil, the cells lose their original shape at certain points of the vegetable structure, and assume a greatly elongated form. Or again they may grow end to end, in series, when, in order to communicate one with another, they open at the extremities, thus making conduits of varying length. From this process result two further kinds of elementary organs : fibres and tubes.

Fibres are elongated cells which diminish in diameter toward their extremities, so that such cells are shaped

FIG. 15.—Speckled fibres.

like a spindle. They form the greater part of the woody substance of the plant. Like the ordinary cells, of which they are merely a variety, they assume various appearances, resulting from the breaches of continuity in their innermost strata, with which the outer membrane is lined. We have therefore speckled, striped, reticulated fibres, and so forth. But the most remarkable characteristic of the fibres is their tendency to heap up layer upon layer in the interior of the cell; with the result that sooner or later the added strata entirely fill their central cavity. Moreover, the fibres may become imbued with colouring matter, or encrusted with mineral substances, and above all, they may become impregnated by a remarkable substance known as lignin. You may remember the hard granulations which occur in the pulp of certain pears of inferior quality. You will also remember the stone of the Peach and the Apricot; whose hard, thick shells will turn the point of a knife. Well—these hard granulations and this stone consist of almost pure lignin. Once encrusted with this hard substance— petrified by it, so to speak—the fibres can no longer play any part in the vital activities of the plant, for the first condition of any vital activity is the faculty of imbibing liquids—in other words, sap, which is the blood of the vegetable organism. They are thenceforth merely building-material, capable of consolidation and resistance. As long as their cavity is free and their walls permeable, the fibres are still constituents of the living wood, which lies immediately beneath the bark; but when they are fully obstructed and encrusted they form the central portion of the trunk, harder than the rest, and darker in colour. The lignin with which they are saturated gives the wood its hardness, its power of resisting rot, and its value as a fuel. It is the larger proportion of lignin in its wood that makes the Oak preferable to the Willow as a fuel, and the centre of the trunk preferable to the outer strata for the purposes of the cabinet-maker.

In order to convey, underground, the water that fills our cisterns, we place a certain number of pipes, of varying length, end to end. Similarly, the plant, in o·der to convey the moisture of the soil to its buds, piles cell upon cell, turning them into conduits, commonly known as hydroids. In its ordinary forms the cell is closed. When it forms part of the vascular system its extremities open out in order to leave a free passage. Here are two short lengths of conduits surrounded by fibres. From the constrictions which occur at intervals we can see that these two tubes are made up of an assemblage of cells. One of them is striped and the other speckled, just as ordinary cells are.

In other cases all such constrictions disappear, and an

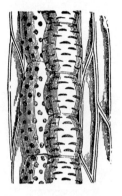 

Fig. 16.—Two conduits amidst fibres.　　Fig. 17.—Annular and Reticulated tubes or conduits.

examination of such tubes, whose bore is equal throughout, will fail to reveal the slightest trace of demarcation between their constituent cells. Such are the two tubes shown in Fig. 17. The first is reinforced, at intervals by rings, and is therefore known as an *annular* tube ; the second is lined with a sort of network, and is known as a *reticulated* tube. We have already found these two formations in the ordinary cells, which is only natural, since the tube is derived from the cell.

These tubes or conduits never branch off and never coalesce. Scattered here and there throughout the wood of the plant, commonly assembled in small bundles, they run direct from the roots to the leaves, without putting forth secondary tubes and without mutual inter-communication. Their length is indefinite, and their diameter is commonly almost too small to permit of their detection by the naked eye. In some kinds of wood, however, the sap conduits are visible without a lens. In a clean-cut section of a branch of an Oak-tree, for example, we may easily distinguish, above all near the junction of two adjacent rings of wood, a host of very small openings, which are the orifices of so many sap conduits. In a section of a well-dried Vine-stock they are even more plainly visible. Such a section is riddled with orifices large enough to admit a fine horse-hair.

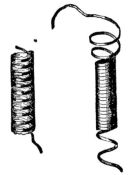

To complete the series of elementary organs, I must mention the *spiral* or *tracheal* tubes. These are tubes which are lined internally with a ribbon coiled into a spiral form, like a spiral spring. The tracheal tubes are never found in the wood, unless perhaps in the immediate neighbourhood of the

FIG. 18.—Tracheal tube and lining.

pith ; but they occur very frequently in the leaves and flowers. If we carefully tear the petal of a Rose in two we shall see, connecting the two shreds, certain very fine filaments, surpassing in delicacy the finest filament of a spider's web. These are the spiral threads lining the broken tracheae, uncoiling as we draw the two fragments of the petal apart. In order to observe all these things—tubes, fibres, cells, tracheae—the aid of the microscope is indispensable ; but under the lens you will discover, in the smallest particle of leaf or bud, a frail magnificence which will fill you with wondering amazement.

Of the elementary organs of the plant we have hitherto considered only the shape of sap-vessels and tracheae ; we must now inquire into the nature of the substance of which their walls are made, and of the materials contained in their cavities.   Let us first take the walls of these organs.   Here the process of paper-making will give us some useful information.   To begin with, all sorts of filthy rags are collected.   Some are picked out of the gutter ;   some are stained with all manner of filth.   A process of sorting is gone through ;   some of the rags are set aside for the making of fine paper ;   others are used in making the commoner sorts.   First the rags are washed, and with great thoroughness ;   and they are indeed in need of a thorough washing.   Next, they are fed into machines which seize them with steel claws, tearing, cutting, masticating them, and reducing them to fine shreds.   Again they are seized by special machines, which masticate them further, grinding them under water and reducing them to a pulp.   But the pulp thus obtained is grey in colour and has to be bleached.   It is now subjected to the action of chemical agents, which attack everything they touch, and make it as white as snow. The pulp is now fully prepared.   Other machines now spread it in thin layers on special sieves.   The water drains away and the pulp of rags becomes a kind of felt. Cylinders compress this felt ;   other cylinders dry it and polish it, and the paper is made.   Before it was paper the raw material of the paper was rags, and these rags were shreds and tatters of woven fabrics that were past use.   And in how many ways were these rags not employed before they were at last thrown away, and to what processes were they not subjected ?   Washing with caustic lyes and acid soaps, repeated boiling and mangling, and exposure to the sun, air and rain.   What is this material, which endures the destructive activities of soap and sunlight and air : which remains intact though steeped in filth ; which survives its treatment by the machinery and the chemical agents of the paper-mill and emerges from these ordeals still more pliant, and whiter than before ; becoming at last a sheet of paper, a sheet of that beautiful, glossy substance to which we confide our thoughts ?

Well !—the material of paper is precisely the material of which the envelope of the vegetable cell is constructed. Cells, fibres and tubes are composed of a substance which is, in all plants, precisely the same. Science has named it *cellulose*, in order to remind us of the cell. Raw cotton, hemp and flax consist of cellulose more or less accompanied by foreign matter which disguises its beautiful whiteness. This cotton-wool, these fibres, are converted into various tissues, being subjected to the processes of manufacture ; but when the linen or cotton fabric is worn out it undergoes yet one more metamorphosis and becomes paper. But this time the cellulose, which on its journey to the mill is subjected to numerous and extremely effectual processes of cleansing, is set free from any trace of foreign matter. Paper, in short, is composed of pure cellulose.

So much for the wall of the cell, and its derivative forms, the fibre, the tracheal thread and the vein or artery. Now let us consider the contents of the cell. The veins contain only air and water. Their purpose being to convey the moisture of the soil to the opening buds, it is a very long time before they become choked ; they do not, indeed, become obstructed until the wood is already changing its character. The wood, long after it has ceased to play any part in the vegetable economy, still contains a certain number of veins whose passage is still unobstructed. The fibres play quite another part : that of strengthening the vegetable structure.

Accordingly, at a comparatively early stage in their history, we shall find them impregnated with a tenacious cement, and they become incrusted with that hard substance to which the adjective lignous is applied. The cell has other functions, but this does not always prevent it from becoming indurated, from turning into wood. It is the cell, which, mysteriously filled with this hard substance, forms granulations, almost like grains of sand, in the flesh of certain pears ; and once again it is the cell that builds the impregnable stone of the peach and the apricot to protect the kernel. But as a general thing the cell contains no lignous elements ; its walls remain elastic and permeable, so that it continues capable of preparing and storing up within itself an enormous variety of substances, for the cell is above all the factory of the plant.

Some cells contain nothing but air : for example, the cells occurring in the dry pith of the elder ; others are full of a liquid consisting almost entirely of water. Some contain resinous varnishes (the Pine and the Fir), gums (the Cherry-tree), acid liquors (the Vine of the green Grape), acrid, milky fluids (the Fig-tree), syrups sweet as honey (Sugar-cane), farinaceous powders (the Potato), aromatic oils (Orange peel), tiny globules of oil (the Olive), deadly poisons (certain Toadstools), green granulations (all true leaves), and colouring matter, red, blue and yellow (flowers). We shall also find cells containing crystals ; in some cases excessively slender and grouped together like bundles of sewing-needles, while in other cases we find crystals of tablet form, heaped together in disorderly fashion, or massed together like a glittering head of cauliflower. None of these materials, so different in their composition, appearance and properties, are obtained by the plant from without all ready prepared. They are formed in the cells, from the sap that oozes

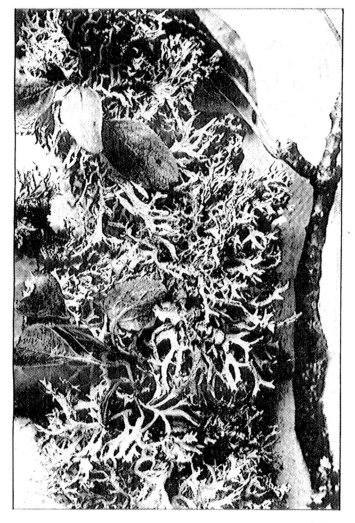

BRANCH OF PLUM-TREE INVADED BY LICHEN.

To face p. 40.

through the membranous envelope. Sugars, acids, resins, oil, essences, gums, starches and poisons, are all derived from the wonderful liquids elaborated in the incomparable laboratories of the cells.

Now, of all the materials elaborated in the cellular cavities the most remarkable is *fecula.* You must be familiar with the appearance of starch—that beautiful white substance which is used to give stiffness to our shirt-fronts or other garments. Starch is pure fecula. Fecula is extracted, by mechanical and chemical treatment,

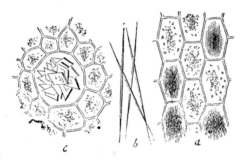

Fig. 19.—*a.* Cells, four of which contain bundles of the crystals or needles known as raphides. *b.* Isolated raphides. *c.* Central cell contains a mass of tabular crystals.

from cereals. This substance is found in the form of minute granulations, in the cells of a great number of plants ; now in the roots, now in tubercles, now in the fruit or seed. It occurs in especial abundance in potatoes. To extract it, it is enough to tear open the cells that contain it, and then to separate the grains of fecula thereby set at liberty. For this purpose the potato is, by grating, reduced to pulp. This pulp is spread upon a piece of linen stretched across the mouth of a glass beaker and watered by means of a fine jet of water, which has the effect of stirring up the pulp while washing it. The grains of fecula washed out of the broken cells are washed

by the water through the meshes of the linen strainer ;
the pulp, too coarse to pass the improvised filter, is left
behind.   You will now have a beaker full of turbid water.
Let us examine it, in a strong light.   A crowd of tiny
white specks are falling through the liquid like snow and
collecting at the bottom of the beaker.   In a few moments
the whole of the sediment is deposited.   You can now
pour the water away ;   it will leave behind it a finely
divided substance, dazzlingly white, which, on being dried,
becomes a fine powder.   This is fecula.

The grains of fecula are excessively minute.   The largest
are those of the Potato.   It would take about one
hundred and fifty to fill a cubic millimetre.   Those

occurring in corn are much
smaller.   It would take something over ten thousand to fill
a millimetre cube.   Maize yields
a grain of which sixty-four

FIG. 20.—Fecula in Potato-cells.   thousand would be needed to
A. Single grain of fecula.   B.   fill the same volume ; while ten
Cell full of grains.
million granulations of the
fecula obtained from the Sugar-beet would be required.
Minute [as they are, however, these granulations are
quite complex in form.   Each begins with a tiny speck
around which a flake of fecula is deposited, followed
by a second flake, a third, a fourth, and so on
indefinitely ; so that by the time it reaches maturity
it consists of a series of sacs, one within another.

The fecula is an elementary reserve, intended as the
first form of nourishment for the young plant.

Every seed that is destined to develop itself in isolation
is provided with its ration of fecula.   When life awakes
within the germ, this substance, in itself inert, insoluble
and innutritious—since its insolubility deters it from
spreading itself through the nascent tissues, and impreg-

nating them—is transformed into another substance, which is soluble in water, and is therefore able to penetrate wherever the work of organization calls for building-materials. The result of this wonderful transformation is known as *glucose*. This is a sweet-tasting substance, very closely related to sugar in its composition and its properties. Place a little Wheat in a saucer and keep it moist. In a few days the corn will germinate. When the green tips of the young shoots begin to show, you will find the grains of wheat quite soft if you examine them. You will find that you can crush them between your thumb and forefinger, and that they will yield a milky sort of liquid of an extremely sweet flavour. In order, so to speak, that the young plant may be given suck, the fecula of the Wheat has become glucose, which dissolves in the moisture of which the wheat-berry is full, and, being mixed with starchy granulations not as yet transformed, provides a sort of milk diet. With the materials contained in this diet cells are built up, and also fibres and tubes. This work of construction is rendered easier in that glucose contains precisely the elements contained in the fecula, which in turn contains precisely the elements contained in cellulose. These three substances, greatly as they differ in respect of their properties, contain precisely the same elements. A mere re-arrangement, which adds nothing and takes nothing away, is enough to convert into fecula that which otherwise would have become cellulose and also to convert into a kind of sugar that which was fecula. A slight modification in the opposite direction will cause a retrograde metamorphosis: the sugar will be turned into fecula if such is needed, or in case of greater urgency it will be turned into cellulose or lignin.

These transformations, strange as they may appear to you, have in part been effected in our human laboratories and factories. From fecula the scientists have made the sugar known as glucose : the same sugar that occurs in honey, in ripe grapes and in germinating corn ; they can even make glucose, or grape-sugar out of cellulose ; they can make it out of the paper on which these words are printed ; or, if you prefer, of cotton rags ; at a pinch they can make it out of wood, out of shavings, or the leg of the chair you are sitting on. For such strange transformations the scientist will employ one of the most powerful of chemical re-agents—sulphuric acid, commonly known as oil of vitriol. But the plant's methods are greatly superior to these rather crude operations. Silently, without the employment of heat, without sulphuric acid, it turns into a milky solution of grape-sugar the reserves of fecula that accompany the vegetable germ. And how does the plant do this ? I do not know, and I am not alone in my ignorance. Here the genuine scientist modestly confesses : I do not know. It is among the designs of the Eternal Wisdom that at a given moment the fecula in the seed, a dry substance, innutritious, savourless and insoluble, becomes a sweet milky liquid, highly nutritious ; and it is done. If some day, having grown pale with much study of books, you can discover some better explanation, please do me the kindness of imparting it to me. I am waiting for it.

CHAPTER V

THE THREE DIVISIONS OF THE VEGETABLE KINGDOM

Tissues—The Protococcus of the Snows—Cellular vegetables—Their importance in Nature—Conifers—Vascular vegetables—The order of appearance of the various vegetable species on the earth—General differences in the structure of the stalk, leaf, flower, and seed—The number of seed-leaves—The inferior vegetables—The three divisions of the vegetable kingdom—Dicotyledonous compared with monocotyledonous plants.

THE fabric of our cloths consists of textile filaments —cotton, wool, silk, hemp, flax—which are first twisted into threads and then woven—that is, made to cross one another ; and by an etymological extension we employ the same term—tissue—to denote the structure that results from the assembly of the elementary organs of plants—cells, fibres and tubes. Vegetable tissue may consist merely of juxtaposed cells—when it is known as *cellular tissue.* There are also tissues in which the cells come into contact only at one point, or over a strictly limited surface, retaining their original globular form, and forming a fragile and rather spongy sort of complex ; there are also tissues in which the cells, distorted by mutual pressure and adhering to one another by extensive facets, assume a great variety of polyhedral forms. The unoccupied intervals which sometimes occur between adjacent cells, especially in soft and yielding tissues, are known as *intercellular meatuses.* Sometimes empty intervals of different sizes occur, which are surrounded by cells : these are known as lacunae. If the tissue consists of fibres it is known as fibrous tissues ; if it consists of fibres and tubes it is known as fibro-vascular tissue.

You will remember the chestnut-tree on Etna, that colossus which thirty men holding hands could not manage to span ; you will remember too the gigantic

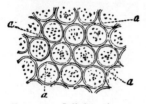

FIG. 21.—Cellular tissue ; *aa.* Intercellular meatuses.

Conifers of California, one of which yielded a section of bark in which a hundred and forty children found a place. To make the tissues of their gigantic frames, how many fibres are required, fibres finer than hair, and how many cells, so minute that many could find lodgment on the point of a needle! Other marvels await us, but in inverse order. One cell, one single cell, a mere vesicular speck, may form a complete vegetable. And you must not suppose that these living atoms are fragile in proportion to their minuteness. On the contrary, they are full of robust vitality ; they prosper under conditions which would be fatal to more highly organized plants.

One such vegetable, the *Protococcus nivalis*, braves the harshness of the Polar climate ; if it ventures into our latitudes it takes refuge on the highest mountains, amidst the eternal, frozen snows. It seeks out the cold and must have snow-fields for its soil. On this frozen bed it is born, develops and brings forth fruit. It consists of the merest speck, of one single reddish cell. Reproducing itself profusely, it gives the snows amidst which

FIG. 22.—Fibrous tissue.

it lives a beautiful rosy tint ; and it is this tiny plant that is the cause of the red snows which are sometimes seen in the Arctic regions and amidst the Alps. Having reached maturity, the cell of the *Protococcus* produces, within its cavity, a family of smaller cells; it then bursts open and flings to the winds its posterity, which goes forth to people other snowfields.

Life leaves no point of vantage unoccupied. In order to people the snows, and to wash them with red as it reddens the harvest-field with the red Poppy, it creates a special creature, the humblest of the humble, a plant reduced to one simple cell. In order to cover with living things the naked rock, the lava-stream but lately cooled, the stagnant pool, the bark of ancient trees, decaying wood, rotten fruit, and all sorts of putrifying animal and vegetable tissues, it creates, by means of cells piled upon cells in an infinite number of ways, myriads of vegetable types, the first rough sketches, in a sense, of organized matter. The fundamental structure of these vegetables contains nothing but cells; it includes neither fibres nor tubes. They are therefore known as *cellular vegetables*. We shall find them in the green slime that floats upon stagnant waters and the filamentous tresses of certain Algae; on the bark of trees, on rocks, on streams of congealed lava, on the leprous incrustations of the Lichens; on aged trees, on rocks fissured by the inclemencies of winter, on ruined walls; on velvety cushions of moss; on rotten wood, dead leaves and fungi of fantastic shape; on rotting fruit and tufts of Mildew; in fermented liquor when turning sour; in the slimy scum known as " mother of vinegar "; in the scum floating on the surface of soured wine and the white deposit known as " flowers " of wine; in short, in all decomposing substances, in the vegetable moulds and scums that are the inseparable companions of filth.

These rudimentary vegetables, Algae, Lichens, Mosses, Toadstools, Mildews, composed entirely of cells, and often quite a small number of cells, and even one single cell, none the less have an enormous part to play. They crumble the rock, turning it into vegetable mould ; they act as scavengers, turning dead matter to living, and sterilize corruption.   Multiplying with amazing profusion they break down dead matter and restore it to the condition in which it is able to re-enter the cycle of living matter.   Let us suppose that a tree is lying prostrate upon the ground.   Before it can feed with its lifeless remains the plants which, in a sense, are its inheritors, and in them live again, it must be reduced

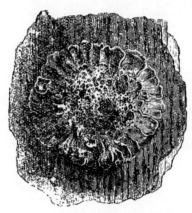

to powder.   The cellular artisans will now set to work upon it.   Mosses, Lichens, Toadstools, Fungi, Moulds and Mildews take possession of its carcase. With the help of insects and the air, their powerful auxiliaries, they dissect the dead tree, cell by cell, fibre by fibre, and by continual subdivision they reduce it to vegetable

FIG. 23.—Lichen on a tree-trunk.

mould.   The great task is accomplished, for now, with this mould, the dust of death, life reappears, and a new vegetation is created.

I can assure the reader that it is no paradox to say that Moulds and Mildews that live but a few days are of greater importance in the harmony of living creatures than the Oak-trees whose life is measured by centuries ; for without all these plants, these fragile assemblies of cells, without all these rudimentary vegetables, which multiply so profusely in the midst of filth and decay, life would be impossible, because the work of death would be incomplete.   In this world the humble have always prepared and are still preparing the way for the

life of the great. Geology, that impressive, dignified
science, is able, with the relics exhumed from the
bowels of the earth, to return, in imagination, to the
early youth of the world.   Now what does geology tell
us on the subject of vegetable life ?   It tells us that the
Oak, the Beech, and the other large and imposing forms
of vegetable life, were unknown among the first-comers.
On the calcined rocks vomited by the subterranean fires,
how could they have lived, with no vegetable mould to
nourish their roots ?   In order to prepare the way for
them the minuter forms of vegetable life appeared, in
chaplets and filaments and sheets of cells, some living
in the water and some on the naked rock.   Granite
crumbled at their touch, and they made the resulting
dust more fertile with their own remains.   Their efforts,
continued through century after century, resulted in a
little vegetable mould, in which fresh workers—still
cellular—such as Mosses and Lichens, contrived to establish
themselves.   To these yet others succeeded : from day
to day the soil became more fertile, and finally, the
Moulds and Mildews having done their work, the way
was opened for the Oak to appear.

Three principal phases may be distinguished in the
evolution of the plant through the ages. Generally
speaking, during the first phase the cell alone appears ;
during the second the fibre is associated with the cell ;
during the third phase the tube completes the series of
elementary organs, and the vegetable reaches its first
stage of perfection.   In our days the vegetable world is
a mixture of the three categories ; its innumerable
species are composed, some of cells alone, some of cells
and fibres, and some of cells, fibres and tubes.

I have just told you something of the cellular vegetables
—that is, those plants whose substance consists of cellular
elements alone : such are the Fungi, the Algae, the Mosses

and the Lichens. Vegetables consisting of cells and fibres, but without tubes, go to make up the group of Conifers or resinous trees, whose fruit takes the form of cones. To this group belong the Pines, Cedars, Firs and Larches. The Conifers are conspicuous, amidst the vegetation predominant at the present time, by their peculiar and individual physiognomy. The Conifers are dignified trees of pyramidal form ; their branches project in horizontal strata ; their slender, needle-like leaves allow the light to filter through them, but do not cast a gloomy shadow beneath them ; the wind in their boughs gives rise to wild, harmonious strains that one might well take to be the distant acclamations of a people making holiday ; their bark, dripping with tears of resin, gives forth an aromatic fragrance ; in short, everything about them tends to make them conspicuous amidst the other trees of our lati-

FIG. 24.—Branch of Fir.

tudes. They are veterans, outcasts amidst plants of a more recent creation ; they belong to another epoch ; they are descended from the first lignous vegetation of the world ; that ancient vegetation, which, long before the coming of man, covered the globe with strange-looking forests, which to-day are buried in the bowels of the earth, and converted into coal-measures. To the cell of inferior forms of plant life the Conifers added the fibre, but did not advance so far as to add to these the tube. Even in our days, faithful to their old custom, the tube is not included amongst their elementary organs.

The vegetable species which predominate at the present time, from the lowly blade of grass to the tallest of our trees, contain, in their structure, the three categories of elementary organ. They are given the name of vascular plants, with reference to the sap-vessel (*vasculum*) by whose presence they may be known. Every plant begins its life as a humble cell. Whether it is destined to become an Oak-tree or a mere weed, at a certain stage it is wholly

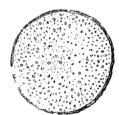

FIG. 25.—Cross-section of a dicotyledonous stem.

FIG. 26.—Cross-section of a monocotyledonous stem.

composed of cells. But scarcely has it rid itself of the husk surrounding the seed, when the young plant, if it is destined to become a vascular plant, adds fibres and sap-vessels to its original cellular structure ; or, if it belongs to the Conifers, it at least adds fibres to the cells. Here we find two groups, readily classified by the manner in which they employ these new elementary organs in the structure of the stem. One group assembles the fibres and tubes in uniform and concentric rings, which go to make up the annual strata of lignin, of which you have already learned something ; the second group scatters them here and there without any methodical arrangement.

Here, side by side (Figs. 25, 26), we have the cross-section of a stem of either group. In the first section, we shall note, in addition to the concentric rings which consist mainly of fibres, a number of tiny black specks arranged along the dividing line between two consecutive strata. These are the orifices of the tubes or sap-vessels. In the second figure the dark points correspond with the bundles of fibres and tubes ; the blank portions consist of cells only. The first structure is

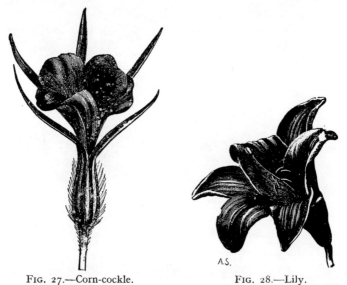

FIG. 27.—Corn-cockle.   FIG. 28.—Lily.

found in the Oak, the Elm, the Beech, and indeed in all our trees. We should find it likewise, but in one ring only, in many of our species that live only one year, such as the Campanula, the Peruvian Balsam, and the Potato The second structure will be found in the trunk of Palm-trees, in the Reed, in Asparagus, in the Lily and Iris.

These different methods of the organization of the stem are accompanied by corresponding differences in the flowers, leaves and seeds. Let us compare the flower of the Corn-cockle with that of the Lily. The Corn-cockle belongs to the category of the plants that assemble their fibres in regular circles ; the Lily belongs to that of the plants which do not arrange them according to any particular method. The flower of the Corn-cockle consists of five *petals*, of a reddish purple, and these five petals form what is known as the *corolla*. The petals consist of an extremely delicate tissue, which under rough handling is soon bruised and torn ; but while in

FIG. 29.—The Paper Mulberry. Leaves with reticulated nervures.

the bud they are safely wrapped up, and when the flower has opened they are protected against injury from without by five other leaves, long and sharp-pointed, green and moderately rigid, which form what is known as the *calyx*. Thus the flower of the Corn-cockle comprises two different envelopes : one, the inner envelope, the corolla, is fine in texture, fragile and richly coloured ; the other, the exterior envelope or calyx, is green in colour, robust in texture, and protects the inner envelope. The flower of the Lily, on the other hand, consists of six petals, all of an ivory white, all equally delicate, but has no green external envelope; it has a corolla but not a calyx. The Rose, the Mallow, the Violet have, like the Corn-cockle, a twofold floral envelope, calyx and corolla; the Iris, the Hyacinth, the Tulip have, like the Lily, a single floral envelope, known as a corolla.

A leaf consists mainly of a thin, flexible sheet of cellular tissue. In order that it may resist the wind and the rain, this thin sheet of tissue is strengthened by means of tough, inelastic bundles of fibres and tubes, enclosed in the thickness of the leaf, and known as *nervures*. Now, if you compare the leaves of the Pear-tree with those of the Iris, you will find that, in the first, the nervures are subdivided, branching forth and rejoining one another so as to form a fine network; while in the second the nervures display no ramifications, but run along more or less parallel lines, without forming meshes. You will find the same difference of structure between the leaves of the Elm, the Poplar and the Plane-tree, and those of the Narcissus, the Lily and the Tulip. When the cellular tissue of the leaf has rotted away, the nervures, more refractory to decomposition, still remain, making a

FIG. 30.--Orchis. Leaves with parallel nervures.

fine lacework in leaves of the first category, and a
bundle of parallel threads in those of the second.

Let us now consider the fruit of the Almond-tree.
We break the stone in order to obtain the germ which
is the seed. The seed is covered with a brown skin,
and under this is another skin, finer and lighter in colour.
These are the envelopes of the germ. When we remove
them we have the kernel, hard, white and glossy, with
a pleasing flavour ; and from this we should obtain an
Almond-tree. This white, glossy kernel is divided into
two equal parts ; and on separating these halves, we see,

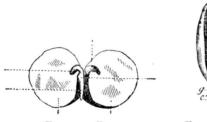

FIG. 31.—Pea.   FIG. 32.—Almond.
c, cotyledons ; r, radicle ; g, gemmule ; t, tigellus.

at the pointed end of the kernel, a small, conical
prominence, pointing outwards, and a tightly compressed
bundle of very minute, undeveloped leaves, a sort of
bud, pointing inwards. The conical prominence will
become the root ; and the bud will expand into leaves,
and will also stretch upwards until it becomes a shoot.
As for the two plump, well-nourished organs, which by
themselves make up almost the whole of the seed, they
are the first two leaves of the plant, but leaves of a
special structure : two elementary reservoirs, supplying
food to the developing plant. At the moment of
germination, these two thick leaves, bursting with
fecula, provide the first nutritive material for the young
plant, which is still too feeble to fend for itself. One

might call them the food-leaves, the vegetable feeding-bottles. Botanists have given them the name of *cotyledons*.

The fact is easily verified that Peas, Beans, Acorns and many other seeds have likewise two food-leaves, two cotyledons. You will find that all those vegetables in which the fibres in the stem are arranged in concentric circles, from the smallest to the largest, provide their germs with two food-leaves. But the seed of the Lily, the Tulip, the Iris, and all those plants in which the fibres in the stem are arranged without regular order, contain only one cotyledon.

You will not always find it easy, above all when the seeds are very small, to discover whether the seed contains two food-leaves or seed-leaves or only one ; but if you enable the seeds to sprout the difficulties of observation no longer exist. You will find that the seeds with two cotyledons will appear above ground with two leaves, the first of all to appear ; you will find also that they are attached to the stem at the same level, and are often quite different in form from those that follow. In the Radish, for example, they are heart-shaped. These two leaves, that appear before any other leaves, and are known as seed-leaves, are simply the two cotyledons, which expand and turn green, while, at the same time, they feed the infant plant with a portion of their own substance. On the other hand, seeds that contain only one cotyledon appear above ground with only one seed-leaf, and this is usually long and narrow. This observation you can make by allowing wheat to sprout in a saucer. Lastly, far beneath these two groups of vegetables, one of which yields a seed with two cotyledons, while the seed of the other group contains only one, there is a third group, which propagates itself by means of seeds which have nothing in common, as regards their structure, with the seeds which I have briefly described. Here we do not find the tiny conical process which becomes a root, nor the bundle of tiny undeveloped leaves, nor the cotyledon. The seed is a simple cell, with no visible division into various organs. The plants of this group are, as a rule, composed entirely of cells. Such are the Fungi, the Lichens, the Mosses and the

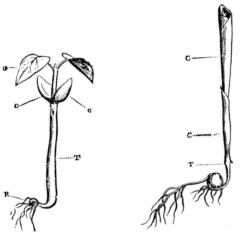

FIG. 33.—Kidney-Bean, in   FIG. 34.—Maize, in state of
   state of germination.   germination.

C, cotyledons or seed-leaves ; G, the first ordinary leaves ; T, tigellus
R, radicle.

Algae. Some, however, like the Ferns and the Horsetails, contain fibres and tubes, but none of them have flowers, and sometimes, as in the Fungi and the Lichens, there is nothing that we can possibly liken to leaves, or roots, or stems.

The vegetable kingdom is thus divided into three sub-classes, according to the number of cotyledons contained in the plant, namely :

1. The *Dicotyledones*, whose seed contains two cotyledons and sometimes more. To this class belong the Oak, the Almond-tree, the Rose-bush, the Lilac-tree,

the Mallow, the Pink or Carnation, the Radish, the Pine, the Cedar.

2. The *Monocotyledones*, whose seed contains a single cotyledon ; such as the Palm-tree, Wheat, the Reeds and the Rushes, the Lily, the Tulip, the Hyacinth and the Iris.

3. The *Acotyledones*, whose seed contains no cotyledons. This category includes the Ferns, Mosses, Horsetails, Algae, Lichens and Fungi.

Let us for the moment set aside the acotyledones, whose organization cannot be compared with that of the other plants ; and let us consider the dicotyledones and monocotyledones together.

DICOTYLEDONES.	MONOCOTYLEDONES.
The seed contain two cotyledons.	The seed contains only one cotyledon.
The plant, on germination, sends up two seed-leaves.	The plant, when sprouting, possesses only one seed-leaf.
The nervures of the leaves are commonly reticulated.	The innervation of the leaf is usually parallel.
The flower, as a rule, comprises a calyx and a corolla.	The flower, generally speaking, has only a corolla, without a calyx.
The fibres and tubes in the stem are arranged in concentric circles.	The fibres and tubes are distributed in the stem without definite order.

CHAPTER VI

STRUCTURE OF THE DICOTYLEDONOUS STEM

The herbaceous stem—Central pith—External pith—Medullary radii—
Lignous bundles—Lignous stems—Cambium—Liber—Suberose envelope
—Epidermis—Descending sap—The second year's growth—Subsequent
growth—Proofs of the downward movement of the sap—Result of
annular decortication and of a ligature—Proofs of the annual formation
of a lignous stratum.

THE stem, the common support of various portions of
the plant, is known as annual or herbaceous when it
lasts only one year. This annual stem consists, in the
dicotyledonous plants, of a mass of green cells, traversed
by a few bundles of fibres and vessels forming a narrow
ring, which may be easily recognized by its dull white
hue. Here the predominant element is the cell, the
simplest of all, the most rapidly formed and the best
adapted to an active but brief existence.

In the cellular mass of a herbaceous stem two regions
may be distinguished (Fig. 35). The region marked *m*,
which lies inside the lignous ring, is known as the central
pith ; the portion lying outside this ring, upon the
circumference of the stem, is known as the external
medulla. Other portions, likewise of a cellular character,
connect the central pith with the external medulla, and
are called the medullary rays. Finally we come to one
layer of robust cells, tightly packed, which envelops
the stem, in order to protect it against the heat of the
sun, and the inclemencies of the atmosphere, and to
prevent the waste of the fluids which it imbibes. This
stratum is known as the epidermis. In the case of young

saplings it is easy to remove it by shreds and flakes, in the form of a colourless pellicle.   In Fig. 35 the herbaceous stem is completely surrounded by a heavy black line.

Some herbaceous plants go no further than this in structure of their stem ; others more or less complete their lignous circle.   Then, between the original columns of fibres and vessels, fresh bundles of these elements come to reinforce them ; the medullary rays diminish until nothing is left of them but thin, fragile partitions,

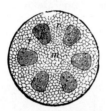
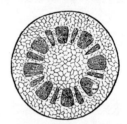

FIG. 35.—Dicotyledonous or   FIG. 36.—The same stem,
herbaceous stem.   further advanced.

while the lignous belt is becoming almost continuous (Fig. 36).

Every stem, no matter how long its life, its size, or its eventual texture, begins by passing through such phases as I have been describing ; then, at the end of its first year, its structure is already sufficiently far advanced to justify our description of it as a lignous structure. Fig. 37 shows, in its natural dimensions, the section of a stem of a Chestnut sapling, and also, a segment *a*, *b*, as it appears enlarged under the microscope.

In Fig. 38 we see that this stem has a central medulla (1), which is always composed of cells alone ; we may also perceive a lignous belt (3), divided into a large number of extremely narrow medullary radii, which are likewise cellular in structure.   In this circular zone we shall see the orifices of the large sap-vessels, in the form of black specks ; while in the area (2), closely adjacent to the pith, there are other openings which correspond with the tracheae. It is only here, in actual contact with the central medulla, that the stem is provided with tracheae ; they will not be found in any other part, whether of the bark or the wood. Outside this lignous zone we find a thin stratum (4) consisting of a viscous liquid and nascent cells. However inconspicuous it may be, this semi-fluid layer is of the greatest importance, for it is the permanent laboratory of the elementary organs. It is known as the *cambium*.

Beyond this the bark is found. It comprises—still

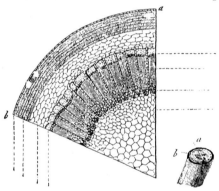

FIG. 37.—Cross-section of a stem of a young Chestnut-tree.

progressing from the interior to the exterior—a layer (5) known as the *liber*, consisting of long, tough fibres ; then a zone (6) of cellular tissue forming the external medulla or cellular envelope, analogous to that of the stems of herbaceous plants, and communicating with the central pith by means of the medullary radii, which completely traverse the liber and the ring of lignous tissue. A little further on we find a dark, brownish ring (7) which is likewise cellular, and is known as the *suberose envelope* ; and finally we come to the epidermis (8), a layer of protective cells.

Here, the reader may think, is a fine collection of

materials and strata, in relation to a scrap of some
vegetable stalk no more than a year old ! In order to
help you to engrave them in your memory I shall
recapitulate these terms, at the same time showing you
the scrap of Chestnut stem under another aspect and a
greater magnification.   Fig. 38 shows us a vertical section
of the same stem.

The central medulla is indicated by the figure 1.   It
consists of cells of irregular form and varying dimensions.
On the outer circumference of the medulla we shall see

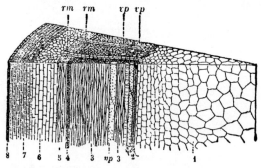

FIG. 38.—Vertical section of a wedge-shaped slice of the same tree.

a certain number of tracheae (2), whose spiral threads
have begun to unroll themselves slightly where the tube
is cut through.   Immediately after this ring the lignous
belt begins.   You will see a few large vessels (*vp*, *vp*)
sprinkled about the surface of the cross-section, and a
multitude of fibres (3), all parallel to the surface of the
stem.   Two medullary radii, *rm*, run in a straight line
from the external (6) to the central (1) medulla, connecting
the two by means of their thin plates of cells.   The layer
of wood in process of formation, and finally the cambium (4), form the external boundary of the lignous
ring.   Then come the fibres of the bark, the liber (5).
Beyond this we have the external medulla (6), consisting
of cells of a pale green, and the suberose envelope whose

cells are encrusted in a sort of brownish cement (7). Lastly, the epidermis (8) surrounds the whole.

The above remarks refer to a stem but a year old, no thicker, at most, than one's little finger. What happens the second year, and the subsequent years? To begin with, we must remember that all plants derive nourishment from the air and from the soil, by virtue of their leaves and of their roots. But as the substances extracted from the soil are not the same as those derived from the air, the two modes of nourishment are not interchangeable ; both forms of nourishment being equally necessary. Every bud, whether buried beneath the surface of the soil or exposed, on the tree-top, to the open air, must, when the time has come for it to accomplish its task, exploit the atmosphere by means of its leaves and the soil by means of the roots with which it is indirectly connected. At this stage the young shoots—that is, the buds in process of development— inject under the bark a liquid substance of which I shall presently tell you more. The thousands upon thousands of tiny drops furnished by the whole community result in a flow of living sap between the bark and the stem, which creeps gradually from the top of the tree to its roots, growing thicker and undergoing a process of organization, finally becoming a layer of wood super-imposed upon a similar layer formed in previous years. At the time of this flow, in the spring, we say that the tree is in sap. At this season the bark, made pliable by the liquid secretions that are flowing beneath it, may readily be detached from the twigs, when it is excellently adapted to the manufacture of whistles, the delight of early childhood. This liquid secretion, elaborated by all the buds in common might well be called the blood of the plant, since it serves to build up every part of the developing organism just as blood builds and nourishes every part of the animal organism. We call it the descending sap, on account of its path from the top of the tree to its roots. The cambium is merely this selfsame sap which has grown turgid and is beginning to organize itself into cells, fibres and tubes.

Thus, on the return of spring the young buds set to work in order to add a further layer of wood to the stem of the preceding generation, and thereby to exploit the soil through the medium of the roots. They pour into the space between the bark and the stem the sap which they have elaborated in common, the sap which solidifies

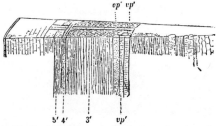

Fig. 39.—Vertical section of the layers developed during the second year.

into cambium, undergoes organization, and gradually forms, on the surface of the stem, a fresh ring of wood like that of the preceding spring, and on the inner face of the bark a fresh layer of fibres, superimposed from within upon the first layer of liber. This operation being completed, the stem will comprise two rings of wood, one within the other, the older ring lying within the newer; the liber too will comprise two fibrous linings, the older lying outside the younger. Fig. 39 will show you the growth of the stem during the second year. That part of the section which is produced downwards is of recent formation; that part of the section shown on the right-hand side of the figure is the old wood; that on the left-hand side is the old bark.

The recent deposit of wood (3′) is formed in the same

fashion as the preceding layer. It consists of a close-packed mass of fibres and tubes (vp'), but there are no tracheae, nor will there be in any future deposits of woody substance. It is completely traversed, here and there, by medullary radii. One of these will be seen in the figure. If you look at this carefully you will see that in one direction it is produced far enough to make contact with the external medulla, but in the other direction it stops short at the old lignous ring, without reaching the central pith. The same thing, it will be found, will be true of all future medullary radii : they will all reach the external medulla, and all stop short at the ring of lignous tissue deposited the previous year. The liber or bast, that is, the sheet of long, tough fibres, is also increased by a second layer ($5'$). Lastly, a layer of cambium ($4'$) is interposed between the bark and the wood, in order to foster the process of growth as long as the weather is favourable thereto.

Thus, every year, the bark, no less than the stem, is increased by a fresh stratum ; only the strata thus acquired have a twofold and contrary aspect : in respect of the wood being added from and on the outside, but in respect of the bark from and on the inside. The wood, enveloped yearly by a fresh lignous jacket, grows old at the centre and is rejuvenated on the surface ; the bark, which receives every year an additional lining of liber or bast, is rejuvenated internally but grows old externally. The wood hides its lifeless and encrusted strata in the centre of the trunk ; the bark rejects its old lignous deposits, which, as they are thrust outwards, split and fall to the ground in shapeless flakes. Old age attacks the tree simultaneously at its outer surface and at its heart ; but within the confines of the wood and the bark the life of the plant is always at work preparing the way for fresh formations.

The materials necessary for these annual formations are furnished by the nourishing sap of the plant—by the descending sap or cambium. If we remove a small area of bark from the trunk of a tree and cover the wound with a plate of glass to prevent dessication, we shall see on the upper part of the stem thus laid bare a number of small sticky drops, which increase in number and in volume, finally spreading and amalgamating and covering the wood with a continuous varnish. This is the descending sap, the materials with which this year's buds are building a layer of wood, a wooden scaffolding which puts them in touch with the soil. This humour is so much liquid wood, just as the blood of animals is liquid flesh ; as it proceeds upon its way it grows thicker and takes the name of cambium ; then, becoming more highly organized, it solidifies, and on the one hand becomes a layer of wood and on the other a sheet of bast.

A very simple experiment will demonstrate its downward progress. By means of a double incision we remove from the stem of the plant a wide ring of bark. In this manner all communication between the top and the bottom of the stem is interrupted, an insuperable obstacle having been placed in the path of the sap ; so that the latter, constantly dispatched downwards, from the top of the tree, by the buds, accumulates at the upper edge of the wound, proceeds to organize itself, and becomes a cushion-shaped fillet of wood. The lower edge of the wound, on the contrary, shows no such ridge of lignous tissue. The fillet of wood at the upper edge of the wound is composed, structurally, of a mass of twisted and interlacing fibres, as though the materials from which the wood was elaborated had all done their utmost to find a thoroughfare and continue their downward progress on the farther side of the obstacle. As a matter of fact, in its present state the tree is doomed to extinction, as the young shoots can no longer communicate with the soil. The tree may linger for a time, but is bound, eventually, to wither away and die.

Similar results may be observed if we forcibly constrict the stem by a ligature. Above the ligature a circular ridge is formed, and then the tree dies. Here again the compression obstructs and prevents the descent of the sap ; it prevents the buds from establishing communication with the soil, and the vegetable community dies. But if the ring of bark thus removed, if the constriction, involves only part of the circumference of the stem, the sap will find its way round the obstacle and will make a path for itself where the bark is still intact, and will thereafter resume its ordinary progress. In this case the tree will not die ; it will only be seriously weakened.

We find, then, that from the buds, taken as a whole, the special fluid, in order to place them in communication with the soil, makes its way downwards, under the bark, and on its way to the ground it is in part transformed into a layer of wood deposited on the layer of the previous year. This woody layer connects the buds with the soil, for having reached the base of the stem it is distributed amongst the roots already formed, or it may produce yet further roots by subdivision and expansion beneath the surface of the soil. As this process is repeated with each generation of buds—that is, every year—we find that a tree consists of a succession of concentric lignous strata ; the oldest near the centre of the stem and the most recent on its outer circumference. A branch will contain so many lignous rings, according to its age, while the stem or trunk, the central point of the vegetable community, contains them all.

Here are some experimental proofs of this annual formation of a layer of woods. A strip of bark is removed from a tree while the sap is flowing, and a thin metallic plate is placed upon the denuded wood. The bark is restored to its place and bound in position in order that the wound may heal. Ten years or so have elapsed ; and the bark of the tree is removed at the same point. The metal plate, however, is no longer visible ; in order to recover it one must delve deeply into the wood. Now, if we count the lignous strata removed before the metal plate is reached, we shall find that they are precisely ten in number ; just as many as the years that have elapsed.

Observations like the following are legion : Some woodcutters felled a Beech-tree, on whose trunk the date 1750 had been carved. The same inscription was visible deep in the trunk, and in order to reach the earliest trace of the figures, it was necessary to dig down through 55 layers in which there was no sign of them. Now, if we add 55 to 1750, we obtain the date when the tree was felled—1805. The inscription carved on the trunk in the year 1750 had penetrated the bark and had involved that layer of woody fibre which was then the outermost. Thereafter fifty-five years had elapsed, and fresh layers of wood, precisely fifty-five in number, had covered that affected by the inscription. I have already told you how an observation of this sort enabled Adanson to estimate the enormous age of the Senegambian Baobabs. We may therefore take it as proven that in our climate at least trees produce one layer of wood each year.

CHAPTER VII

THE ANNUAL LAYER OF WOOD

Vitality of the superficial lignous deposits—Decrepitude of the central strata—Sap-wood and heart-wood—Characteristics of heart-wood—White woods—Hollow trunks—Why the disintegration of the central part does not involve the death of the tree—Deductions derived from inspection of the annual rings of wood.

WE have just seen that a tree in great part consists of a series of lignous layers or sheaths, lying one within another. The trunk of the tree includes all these rings ; the boughs, according to their age, contain a varying quantity. Each ring is the product of a generation of buds. The woody stratum of the present generation will be found outside the stem, immediately beneath the bark ; those of the bygone generations are found in the interior of the trunk, their nearness to the centre being in proportion to their antiquity. The buds of the future will produce, year after year, their respective layers of wood, which one by one will be superimposed upon their predecessors, and the outermost layer, the contribution of the current year, will in its turn be buried in the thickness of the trunk.

Of all these layers of woody fibre whose age varies so greatly, the most essential to-day is obviously that on the surface, since it places this year's buds and shoots in communication with the soil. The destruction of this layer would result in the death of the tree. The layers of wood inside the tree, when newly organized on the surface of the trunk, all played the same part, each in its turn, in respect of the buds contemporary with them ; but to-day, now that the buds have become branches, the deeper strata play only a secondary part, or possibly none at all. Those nearest the surface still retain a certain capacity for work, and come to the assistance of the year's deposit of wood by conveying water and various necessary salts from the soil to the branches. As for those layers that lie nearer the centre, they are henceforth incapable of any activity whatever ; they have become hardened, choked with lignin, and are dry and sapless. These woody rings in the depths of the trunk become useless as they grow older ; at most they add to the strength of the general structure by means of their tough woody fibres. Consequently the activity of a tree increases as we move from the centre to the surface. On the surface we have youth, vigour and active labour ; at the centre of the trunk we find decrepitude and inertia.

The lignous layers, taken as a whole, are thus divided into two categories : (1) those near the centre, from which life has completely withdrawn, and (2) those near the surface, in which life is still extant, in varying degrees. These two portions are distinguished, in the section of a moderately ancient tree-trunk, by a difference of colour : the lifeless portion is dark in hue while the second is whitish. The first is known as heart-wood ; the second is known as sap-wood. Sap-wood is pale in colour, soft and impregnated with sap ; it is living wood. The heart-wood, on the other hand, is dark in hue, hard and dry ; it is dead wood.

Decrepitude is far from being an improvement ; yet in French the wood from the heart of the trunk is known not only as heart-wood, but as *bois parfait*—complete, finished or mature wood. Yet it would seem more reasonable to call it imperfect wood ; for in respect of the tree, which it no longer nourishes, the heart-wood is anything but perfect ; but in respect of the uses to which man is able to put it, we may well call it perfect —the cabinet-maker, for example, needs a richly coloured wood with a close texture Well !—these qualities will not be found in the sap-wood, but we shall find them in the heart-wood. Ebony, valued for its hardness and its glossy blackness, and mahogany, with its rich, deep reds and fine texture, are derived from two trees whose sap-wood is soft and white. Sandalwood and Logwood, which provide the dyer with colouring materials, have an outer wrapping of sap-wood which is colourless. A wood so hard that it is compared with iron, and is for this reason known as Ironwood, is the heart-wood of a tree whose sap-wood is by no means remarkable. Lastly, who is there who is unfamiliar with the variations of hardness and colour between the heart-wood and the sap-wood of the Oak, the Walnut and the Pear-tree ? No one would ever employ the sap-wood for the sake of its colouring materials or its value to the cabinet-maker. It has to be chopped away in order to uncover the heart-wood, for in this alone shall we find dye-stuffs and a close-grained timber.

The heart-wood itself is sap-wood to begin with, and the sap-wood of to-day is destined to become heart-wood as it grows old and fresh layers of wood are deposited over it. Colour and hardness are therefore qualities that spread from the centre to the circumference, while at the circumference fresh layers of soft, white wood are being formed. In some trees the transformation of the sap-wood into heart-wood is very incomplete ; the heart of the tree decays before it has properly hardened. These are known as whitewoods. Of this number are the Willow and the Poplar ; their quality is poor ; they are deficient in toughness and soon decay.

Having reached an advanced age, certain trees, and

above all those whose heart-wood does not grow hard, often exhibit a hollow trunk. Sooner or later the central strata, eaten away by a dry rot, are reduced to vegetable mould, until the trunk of the tree becomes hollow : which does not deter it from producing a vigorous outgrowth of branches. At first sight nothing could be stranger than those ancient Willow-trees, riddled by the larvae of insects, hollowed by decay, broken open by the years, which nevertheless, despite the ravages of time, clothe themselves with a crown of vigorous foliage. Inwardly they are corpses in a state of decomposition, but outwardly they are still rejoicing in the fullness of life This peculiarity becomes intelligible if we remember that the central rings of wood are now of no service to the prosperity of the tree. Ancient relics of bygone generations, though they are consumed by decay the rest of the tree will not suffer thereby, so long as the outer strata remain healthy ; for in these alone does the vitality of the tree reside. Destroyed, as regards its central portions, by the assaults of time, and yearly rejuvenated by fresh generations of buds, the tree lives on through the centuries, with its will to live unimpaired. Thanks to a prerogative inherent in its organization as a collective being, it combines in itself the most contradictory qualities. It is at the same time old and young, dead and living.

The lignous rings accumulated in the thickness of the trunk are in some sort the pages of a book on which the life of the tree is recorded. Here are the principal data to be found in these vegetable archives : if we count in the section of a tree one hundred and fifty rings, we know that the tree was one hundred and fifty years old, since each ring corresponds with a year. If we know when the tree was cut down we know, likewise, in what year the seed that produced it germinated.

The several rings of wood are not all of the same thickness ; some are very much thinner than others. The thin rings correspond with years in which the tree produced a large crop of fruit ; the wide rings to years when it yielded little fruit or none. If the tree employs, in producing fruit, the greater part of the materials at its disposal, it will inevitably be compelled to reduce the formation of wood. On the other hand, if it converts it into wood it will be compelled to diminish the quantity of fruit produced. All trees that produce large crops of fruit—that is, crops representing a considerable weight and volume—will be found to exhibit such variations in the thickness of their lignous deposits. If an Oak-tree or Apple-tree should produce, in any given year, an abundant crop of apples or of acorns, its young shoots will show a smaller growth than usual in order to balance this excess ; on the other hand, if it grows an excess of fresh wood it must reduce its production of fruit. All trees accustomed to yielding heavy crops of fruit of a certain bulk reveal such variations in the thickness of their annual deposit of wood. Let an Oak-tree or an Apple-tree produce an abundant crop of fruit, and it will show but little growth of its shoots, or " green wood," that year.

The fruits will prosper, but the wood of the tree will be starved. Thus, in order to restore the stem to a healthy condition, the tree periodically rests awhile, ceasing, more or less, to produce any fruit. Almost all our native fruit-trees pass through a year's interval between two abundant crops ; in the Oak and the Chestnut the interval is one of two or three years, and in the Beech five or six. On the other hand, such trees as produce seeds of very small dimensions, requiring only a small store of material, will produce their seeds year after year, but will still deposit lignous rings whose diameter is almost invariable. Such are the Willow, Elm and Poplar.

But the unequal thickness of the rings of wood is due to yet another cause. There are years of universal hardship in the vegetable world ; there are the years of abnormal drouth. The roots contrive to obtain only very little moisture from the soil ; the new wood is affected by the results of the drouth, so that only a very shallow ring is deposited. On the contrary, thick rings of lignous tissue are a record of years when the soil was comfortably moist.

In the midst of healthy rings, some thick and others thin, we may here and there detect others of a dark, brownish hue, half disintegrated, and even revealing spots of decay. These correspond with winters of exceptional severity. The year's deposit of lignous tissue, then placed on the outside of the stem, was at various points killed by the frost ; during subsequent years, however, the damaged rings were covered up and hidden away under layers of healthy wood. If, on counting the rings from the outside, we hark back to the date of a disintegrated ring, we shall find that this date corresponds with a year noted for its frosts.

A layer of uniform thickness throughout its circum-ference announces a normal and regular growth. In that year everything favoured the tree ; both the air and the earth were kind to it ; its roots and branches met with no obstacle to their growth ; throughout the whole tree there was a plentiful flow of nourishing sap. A series of such layers testifies to favouring conditions continuing through a term of years.

A ring of irregular dimensions, here narrow and there wide, speaks of uneven development. A scanty deposit of lignous tissue means that on the corresponding side the tree was beset with difficulties ; the roots may have met with a poverty-stricken soil, a stratum full of pebbles ; or the growth of its branches was impeded by neighbouring trees ; or it may have been over-shadowed, which would tend to starve its foliage. If the irregularity of the annual rings disappears suddenly, giving place to regular growth, this means that the natural order of things was re-established. The obstacle was surmounted or circumvented, and the roots were able to resume their outward growth ; its neighbours were felled or overturned, and the boughs half-stifled in the shade were able to resume their usual vigorous growth.

CHAPTER VIII

THE BARK

*Epidermis—The suberose envelope—Cork—The Cork Oak—The cellular
envelope—Laticiferous vessels—Latex or essential juice—The Cow-
tree—Caoutchouc—Guttapercha—Liber—Its structure—Textile fibres
—Flax and hemp—Preparation of textile fibres.*

WE have seen, in the foregoing chapters, that the bark
consists of four distinct strata: the epidermis, the
suberose envelope, the external pith or cellular envelope,
and the liber. This, at least, is what we shall observe
in young stems; with age profound modifications may
occur, and some of these layers may entirely disappear.

The epidermis is the outermost layer of the bark.
It is a thin, transparent membrane consisting of one single
layer of cells. We find this upon stems of every kind—
that is, if they are young enough—for its existence is
merely temporary. As the stem grows the epidermis is
stretched until it tears, when it falls to the ground. It
is not renewed. It is well adapted, by virtue of its fragile
pliability, to envelop the young stem; but as the sapling
increases in bulk and stature it provides itself with a
very much thicker and stronger overcoat. Some trees
employ, as their superficial envelope, the second layer of
the complete bark, otherwise known as the suberose
envelope, of which cork—the familiar cork which we
employ to stopper our bottles—is merely one variety.
This layer derives its name from the Latin word *suber*,
which signifies cork. As the tree grows this suberose

76

sheath, thrust outwards by new formations, becomes
rent and cracked and gradually falls to the ground in
the form of large flakes and tatters ; but beneath these
discarded rags a brand new envelope has already developed.

The suberose layer of all trees is analogous to ordinary
cork ; like the latter, it consists of a spongy tissue of
cells of a brownish colour.   But the sort of cork of which
we use to make corks for bottles is produced by a particular species of Oak-tree, known as the Cork Oak.   This
is a handsome tree, an evergreen, not unlike the Evergreen
Oak or Holm Oak of Southern France.   Like the Holm
Oak, it is a native of the Mediterranean, but is not
found very far north.   It is found, in particular, in the
department of Var, in some parts of the Pyrenees, and,
above all, in Algeria.   It can be distinguished from
other Oak-trees by a thick suberose jacket which gives
the trunk of the tree a swollen appearance.   In our colder
latitude we have a variety of Elm whose young twigs
are covered with a cork as fine and elastic as ordinary
cork ; but this cork grows in irregular longitudinal
ridges or shapeless excrescenses which cannot be profitably
exploited.   In order to obtain the suberose jacket of the
Cork Oak one makes a circular incision at some distance
from the ground, and another at the base of the tree,
while the two incisions are joined by a longitudinal
incision.   The suberose sheath of the trunk is thus
removed, all in one piece, by a process of gradual leverage.
If the deeper strata of the bark have suffered no injury,
the tree thus flayed survives the operation ; and it proceeds to make for itself a fresh jacket of cork, which in
turn is removed a few years later.   In order to make cork
stoppers of this jacket, it is cut into small pieces, which
are rounded off, one at a time, with a very sharp knife.
In the form of cork stoppers, cork is in many ways of
the greatest value to us.   No other substance could

replace it for this purpose, for no other substance is at
once as firm and as pliable, as tough and elastic. Cork,
again, is eminently adapted to guard against cold and
moisture. Thus, in order to keep our feet dry, we inter-
calate a thin slice of it in the soles of our boots or employ
it in actual contact with the sole of the foot. In addition
to this familiar example I will mention another, of greater
significance.

A certain ship entered the inhospitable seas about
the Pole intending to winter there. The praiseworthy
desire to enlarge our knowledge of the history of our
planet had led her into these fearsome regions, where the
sea becomes hard as iron and where a night prevails
that is several months in length. Do you realize what
sort of cold one meets with in those dismal regions?
I will tell you. As soon as one goes out into the open
air the breath exhaled crystallizes into needles of white
hoar-frost around one's nostrils ; the tears that rise to
one's eyes freeze upon one's eyelids, cementing them
together ; the wind lashes one's face as though with
leathern thongs and ploughs deep furrows in the skin ;
the blood seems to be congealing in one's veins ; one's
flesh, where exposed, turns purplish and then white, and
loses all sense of feeling. If one did not quickly take
shelter one would be lost. What do the intrepid explorers
do, in order to protect themselves against the terrible
cold below decks of the vessel thus embedded in the ice ?
They line the whole of the interior of the vessel with a
thick layer of cork.

Not every tree has the power of increasing the thickness
of its suberose envelope in order to make such an effective
defence against the cold ; the majority of trees lose this
capacity at a very early age, just as they lose the epidermis. They then rely on the deeper layers of the cortex,
thus obtaining a sort of substitute for cork : that is, a

J. Boyer.

STRIPPING A CORK-OAK: ALGERIA.

To face p. 78.

sheath of spongy substance, more or less adapted to defending them against the inclemencies of the seasons. In addition to the epidermis, which we need not take into account, since it is shed by the tree at a very early stage, the bark includes the suberose envelope, the cellular envelope, and the liber. Each of these structures may in turn, according to the species of the tree, become the site of activities which multiply its strata, while the others go to work more slowly, or they even remain inactive, or gradually decay. Hence many varieties may be noted in the character of the tree's external covering.

If it is the suberose envelope that is most active in multiplying its cells, the tree will be clad in actual cork ; but if it is sluggish it will sooner or later disappear, thrust outwards and discarded by the expansion of the layers immediately beneath it. Its place will then be taken by the cellular envelope. With its external cells, indurated and dark in colour, it manufactures a false cork, which will sometimes occur in thick plates, as in the Pine, and sometimes is reduced to thin sheets which are renewed each year, as in the Plane-tree. In other cases the liber alone betrays such activity. It thrusts outwards and rejects the two external layers and itself envelops the stem with a strong, coarse tissue of fibres. Such is the case with the Vine, which every year replaces its bark by a sheet of liber, discarding the old envelope in the form of stringy tatters. In other trees, for example, the Oak and the Lime, the liber and the cellular envelope co-operate in the business of making the bark. The liber, with its bundles of fibres, provides the warp of the fabric ; the cellular envelope, with its layers of cells, provides the web. Their common labours result in a complex envelope, which, as it ages, falls away from the trunk in large flakes of associated cells and fibres.

Of the various zones of the bark, the cellular envelope is, as a rule, that which displays the greatest activity ; if not in its outer layers, which, in a dry and withered state, form a rough sort of sheath, at least in its inner strata, which are always full of sap. This sap is to a great extent absorbed by the spongy tissue ; the twigs and boughs send thither the compound partly elaborated in the leaves, there to undergo a final process of preparation, and to undergo transformation into various substances. It is, together with the leaves, the great laboratory of

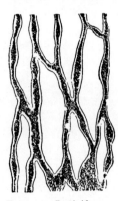

FIG. 40.—Laticiferous vessels.

the tree, the vegetable factory into which materials are constantly flowing, to emerge thence with fresh properties. It is there that the plant makes and stores its drugs—by which I mean those special substances which vary, according to the species of the plant, and are endowed with properties for which they are sought out by medicine, the arts and industry. It is there, to take only a few examples, that the Cinnamon-tree elaborates the aromatic essence of its bark ; it is there that the Quinquina-tree prepares its quinine, one of the most valuable of medicines ; it is there, too, that the Oak-tree prepares its tannin, that a stringent substance which enables the tanners to preserve the raw hide and to turn it into leather.

The preparation of these drugs calls for a special equipment, consisting of conduits of a peculiar form, known as laticiferous vessels. They occur in the thickness of the bark, at the junction of the cellular envelope and the liber. They differ from the liber, whose acquaintance

we have already made, as much in their form as in their
contents. They do not consist of a series of straight
tubes, unrelated to one another and without ramifications,
but are subdivided, like the veins of an animal, flowing
one into another, and forming an irregular network with
inter-communicating branches (Fig. 40). The ordinary
vessels form part of the wood ; it is through them that
the liquids drawn from the soil by the roots ascend to the
top of the tree. The laticiferous vessels form part of the
bark. They imbibe the descending sap, that is, that
species of vegetable blood elaborated by the branches
which flows downwards between the bark and the wood.
In this way they fill themselves with a liquid, often milky
in appearance, which is known as the latex, or quintessential sap, because every vegetable species elaborates one
of an individual character, which is peculiar to it. The
latex is white as milk in the Fig-tree, the Spurges, the
Poppy and the Dandelion ; it is a reddish-yellow in the
Swallow-wort, an unpleasant, nauseous-tasting weed that
grows on heaps of rubbish and old walls. Woe to him
who is seduced by the tempting, milky appearance of the
quintessential sap ; this apparent milk is often a most
noxious liquid. The latex of the Spurges is so corrosive
that if you taste it you will feel as though you had filled
your mouth with liquid fire ; the milk of the Fig-tree is
so acrid as to be painful to the tongue, and even to
delicate fingers that go picking the figs when they are
ripe ; the milk of the Poppy contains opium, of which a
small dose will send you to sleep, and a stronger dose
would kill you ; while the latex of the Javanese Antiar
is the terrible liquid with which the natives of the Sunda
Isles poison their arrows and the points of their krisses.
By a curious paradox, the latex, which is almost always
poisonous, becomes, in certain instances, a pleasant and
wholesome article of diet. In South America—to be

7

exact in Colombia—there is a tree known as the Cow-tree. Its botanical title is Galactodendron, which means, a tree that gives milk. It is treated much as we treat a milch-cow, or rather, this vegetable cow is bled ; its veins are cut—that is to say, the bark of the tree is incised. Immediately the laticiferous vessels thus bisected yield an abundant flow of a white liquid which, as regards its appearance, taste, and nourishing properties, hardly differs from ordinary milk. Evaporated by gentle heat, this vegetable milk yields a delightful sort of marzipan with a slightly aromatic odour.

The substance most commonly contained in the latex is caoutchouc, or elastic gum, not in the solid state, as in the slabs which we employ in erasing pencil-marks, but in a state of solution. The latex containing caoutchouc in a state of suspension is viscous ; but exposure to the air gives it consistency, and it sets into a solid but elastic mass. Our Spurges, and above all the larger species that occur in the south of France, contain a latex of this character. They, however, would prove but a scanty reservoir of " gum-elastic " ; a much richer latex is found in many foreign trees, and especially in the *Siphoniae*, plants belonging to the Euphorbia family, which occur in Guiana and Brazil, in the " Elastic Fig " of India, and the Urceolus, a rubber-yielding shrub of the Malay Archipelago. In order to obtain the caoutchouc, the collector makes a deep incision in the bark of the trunk, the milky sap which oozes from the wound being caught by calabash-shells, or large leaves, folded in such a way as to form a cone-shaped receptacle. This sap is at first liquid, but very soon assumes the appearance and the consistency of cream, while it finally becomes wholly coagulated. While still in a liquid state it is applied, layer upon layer, to earthenware moulds, shaped like a gourd or a pear ; and as each layer is applied it is put in the sun to dry before another is added. The various super-imposed layers are completely amalgamated, and form an indivisible whole. When the thickness of the layers is sufficient the fragile earthenware mould is broken between the hands and the fragments extracted through a sort of bottle-neck expressly contrived for that purpose, and the operation is completed. The rubber is then in the form of hollow, pear-shaped masses ; again, the latex may be moulded in sheets of varying thickness on flat plates of earthenware.

The latex of *Isonandra gutta*, a tree of the Malay Archipelago, yields guttapercha, a substance closely related to rubber, which to-day is of the greatest service to industry. It is a dark-brown material, heavy, tough and pliant as leather, but less extensible than gum-elastic. In boiling water it may be softened sufficiently to assume any form imposed upon it ; it may be moulded by pressure, when it will reproduce the finest details. Removed from hot water and chilled, it becomes harder than wood, while still retaining the form impressed upon it. It is used for the purpose of making belts for the transmission of power to machinery, tubes of every bore for conveying liquids, walking-sticks, whips, switches, rollers (in printing-presses), surgical implements, and a host of useful or ornamental objects. As it is as bad a conductor of electricity as resin or glass, it is employed in protecting and insulating the wires of submarine telegraph-cables.

Beneath the cellular layer, where the drugs of which I have just told you something are elaborated, you will find the liber, consisting of fibres of varying length. These filamentous fibres are arranged in bundles which combine, divide and combine again, forming in this way a rough network, whose meshes are filled by the outer ends of the medullary rays, which traverse this stratum of the bark from side to side. Here (Fig. 41) is a slip from the liber of a Chestnut-tree. At *f* we see the fibres neatly lying side by side ; and at *r* the medullary rays, whose cellular partitions run deep into the wood. Every year, at the expense of the descending sap, the liber is increased in thickness by a thin layer which is deposited on the inner surface of the preceding layers. Hence this part of the bark has a laminated texture, which has led to the comparison of the liber to a book, and has earned it the name of *liber* (*liber*, book). It would be possible to determine the age of the tree, by counting these strips of liber, but they are too thin, and too closely packed, to lend themselves to enumeration.

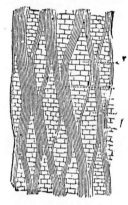

FIG. 41.—Liber of the Chestnut-tree.
r, medullary rays. *f*, fibres

In some plants the fibres of the liber are long, flexible and tenacious : a combination of qualities that makes them of the greatest value to us. Our most luxurious fabrics—lawn, cambric, nainsook, gauze, and the like—are obtained from the outer husk of the flax-plant ; the stouter fabrics, down to thick sack-cloth, are made of the outer fibres of hemp. I shall not here say anything of those fabrics whose raw material is cotton, since the cotton-bush, the champion spinner, produces its textile fibres not in its liber, but in the shell or pod containing its seed.

The Flax-plant is an annual ; a slender plant with small flowers of a soft blue. Its original home was the central plateau of Asia. To-day it is widely cultivated in the North of France, Belgium and Holland. It was the first plant on which man levied toll for his clothing.

The Egyptian mummies, who have been slumbering in their tombs for two or three thousand years, are swathed in linen bandages. The fibres of the Flax-plant are so fine that an ounce of thread from the spinning-wheels will be some three miles in length. Only the spider's web can rival certain tissues woven of the flax fibre.

FIG. 42.—Hemp.

Hemp appears to be a native of the East Indies, but it was naturalized in Europe centuries ago. It is an annual, with a noxious odour, putting forth small, rather dingy flowers, whose stem, no thicker than a pencil, rises to a height of six or seven feet. It is cultivated, just as Flax is cultivated, both for its stalk and for its seed.

When Hemp and Flax have reached maturity, and their seed is ripe, they are harvested, and the seed extracted by threshing. The plants are then subjected to a treatment known as *retting*, the object of which is to facilitate the separation of the fibres of the liber from the woody tissue. These fibres are actually glued together and cemented to the stem by a very tough, gummy substance, which makes the isolation of the thread impossible until it has been destroyed by decomposition. Sometimes the retting process takes the form of leaving the plants outspread on the ground for some six or seven weeks, turning them over from time to time until the bundles of fibre become detached from the stalk. But the quickest method is to steep the plant, tied into bundles, in a trough or tank. A state of fermentation very soon appears, which gives off unpleasant effluvia ; the bark soon rots, and the fibres, which possess exceptional powers of resistance, are set free. The bundles are then dried and crushed between the jaws of a machine known as a crushing-mill, in order to break the stalks into small fragments and divide them from the " tow." Finally, in order to rid the " tow " of all woody refuse, and to subdivide it into finer filaments, it is passed through the iron teeth of a sort of great comb or " hackle." In this condition the fibre is spun, either by hand or by machinery. The thread thus obtained is woven on a loom, and the transformation is completed : the bark of the hemp has become sacking ; the fibres of the Flax-stem have been made into lace fit for a princess to wear, worth its weight in gold.

CHAPTER IX

THE MONOCOTYLEDONOUS STEM

Organization of the trunk of a Palm-tree—Structure of a lignous bundle —The progress of vegetable organization through the ages—The primeval forests—Tree-ferns—The structure of their stems—The origin of Coal.

IN the stems or trunks of the monocotyledons there is no definite line of demarcation between the wood and the bark. It is true that we find in the case of tall trees whose seed possesses a single cotyledon, a thick envelope of indurated cells and the bases of old leaves, but this protective sheath does not in any way resemble the bark of dicotyledonous plants ; it has not the complex structure of the latter, and is continuous with the wood of the stem, being powerless to isolate or detach itself. In our temperate climate we have no tall trees with only one cotyledon, except in our gardens, or under glass ; they are peculiar to hot climates. We have reeds and rushes, which bear a slight resemblance to them. But you will never succeed in detaching a cylindrical tube of bark from the reed ; though in the spring you can easily do as much in the case of our various trees. Its bark and its wood are one and the same substance ; and this is true of all plants possessing only one seed-leaf.

The stem of the monocotyledonous plants are likewise without concentric zones of lignous tissue. A tissue of cells is traversed by small bundles of fibres and vessels which display no orderly arrangement, as will be seen from the segment of a Palm-tree shown in Fig..43. The black specks that are seen in the cross-section correspond to the

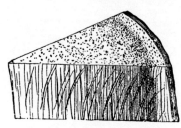

lignous filaments which are seen in the vertical section, traversing the cellular mass. You will see that these lignous bundles are more numerous and more closely set toward the outer surface of the trunk ; and it is there, too, that they are

FIG. 43.—Segment of the trunk of a Palm-tree.

more deeply coloured. Now, as it is these bundles that give the wood its hardness and its colour, the stem of the Palm-tree is hard and dark in hue in its more outward parts, but soft and lighter in shade in its central portions. This is precisely the reverse of that which occurs in the stem of a dicotyledonous plant, whose heart, or centre, is hard and deeply coloured, while the outer part, the sap-wood, is soft and light in shade.

Despite its wholly different architecture, the trunk of a Palm-tree shows us nothing new as to its raw materials. Every one of its lignous bundles contains, in its make-up, all the elementary organs of a dicotyledonous stem. Here is a section, across the grain, and another parallel with the grain, both being largely magnified (Fig. 44). At *a*, we see a little of the cellular tissue which fills in the space between the various lignous bundles ; at *b*, there are several layers of fibres with thickened walls ; at *c*, a trachea ; at *d*, there are striated vessels ; and at *e*, some laticiferous vessels, which, in the case of dicotyledonous stems, will be found only in the thickness of the bark.

In short, this filament, of which thousands would be needed to make up the stem of a Palm-tree, is an abridged

COCO-PALMS : ALGERIA.

To face p. 88.

form of the complete trunk of more highly organized plants. It contains at once the tracheae that occur in the outer limits of the medulla, the laticiferous vessels of the bark, the fibres with indurated walls and the vessels found in the wood.

Let us suppose that a hand endowed with impossible dexterity were to decompose, into its organic elements, the stem of a dicotyledonous plant : for example, the trunk of an Oak-tree. Let us imagine it setting aside the fibres in the wood, and likewise the tracheae ; the large vessels of the lignous rings, and the laticiferous vessels of the bark ; and lastly, let it unite in one common mass the cells of every kind, and of whatever origin. Having thus sorted out these organs, let us imagine this hand gathering up a few of each of these kinds of organs, excepting the cells ; let us imagine it putting them

together, and making a long thread of them, and then another and another, into the hundreds and the thousands, as long as any material is left. Then let it pack these threads together, side by side, in the shape of a column ; and let it unite them all by packing between them the mass of cells still at its disposal. This done, the trunk of the Oak-tree will have been trans-

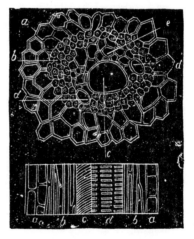

FIG. 44.—Section of a fibro-vascular bundle in a Palm-tree.

formed into the trunk of the Palm-tree. In this transformation would there be decadence or progress ? Decadence : for the dicotyledonous stem, so correct, so geometrical, with its uniform, rectilinear medullary radii, its concentric circles, perfect as though drawn with a compass, its cartical and lignous strata, in which the cell, the fibre and the vessel are methodically assembled, is assuredly superior in organization to the monocotyledonous stem, in which all is disorderly and confused. This inferiority of monocotyledonous plants, and of the Palm-trees in particular, is due, amongst other things, to the progressive advance of creation through the ages. A mysterious power, the mandatory of the eternal purposes of God, leads all living creatures onward, at a pace whose deliberation is mirrored by century piled upon century, toward a more perfect organization. The plants of bygone ages, we are told by geology, were slimy Algae, living in the waters, or incrustations of lichens on the rocks ; and almost all life was confined to this level. Life was making its first experiments ; grouping together the cell of the rudimentary plants preparatory to building up the fibre and the vessel of the tree. Ages went by, and the royal race of the acotyledons appeared on the earth ; the gigantic Horse-tails and Tree-ferns, then, as in preparation for the plants that endow their seeds with seed-leaves, the conifers emerged, still unable to construct the vessel. After the conifers the monocotyledons appeared, and in the front rank were the Palm-trees. Lastly, came the dicotyledonous trees, the Elms, the Willows, the Maples, and all the plants of superior species.

There was a time when the scrap of earth which we now call France was subdivided by three arms of the sea, occupying, more or less, the present basins of the Garonne, the Seine and the Rhone. Between these wide inlets was a country covered by great lakes and volcanoes. There, under the influence of a tropical climate, flourished a lusty vegetation, the like of which cannot be seen

to-day save in the heart of the equatorial countries. In
the selfsame spots that are to-day covered by forests of
Beech and Oak, the Palm-trees bore aloft, swaying upon
their slender trunks, the graceful crown of their enormous
leaves. In our days the virgin forests of Brazil carry us
back to the time of this bygone flora. In the shadow of
the Palm-trees elephants browsed and cats larger than
our lions roared and sought their prey. Beside the lakes
monstrous reptiles, crocodiles and tortoises, plashed
through the tepid mud with their mighty feet. Where
then were the trees of our epoch ? Where was man
himself ? Where those things are that are not yet, but
are one day to be ? They were in the creative thought
whence all things are outpoured in an unceasing flood.
The time came when the colder climate was incompatible,
in Europe, with the existence of the Palm-trees, and with
the animals that were contemporary with them. All
disappeared, and from the Divine treasury other beings
emerged, an advance, structurally speaking, upon their
predecessors. The last comers, and therefore the most
highly organized, were the plants and animals of to-day,
over whom reigns man, himself the latest born of creation.

To discover, in our latitudes, the vestiges of the ancient
race of the Palm-trees, relegated, to-day, to the tropical
zone, to sunnier skies than ours, science must search
underground ; interrogating the bowels of the earth,
where lie the trees of past ages, transformed into coal or
stone. So searching, far beneath the strata in which the
Palm-trees lie, it has exhumed another race, more ancient
still, more unfamiliar, and mingled with that of the
Conifers. This is the race of the Tree-ferns, which,
having once been the predominant vegetation of the whole
world, reaching even to the Poles, are now found, in small
numbers, in islands washed by our warmest seas. The
Ferns that are to-day found in Europe are humble plants,

a yard in height at most, and often a few inches only. Their stem is reduced to a mere stump, crawling underground, but in the islands of the Equatorial seas, Ferns become trees whose bearing may be compared with that of the Palms. Their stem springs at once to a height of twenty to thirty feet, and is crowned with a great bunch of leaves of graceful outline. At the centre of the bunch the youngest leaves are rolled up crozier-wise. This is a characteristic feature of all Ferns.

Amidst the acotyledonous plants, the great majority of which are composed solely of cells, Ferns offer a remark-

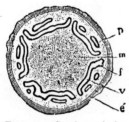

able exception, in their lignous structure, the employment of the fibre and the vessel, and their tree-like formation. We must look to find, in these representatives of the first lignous vegetation to appear on the earth, a special structure. And in sober truth, the stem of a Tree-fern is

FIG. 45.—Section of the stem of a Tree-Fern.

about as unlike the usual organization of the plant as anything the vegetable kingdom could show us. Here is the section of such a stem. In the midst of a cellular mass *m*, constituting the greater part of the stem, are lignous bundles, fantastically curved, making patterns of white edged with black. The white area, *v*, of these bundles consists of a mass of tubes ; the black portion consists of layers of fibres impregnated with a blackish substance. At *p* we see more cellular tissue, communicating, here and there, through breaches in the irregular lignous zone, with the cellular tissue of the central portion. Lastly, *e* is a hard envelope, replacing the bark. It is made up of a basis of old leaves, which have fallen to the ground as the stem has grown. In the stems of the Ferns familiar in some parts of Europe something may be seen of this peculiar structure. For example, the stem of the species of Bracken so often observed, with its bundles of blackish, lignous filaments. Thus the stem of our

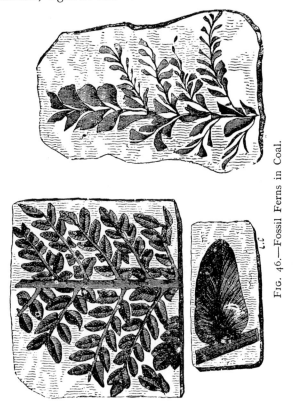

FIG. 46.—Fossil Ferns in Coal.

common Bracken reproduces, in its bundles of blackish, lignous tissue, the rather sketchy design of a two-headed, heraldic eagle, as though to blazon the nobility of its ancient race.

Long before the Palm-trees, the Tree-ferns in particular covered certain tracts of land which, enlarged by the retreating seas, were one day to be the land of Europe. They constituted the greater part of the gloomy forests that were never enlivened by the songs of birds, nor resounded to the trample of the quadruped. As yet the dry land had no inhabitants ; but the sea alone nourished, above and beneath its waves, a population of monsters, half fish and half reptiles, whose flanks were covered with plates of enamel instead of with spangles. The atmosphere must have been unbreathable, for it contained, in suspension, in the state of poisonous gas, the enormous mass of carbon which has since become coal. But the Tree-ferns, like other plants of their day, set to work in order to cleanse it and to render the solid earth habitable. They subtracted the world's carbon from the air, storing it in their leaves and stems ; then, falling into decay, they made room for others, and these yet again for others, which unremittingly pursued, in the silence of the woods, their noble task of atmospheric salubrity. The purification of the atmosphere was at last accomplished, and the Tree-ferns died. Their remains, buried underground, have in course of time become coal-measures, in which leaves and stems, wonderfully preserved as to form, are to-day to be found in abundance, and record, in their archives, the history of this ancient vegetation, which has given us an atmosphere that we can breathe, and has stored up for us, in the bowels of the earth, those strata of coal which are the wealth of nations.

STRUCTURE OF THE MONOCOTYLEDONOUS STEM—THE CARBONIFEROUS PERIOD.

(From *La Terre avant l'Homme*. P. RAMBAUD. Delagrave.)

To face p. 94.

CHAPTER X

THE ROOT

*The structure of the root—Absence of leaves and buds—Mode of extension—
Radicles—The Beard—Direction. An experiment of Duhamel's—
Direction of the root Mistletoe—Pivoted root—Fasciculated root—
Dimensions of the root—Rest harrow—Lucerne—The use of deep
roots in agriculture—Rotation of crops—How a tap-root is transformed
into a spreading root.*

THE structure of the root hardly differs from that of the stem ; it consists of the same elementary organs—cells, fibres and tubes—arranged in a precisely similar order of precedence. Thus, in plants with a single cotyledon the root comprises bundles of fibres, and of vessels submerged in a homogeneous cellular mass ; while in plants with two cotyledons it consists of a lignous portion and a cortical portion, in which we shall find again the different divisions of the stem, the concentric rings and medullary radii corresponding with the wood, while corresponding with the bark we have the liber, the cellular stratum, the suberose stratum, and lastly, the epidermis. These two portions increase in thickness by annual layers, which are mutually superimposed precisely as in the stem.

The most definite of its individual characteristics consists in the absence of buds and leaves. Never, save in the most exceptional circumstances, does the root put forth buds ; never does it cover itself with leaves, not even with the meagre scales which are, after all, leaves transformed with a view to special functions.

Another very characteristic difference is furnished by
the mode of extension. Throughout its length, the stem
shares in all increases of length. If we make a series of
marks upon its surface we perceive, after the lapse of a
certain time, that the distance between any two marks
has increased in the same degree at the base of the stem
as half-way up or at the top. The root, on the other hand,
adds to its length only at its extremity. This may be
verified by observing that the marks made upon its
surface preserve their respective distances unaltered, with
the exception of the extreme end, which gradually but
steadily increases its distance from the tap-root. The
end of the root is therefore in a permanent state of growth
and its tissues always young, exclusively cellular, and
therefore especially calculated to imbibe the liquids with
which the soil is impregnated, very much as a fine sponge
would do. As a sort of comment on this faculty of
absorption, the evergrowing tips of the roots, are known
by the name of *spongiole*. Spongioles will be found on
the terminal tips of the radicles, that is, the last subdivisions of the root, subdivisions whose total sum is
sometimes known as the beard of the root, because of
its vague resemblance to a tangled growth of hair.

The stem and the root display tendencies diametrically
opposite in character : the stem demands light and the
root demands darkness. In order to reach the light of
day, the stem, when unable to stand erect or climb unaided,
makes use of a whole siege-train of devices : tendrils,
suckers, hooks and levers. It throws itself upon neighbouring stems, and embraces them with its spiral fingers ;
if need be it stifles them in its coils. The root seeks
subterranean darkness ; and nothing has the power to
deter it from its purpose. In default of vegetable mould
it will burrow through clay or volcanic rock, or it will
force its way through stony soil or disappear into the

crevices of a fissured rock. These contrary tendencies reveal themselves from the very first.

Let us consider a seed germinating in the ground. Hardly has it emerged from its vegetable egg, but the little plant unhesitatingly directs its root downwards in order to plunge it into the soil, while the stem is pointed upwards in order to lead it to the light of day. Now alter the position of your seed ; turn it upside down, the root on top, the stem beneath. The root and the stem of the infant plant turn about until they are twisted into the form of a fish-hook, until the stem is once more pointing upwards and the root downwards. You may repeat the experiment, reversing the seed a second time, but again your move will be checkmated ; root and stem will turn about the second time, each pointing in the proper direction. They seem to be in the grip of an invincible instinct. In spite of all the difficulties which you may put in their way they will, respectively, continue to ascend and descend, and will die rather than abandon their intentions. Of the various experiments which may be made in this connection, here is one of a very striking nature, which was first performed by Duhamel, to whom we owe many valuable investigations of plant life. An acorn is sown in a vertical tube, full of earth. The seed germinates, and, in accordance with the laws of plant life, the young Oak-tree sends its root downwards and its stem upwards. The tube is then reversed, so that up becomes down, and down up. Promptly the tiny root makes a right-about turn ; the tiny stem does the like, and each once more resumes the direction in accordance with its intentions. As often as the tube is reversed, so often do the two opposite extremities of the plant face about and change their direction, thereby giving proof of the indomitable energy that urges the root to burrow downwards and the stem to rise. In short, during the

stubborn struggle to resume its direction despite the
experimenter's interference, the root, if the tube is of
glass, will always turn to the dark side, while the stem
will always turn to that side of the tube exposed to the
light of day.   Light and an upward urge for the shoot ;
darkness and a downward urge for the root : such is the
law.

In this twofold tendency toward the daylight and the
earth is there some vague perception in the plant ; are the
root and the stem capable of seeking and choosing : or
rather, do we not here behold in action that mysterious
power, which, designed, as it is, for the protection of
life, impels the humblest creature blindly and without
prevision to perform actions of incomparable wisdom ?
In the animals we call it instinct.   The newly born
mammifer, without acquired experience, without previous
attempts, without feeling its way, fastens on to the
teat that gives it life ; and so the plant, by an essential
instinct, persistently thrusts its root into the earth, at
whose prodigious bosom all vegetable life must drink,
and lifts its stem above the ground that its leaves may
unfold in the open air.

The vertical direction is followed by the great majority
of plants ; nevertheless, there are those that are exceptional, but thereby they do but confirm the general law,
according to which every vegetable organism plunges its
root into the substance from which it must derive its
food and thrusts its stem in the opposite direction.   This
category includes a certain number of parasitic plants,
the best known of which is the Mistletoe.

The Mistletoe lives on the sap of various trees ; in
especial, on the Almond-tree, the Apple-tree and more
rarely the Oak-tree.   This is the plant that our fathers
were wont to venerate in the forests of ancient Gaul ;
the plant that the Druids, with great pomp, used to cut

from the Oak-trees with a golden sickle. It plunges its root into the wood of the fostering branch, uniting with it thoroughly, and thenceforth it lives upon the sap of the tree. Its fruit is a white berry full of a viscous juice. The Thrushes, which are very fond of it, sometimes carry away its seed, sticking to their feet or their beaks. Such a bird, we may imagine, alights on an Apple-tree, its feet sticky with the juice of the Mistletoe-berry. It rubs its feet, to clean them, on the bough, and there you have the seed of the parasitic plant glued to the Apple-tree, some-times to the upper surface of the bough, sometimes to its side or even underneath it, according to the way in which the bird cleaned its feet. Presently the seed germinates, and without the least hesitation it turns its root against the branch, in order to sink it into the wood, downwards if it is on the top of the bough, sideways if it is glued to the side. As for the stem, it follows precisely the reverse direction.

Here the evidence is complete : the young plant behaves as though it were able to see and choose ; as though it were able to perceive the branch into which its root must be plunged and the air into which the stem must grow. There is, therefore, in plants, a shadowy vestige of the instinct existing in animals. By means which doubtless will forever remain the secret of that inevitable Power that watches over the destinies of creation, the plant is able to discern the environment in which it is destined to live. Certain plants, destined to live as parasites in a position wholly fortuitous, change the direction of their stem and root according to the manner in which the seed is situated at the moment of germination. Other plants, much more numerous, and destined to live with their roots in the ground, invariably turn the root down-wards and the stem upwards ; and in obeying this inflexible tendency they are assured of finding the conditions necessary to their existence. The stem in rising and the root in sinking will find, in the one case air and light, in the other moisture and obscurity.

Generally speaking, the root is that part of the plant which moves downwards, and the stem, the part that climbs upward. The imaginary line, imaginary and somewhat vague, at which the plant ceases to be stem and becomes root, is known as the collar.

The root assumes various forms, which may be referred to two fundamental types. In some cases it consists of a central body or *tap-root*, which throws off ramifications as it plunges deeper into the soil. The plant is then said to be tap-rooted. This form is peculiar to the dicotyledons. Sometimes it comprises a cluster, a bundle of parts, undivided or full of ramifications, and these parts, starting from the same level, are more or less equal in importance. Its resemblance to a cluster or bundle has earned it the name of *fasciculated* root. This form of root belongs to the monocotyledons ; thus, even in the dark realm of the soil, plants with two cotyledons and plants with one cotyledon have adopted different arrangements of their parts. There are, however, many exceptions to this law. Certain dicotyledonous plants— the Melon, for example—lose the tap-root which was theirs on germination and replace it by a fasciculated root ; others, belonging to the monocotyledonous plants, the Lily and the Tulip for example, have likewise a tap-root to begin with, which later on becomes fasciculated.

As a general thing the development of the root is in proportion to that of the stem. Thus, the Oak, the Elm, the Maple and the Beech, and all our large forest trees, have sturdy, deep-delving roots, in order to sustain their enormous mass of boughs and to enable them to stand fast against the wind. Yet there are humble plants whose root is out of all proportion to the rest of the organism, plants which display a vigorous tap-root, such as we shall not find in many other plants far more fully developed as regards their aerial portion. Such are the Mallow, the Carrot and the Radish. Lucerne supports its meagre cluster of stems with a root that sinks to a depth of six to ten feet. Rest-harrow, a weed common in our meadows, with a spindly stem only ten or twelve inches in height, takes hold of the ground by roots so long and tenacious as to bring the farmer's team to a standstill, which has earned it the name by which it is commonly known.

An agricultural operation of first importance is at least in part dependent on the excessive development of certain roots. The plant is a laboratory in which life converts into alimentary substances the filth of our dunghills. A cartload of manure becomes, at the will of the farmer, by virtue of passing through this or that plant, fruit or vegetables or corn—that is, bread. This filth, this manure, is therefore a thing of great value, which nothing could replace, which must be exploited to the last fragment ; for we all depend on it for our food. Enriched by this manure, the soil produces, let us say, the first crop of Wheat. But the Wheat, with its poor little bunch of roots, has exploited the fertilizing principles only of the surface layer of the soil, leaving intact those which the rain has dissolved and washed into the deeper strata. It is true that it has fulfilled its special function with admirable completeness ; it has cleared the table, converting into grain all the manure in the layer of soil which its roots were able to reach ; so much so, that if we were again to sow the land with Wheat, we should not obtain any harvest. As regards the surface the soil is therefore exhausted ; but the deeper strata are still richly impregnated. Well ! what shall we entrust with the exploitation of the deeper strata, in order to obtain

any nutriment that may remain there ?   Not Barley, nor
Oats, nor Rye, whose small clustering roots would find
nothing to glean, were they to follow Wheat, from the
topmost layer of the soil.   Lucerne is the plant that will
plunge its roots as thick as a man's finger, to a depth of
three, six, or ten feet and more, if need be, winning back
the fertilizer in the shape of forage, which, with the help of
the animal whose food it will become, will be transformed
into butcher's meat, dairy produce and wool, or, at the
very least, labour.   This succession of two or more plants
which derive the greatest possible advantage from a
previously prepared soil is known to farmers as the
rotation of crops.

The deep root that is so well adapted to the exploitation
of the deeper strata of the soil might under other circumstances be embarrassing.   Let us suppose that a tree has
to be transplanted.   Its long tap-root is likely to make the
operation difficult and hazardous.   To begin with, it
would be necessary to dig deep into the ground in order
to extract its root, and again in order to transplant it ;
further, the greatest care must be taken not to damage
the root, since it is the only one, and if it does not recover
from transplantation the tree is bound to die.   Now
matters would be better if only the tree had fasciculated
roots, which would not burrow very far underground ;
it could then be uprooted without difficulty ; and if a
few roots were destroyed, enough would be left intact
to insure the success of the transplantation.

Such a result can be obtained ; it is quite easy to
deprive the tree of its tap-root, and to compel it to adopt,
not a regular bundle of roots of equal length, such as we
find among the monocotyledons, but a root much subdivided and of no great length, which offers the advantages
of the fasciculated root although it differs from it in
form.   Thus, in nurseries of young Oak-trees, where the

young trees are kept ten years or longer before being transplanted, we find that two years after the acorns are sown, the spade is driven deep into the soil in order to cut through the principal root, which would otherwise have become a sturdy tap-root. The stump which is then left throws off ramifications in the horizontal plane, but does not burrow any deeper. Or again, the soil of the nursery may, at a certain depth, be paved with tiles. Until the tap-root of the sapling has reached this barrier it may add to its length, but is, having reached it, necessarily compelled to cease its downward growth, and to throw off lateral ramifications.

CHAPTER XI

ADVENTIVE ROOTS

The normal root and adventive roots—Coltsfoot—Ivy. Vanilla—Pandanus and Coco-Palm—The Indian Fig—A contemporary of the elephants of Porus—Propagation by cuttings—The use of the glass bell-jar in propagation by cuttings—Species that best lend themselves to this operation—Propagation by layering—The Carnation—The layering of Vines—Layering with the assistance of a broken jug or a leaden cone—Gradual weaning—Why we earth up Maize, Madder and Liquorice.

THE root which we have just been considering is the primordial, original root which every plant possesses on issuing from its seed ; it appears, indeed, directly the seed germinates. But many vegetables have other roots, which develop at various points along the stem, replacing the original root when the latter has perished, or at least coming to its assistance if it should survive. They are known as adventive roots. Their function is one of the greatest importance, above all in certain horticultural operations of which I shall presently tell you. For the moment, if merely to show how well the plant contrives to adapt itself to circumstances, we will consider a few instances of adventive roots.

Coltsfoot is a weed constantly occurring on cultivated soil, especially on damp, clayey soil. Its yellow flowers bloom very early in spring, long before its leaves appear ; the leaves themselves are green on their upper surface, but white and fluffy underneath. The stem is sub-terranean, constantly dying away at its older extremity, while constantly prolonged at its other end, by means of

fresh buds. This annual segment of a stem, the contin-
uation of an earlier segment, now rotted away, sends
forth adventive roots which replace the primordial root,
which has long since disappeared.

In order to fasten itself upon the bark of trees, and the
roughened surface
of rocks and walls,
Ivy is provided, so
to speak, on that
side only of the
stem which is in
contact with the
supporting surface,
with an arrange-
ment of climbing-
irons set close as
the bristles of a
scrubbing - b r u s h,
and in appearance
not unlike short
r o o t s. However,
they are not roots,
or at least, they do
not do the work of
roots. They are
climbing gear, not
suction-pipes; they
enable the plant to
climb perpendicular walls. But if a favourable oppor-
tunity occurs the climbing-irons of the Ivy become
emergency roots which plunge into the soil and find
food for the plant. This fact it is easy to verify by
examining the ramifications of Ivy wherever we find
it sprawling over the ground.

FIG. 47.—Coltsfoot.

In the tropical forests of South America there is a plant

with a slender stem, remarkable for the pleasant flavour
of its fruits, the Vanilla vine, which is found living as a
parasite on some old, rotting tree-trunk.   Thence, like a
fine network of cords covered with fleshy leaves of a mossy
green, it leaps from tree to tree, in order to escape from
the dense shadow of the forest to the light that bathes

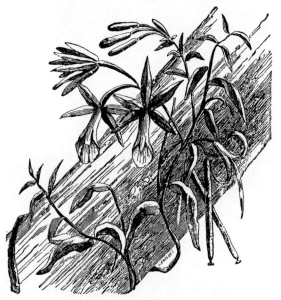

Fig. 48.—Vanilla.

the tree-tops. The distances which it is thus able to
cover, climbing upwards, flinging itself abroad, and again
climbing, finally become so great that the nourishment
absorbed by roots of the ordinary type would find it
difficult to reach the buds. The Vanilla, accordingly,
sends forth a vast number of adventive roots from its
stem and its ramifications. Some of these fasten upon
the bark of neighbouring trees, deriving nourishment
from the mould that has collected in the hollow of some
half-healed wound ; but most of them fall downwards

from the tops of the tall forest trees, hanging loosely in the moist atmosphere of the forest. In this warm atmosphere, always saturated with water-vapour, they find an amount of extra nourishment that is of the greatest value to the plant.

On the islands built by the Coral "insects," in the tropical seas, which have but recently emerged from the waves, there grows a tree which in the first place breaks up their calcareous soil, preparing it for the growth of other plants, and finally rendering it habitable. This is the Pandanus or Vacoua, which shares its benevolent activities with the Coco-Palm; these two trees are the first colonists of the coral island. Their seeds, padded with fibre and protected by strong hard shells, which pro-

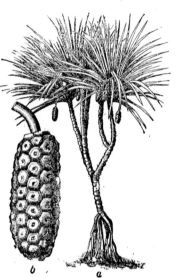

FIG. 49.—Pandanus: a, the tree; b, the fruit.

tect them from the action of salt water, drift thither from neighbouring archipelagos and germinate on these newly created islands, whose soil, consisting wholly of finely divided Coral, would be unfitted for any other form of vegetation. There the two cultivators set to work, their leaves floating in the air and their roots bathed by the salt waves. From this time forward the island is habitable; for man, if he appears there, will find on the Coral-reef food, and materials with which he can build a hut and weave a skirt or petticoat. Now, this soil of finely divided Coral, saturated with saline infiltrations, offers but little food and less support to house or tree. How are these trees to hold out against the squalls that sweep the level surface of the islands and set the breakers thundering on the barrier-reefs ?   How are they to gather the few particles of food that lie hidden in a soil that consists almost wholly of lime ?   The difficulty is over-come by the provision of additional roots.   The trunk of the Pandanus gives off, at different levels, a number of stout adventive roots, which, although aerial in their upper portions, burrow, with their tips, amidst the broken fragments of Coral, thereby doing as much as the normal roots to support the tree and to feed it.   It is not unusual to see the Pandanus lifted high above the ground, on the top of a stout scaffolding consisting of adventive roots. Its fellow-cultivator, the Coco-Palm, without resorting to this curious scaffolding of roots, partly aerial and partly subterranean, none the less plunges into the crevices of the Coral numbers of adventive roots, like so many stout cables.

Certain Fig-trees, peculiar to India and the adjacent countries, have a very remarkable manner of supporting their enormous horizontal spread of branches and of placing them in communication with the soil.   From the principal branches slender columns of lignous tissue hang downwards, first swinging in the air like so many great ropes, then reaching the ground and burrowing into it, finally becoming so many pillars upholding the common edifice.   Year after year the area covered by the spreading branches of the tree grows greater ; the pillars necessary to support them fall downwards and bury themselves in the ground, until finally the Fig-tree becomes a little forest, a dense forest, consisting of one sole tree, supported by hundreds, nay, thousands, of living props.   Yet these props, which fall, straight as a plumb-line, from the branches, are still merely adventive roots, but they are strong and sturdy and sometimes of enormous size, acquiring, as they grow older, the appearance of ordinary tree-trunks. There is in India, on the banks of the Nerbudda, a Fig-tree which is in itself a very forest, whose stupendous growth of branches is supported by three thousand three hundred and fifty living pillars, consisting of adventive roots. Think of three thousand three hundred and fifty trees of different sizes, three hundred and fifty, with trunks of enormous girth, being surrounded by three thousand of lesser dimensions ; reflect that all these trees are connected by their branches, form one stupendous structure, and we may obtain some vague idea of this colossal Fig-tree, which could shelter an army of seven thousand men beneath its foliage, while the area covered by this vast assembly of trunks is no less than two hundred yards in diameter. According to tradition, Alexander the Great saw this Fig-tree, when, yielding to the complaints of his soldiers, he called a halt, on the banks of the Indus, to his extravagant expedition. What can be the age of this veteran of the vegetable kingdom, which saw the phalanxes of Alexander contending against the elephants of Porus ?

*   *   *   *   *

The twig, which has itself developed from a bud, is an individual of the vegetable community ; it is a shoot of a younger generation, implanted in the mother stem instead of in the ground. Being severed from the community, it can, by means of adventive roots, draw its nourishment directly from the soil, develop roots of its own and live an independent life. This faculty is the foundation of two horticultural operations of great importance : the multiplication of plants by *slips* or *cuttings* and by *layering*.

In propagating plants by means of slips or cuttings a branch is detached from the parent plant and is placed in circumstances which will enable it to develop adventive roots. The detached branch is known as the slip or cutting, or the *shoot* when the cutting is made from one of those species of trees that live beside the water : Poplars, Willows, etc. The amputated branch is planted in a cool, shady spot, where evaporation is slow and the temperature mild. The shelter of a glass bell-jar is often necessary, in order that the surrounding atmosphere may be maintained in a favourable state of humidity, and the cutting prevented from withering before it has time to put forth the roots which would enable it to make good its losses. For greater certainty, if the branch is very thickly leaved, the greater part of the leaves nearer the root of the shoot is removed in order as far as possible to reduce the evaporating surfaces, without injury to the vitality of the plant, which resides more especially in the upper portion. But in many cases these precautions are needless. Thus, in order to multiply the Vine, the Willow, the Poplar, one need do no more than thrust the severed cutting into the ground. In any case, the end of the branch, if thrust into damp soil, will presently begin to put forth adventive roots, and thenceforth the branch will suffice to itself and live as an independent plant.

Vegetables whose wood is soft, with tissues bursting with sap, are those that lend themselves most readily to propagation by slips or cuttings ; such are the Willow, whose wood is so soft, and the Pelargonium, an habitual ornament of our flower-beds, whose stem consists chiefly of fleshy, cellular tissue. Those plants whose wood is hard and compact are, on the contrary, exceedingly difficult, if not impossible, to multiply by means of cuttings. Thus, the raising of saplings from cuttings would inevitably fail in the case of the Oak, Box, and a number of other species with close-packed lignous tissue.

Certain plants, amongst which is the Carnation, put forth, at the foot of the parent stem, straight, flexible ramifications which may produce as many new plants. These runners are planted out by forcing them to describe a sudden angle, which is fixed in the soil by means of a wooden peg ; the end is then compelled to stand upright, its vertical position being maintained by means of a supporting stick. Sooner or later the buried elbow puts forth adventive roots ; but until then the mother plant nourishes the offshoot. When the buried portions have produced a sufficient number of adventive roots, all the ramifications between the parent plant and the buried portion of the runner are cut through. Each of these runners, which may now be planted out, is henceforth a distinct vegetable.

This operation is known as *layering*, and the various plants detached from the original plant are known as *layers*. Success is more likely to follow this process than that of propagation by means of slips or cuttings, which, without any sort of preparation, suddenly deprive the plant of the nourishment furnished by the stem, compelling it then and there to suffice to itself. From all times layering has been employed in propagating the Vine.

There are other plants, for example, the Oleander, that do not display sufficient flexibility in their limbs to lend themselves to layering in the manner thus described ; the branch would break were we to attempt to bend it so that it might be fastened down to the ground. Sometimes, too, the branches are sprung too high for such treatment. In such cases a jug or crock with its side partly broken away, or a little cone of sheet lead, is fastened about a suitable twig—that is, a twig growing in such a position that it can be laid along the axis of the crock or cone. The latter is then filled with mould or moss, which is kept moist by frequent watering. Under such conditions adventive roots will sooner or later make their appearance. The twig is now subjected to a sort of weaning process—that is to say, the twig is partially cut through between the leaden cone and the parent stem, and the cut is made a little deeper day by day.

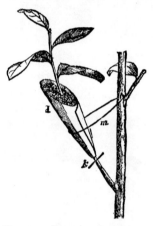

FIG. 50.—Layering by means of a leaden cone.

The object of this procedure is gradually to accustom the plant to dispense with the aid of the parent plant and to lead an independent existence. In the end a snip of the shears completes the work of separation. This gradual weaning is equally useful in the case of layers pinned to the ground, and greatly increases their chances of success.

In provoking the formation of adventive roots the gardener is not always aiming at the multiplication of the plant; sometimes he wants to obtain a number of roots, either to tie the plant more firmly to the ground or to obtain a more abundant harvest. The most effective means of achieving this result is to heap up the soil around the base of the trunk. This is known as *earthing* or *banking* up. The buried portion is soon covered with roots. Maize, to take an example, is, if left to itself, too feebly rooted to resist violent wind or rain, which would beat it to the ground. In order to give it a stronger support the farmer " earths up " his Maize. Bundles of adventive roots are formed in the earth heaped up at the base of the trunk, giving the plant a firm hold upon the soil. Madder contains in its roots a dye-stuff of great value, alizarine. It is therefore in the farmers' interest to induce the plant to develop its roots to the utmost. With this purpose in view the plant is earthed up until it is half buried. Liquorice also is earthed up, in order to increase the number of its roots.

9

CHAPTER XII

VARIOUS FORMATIONS OF THE STEM OR TRUNK

Importance of the longitudinal arrangement of the fibres—The Trunk—The Stipe—The Culm or Haulm—Resistance of hollow formations of circular section to rupture—Tubular bridges—Feathers and the longer bones of animals—Remarkable structure of Wheat-straw—Bamboo— In monocotyledonous stems the exterior is harder than the interior —Stems of climbing plants—Lianas—Volubile stems—Stolons— Colonies of the Strawberry and the Violet—Stems of Creepers—The Moneywort—Vegetation of the Polar Regions—Rhizomes of the Sedges and the Gramineous plants—Dunes—The stabilization of dunes—The stems of the Cactuses.

THERE is not much variety to be observed in the structure of the stem. We have already described what we might call the three fundamental orders of vegetable architecture: the order of the dicotyledonous trees, which build a series of lignous sheaths or cylinders, fitting one inside another; the order of the Palm-trees, which distribute a scaffolding of fibrous bundles more or less at random throughout a cellular trunk; and the order of the Tree-Ferns, which surround the cellular column of the trunk by a fantastically sinuous rampart of fibres and vessels.

In these three orders the fibres and vessels are methodically arranged parallel with the axis of the stem, but never cutting across it. The reason for this is obvious. Let us imagine a bundle of threads, all cemented together. You would find it easy to divide the bundle along the line of the fibres; you would have to overcome only the adhesive powers of the threads. But in order to break it across its axis it would be necessary to snap through the threads, not merely to separate them, so that a violent effort would be necessary. Similarly, on account of the longitudinal arrangement of its lignous bundles, the stem may be split lengthwise without much difficulty, while it offers a stubborn resistance to divide it across its grain, which only the sharp edge of the woodman's axe is able to overcome. The force exerted by a wedge driven into the wood by a sledgehammer will readily split it lengthwise but is powerless to bisect the trunk. The extraordinary value of this arrangement of the fibres is very evident. In order to resist the wind, which would otherwise snap the trunk in two, the stem subordinates everything to its power of transversal resistance ; attributing only a secondary importance to its power of longitudinal resistance, which is less seriously endangered. By arranging its lignous bundles along the line of its axis the plant acquires pliability, elasticity, and, at the same time, resistance to the assaults of the wind ; it bends, but does not break.

Although, as regards their internal structure, the stems may be referred to a small number of types ; although they resemble one another in the arrangement of their fibres and their vessels regarded as the conditions of mechanical strength, they present a very great variety in their external configuration. We use the word *trunk* for the stem of the Oak, the Beech, the Lime, the Pine, and the dicotyledonous trees in general. Impressive in appearance and robustly built, the trunk is peculiar to the giants of the vegetable world. In the ample shade cast by its gnarled branches, one characteristic above al will strike you : namely, the serene majesty of strength. The trunk gradually decreases in diameter from the base upwards, and the upper portion is divided into boughs, branches and twigs. It also increases in diameter by the yearly formation of a layer of woody tissue, super-imposed on those deposited in previous years.

In the case of herbaceous plants, and those lignous plants which, by reason of their small dimensions, do not deserve the name of tree, we employ the word *stem*. The lignous plant is known as a *bush*, when the stem, ramifying almost at the level of the soil, grows to a height which may vary from three or four feet to ten or fifteen. Its buds are enveloped in protective scales, as in the case of trees ; and its shoots become lignous to the tip. Such are the Lilac and the Privet, for example. A *shrub* is a lignous plant which begins to ramify at its base and rarely exceeds three or four feet in height. Its buds do not possess a scaly envelope ; the tips of its shoots remain herbaceous and are destroyed each year by the winter's cold. To this category belong Lavender, Thyme, etc.

FIG. 51.—Stipe of a Palm-tree.

Stipe is the name given to the stem of the Palm-trees and Tree-ferns. It is a graceful pillar, slender and elastic, almost equal in diameter throughout its length, and crowned by a great bunch of leaves, in the centre of which is a large terminal bud. This bud is unique ;

if it dies, the Palm-tree, being decapitated, must also die. The stipe increases in length but never ramifies. The term *stalk* is reserved for the hollow stem of the Gramineous plants—that is, the Cereals, the Reeds, the Bamboos, and the Grasses, including a thousand species of herb or weed, such as form the carpet covering the earth : the prairies, pastures, meadows and lawns.

Let us for a moment consider the wonderful skill with which this stalk is constructed. And in order to consider it we must have some acquaintance with the mechanical theorem which explains its efficiency. Let us suppose that we have at our disposal ten pounds' weight of iron, neither more nor less, and we have to fashion this iron into a stem or prop three feet in length and endowed with the greatest possible powers of resistance to shearing stress. Now, to begin with, what section are we to give this metallic stem or prop ? Shall we make it triangular, circular or square ? Scientific calculation will tell us that in order to give it the greatest strength we must give it a circular section. So much we know ; and now, is the stem to be solid or hollow ? Again calculation will tell us that we must make it hollow, for only then will it offer the greatest possible resistance to fracture by bending. The above-mentioned mechanical theorem may therefore be expressed as follows : A given quantity of material will offer the greatest resistance to fracture if given a hollow and circular cross-section.

Here is one of the most impressive applications, if not of the circular form, for that is not always possible, at least of the hollow cross-section : the tubular bridges, a creation of modern industry due to the genius of George Stephenson, the immortal inventor of the steam loco-motive. These bridges are rectangular tubes, gigantic girders of riveted iron plates, through which the trains are run on certain railways when a river has to be crossed.

One of the most celebrated bridges of this type, the Britannia Bridge, over the Menai Straits, crosses a channel some 1,400 feet in width. The bridge consists of two tubular girders, each weighing between five and six thousand tons, to carry the permanent way across the Straits, the trains passing through these gigantic girders. Three piers, some 460 feet from one another, carry the tubes from bank to bank at a height of 104 feet above the level of high tide. What is the power that upholds these monstrous girders, and, despite such enormous spans, keeps them from bending when the trains go thundering through them ?   It is the strength of the tubular form, the strength of the hollow structure. Life, even more ingenious than Stephenson, frequently makes use of the circular tubular form in order to obtain structures of great strength with a great economy of material. Consider the wings of the bird, that beat the air as it flies. The pinions of these aerial oars must be extremely light, lest they should impede the bird's flight by excessive weight ; they must also be extremely strong, especially at the point of their insertion in the flesh of the wing, in order that the small support to be obtained from the air may be balanced by the force of the stroke of the bird's wing ; they must also be able to endure sudden and repeated stresses. These objects are attained in a wonderful degree by the circular, hollow cross-section of the quills.

All the long bones of the animal organism—the bones of the legs, wings and feet—the bones which enable the animal to walk, run, fly, climb, swim, and grip its prey, are likewise built in accordance with the same principles. In order that they might be at once light and firm, economical in structure, yet rigid, they have adopted the hollow, circular cross-section.

Wheat, the precious seed that gives us bread, carries

its heavy ear at the tip of a stalk long enough to save the ripe grain from contact with the soil, yet slender enough to grow in dense clumps without incommoding its neighbours ; rigid enough to sustain the weight of the ear, and elastic enough to bow before the wind without fear of breaking. This combination of valuable qualities results from the circular, hollow cross-section of the stalk. Moreover, the stalk is further provided, externally, with knots that add to its strength ; and these knots put forth leaves, the bases of which form a sort of sheath which envelops the stem and adds still further to its strength. All these minute precautions are insufficient ; it is impregnated with one of the hardest and most incorruptible of mineral substances, silicon, the material of which the ordinary pebble consists. It would be impossible to imagine a more cleverly devised structure. See how easily the ear of Wheat, heavy-laden with ripe grain, is borne aloft by the straw, though this last is so slender that without a special structure it would bend beneath its own weight ; consider how gracefully the stalks of a field of ripe corn bow before the wind ; consider their pliancy, their elasticity ; reflect how the golden harvest rises and falls like the waves of the sea. From its golden waves, sprinkled here and there with blood-red Poppies and Corn-flowers, a gentle whisper rises, a whisper that tells us of an invisible Stephenson, who, outstripping the calculations of our engineers, gives a round, hollow stem to corn, round, hollow bones to animals, and the round, hollow pinion to the bird.

A hollow stem, provided at intervals with knots that subdivide the general cavity, and leaves springing from these knots, whose base forms a kind of sheath, and tissues impregnated with silicon : such are the general characteristics of the *culm* or *haulm*. In some tropical Gramineous plants the silicon is so abundant that the culm gives off sparks beneath the knife like flint beneath the steel. Certain Bamboos, enormous Gramineous growths found in the tropics, have stems of such large diameter that each segment—that is, the portion between two adjacent knots—constitutes a very useful little barrel or keg, all of a single piece, of the greatest value for carrying or storing liquids.

FIG. 52.—A forest of Bamboos.

The advanced mechanics displayed in the structure of the culm of the Gramineous plants is exemplified likewise, as regards their more fundamental characteristics, in the stems of all the monocotyledonous plants, reinforcing the inner portions of the stem without in any way concentrating upon its centre or axis, but rather in accordance with the mathematical principle of the hollow tube. It is true that the stem is no longer fortified by knots or reinforced by silicon ; it is, however, rendered harder, as regards its external parts, by the accumulation of lignous fibres, while the centre of the stem is sometimes hollow and sometimes occupied by cellular tissue which offers but little resistance to breaking or crushing stresses. We found this structure in the

Palm-tree, and we shall find it again, under various modifications, in all the monocotyledonous plants. The larger acotyledonous plants, the Tree-ferns, exemplify the same principle. With them the irregular lignous zone is situated near the circumference, while the interior of the stem consists of tissue, offering but little resistance, which consists of cells alone. To sum up : to strengthen the outside of the stem and to neglect the centre is the invariable law regarding those plants that do not possess the massive structure of the dicotyledonous stem ; which are obliged, with a strictly limited amount of lignous material, to acquire a sufficient power of resistance to rupture by flexion : a law inspired by the strictest logic, in conformity with the principles of the most advanced mechanics.

One of the chief necessities of the stem is to grow upwards, that it may outspread its foliage to the light of day. The majority of plants are able to rise by their own efforts, but there are some that cannot do so without assistance. Some, known as *sarmentous* stems, depend upon their neighbours ; for example, the lianas, creeping from branch to branch, in the forests of South America, bind the trees of the forests together by an inextricable network of long festoons and hanging cords, which enable the monkeys and the tiger-cats to climb swiftly to the tops of the highest trees, passing from one tree to another without touching the ground, and crossing the rivers as though by so many suspension-bridges. In their unbridled ascent towards the light some of these lianas make use of methods of climbing which are decidedly prejudicial to the trees from which they obtain support. One of these, the deadly liana of the Brazilian forests, flattens its stem and curls up the edges until its section is semicircular, as by such means it is enabled more closely to embrace its support ; it then puts forth, to the right and the left, two strong lignous outgrowths, which meet one another, unite, and embrace the tree as though with a pair of arms. A little higher up, as the liana pushes upwards, a second ligature is made fast about the trunk. These ligatures are repeated at intervals, until eventually the tree is surrounded from base to summit by the lignous fetters of its guest. By this time the sarmentous stem has completed its climbing

FIG. 53.—The virgin forest of South America.

and the two plants, one embracing and one embraced, mingle their topmost leaves together. By this time they resemble a single tree with two forms of foliage, two kinds of fruits and flowers. But if the tree is dicotyledonous the bonds of the liana will soon become so many strangling nooses ; and the trunk thus embraced, being no longer able to expand, withers away and dies. For a time the liana will remain erect, supported by the lifeless tree ; but the latter will soon decay, when the deadly liana and its strangled victim will fall, never again to rise, into the mire of the forest floor.

The Vine, displaying its wealth of foliage on a pergola or trellised wall, will give us some idea of the lianas of the tropics. In the South of France it is by no means unusual to see a Vine embracing with its runners the boughs of a Fig-tree, mingling its fruit and foliage with the fruit and foliage of its host. In the matter of equipment for climbing, the Vine employs tendrils, tough, flexible filaments, which wrap themselves in a spiral round the first object that comes within their reach, providing the spreading branches of the Vine with a firm support.

There are certain other plants, known as creepers, which likewise make use of spiral tendrils in climbing, seizing and holding anything that may come within their reach ; for example, the Pea, the Pumpkin, the Cucumber, the Clematis and the Passion-flower. Other creeping plants develop on one side only of the stem a multitude of tiny climbing-spurs, which finds support in anything they may touch ; such is the Ivy, which climbs trees and walls or creeps over the most precipitous rocks. Its climbing irons are really adventive roots, which do not in any way contribute to the nourishment of the plant when in contact with a dry, hard surface. If, on the other hand, they encounter any vegetable mould, they burrow into it, increasing in length, and fulfil the proper functions of ordinary roots.

There are some plants that possess no climbing appliances whatsoever, neither tendrils nor adventive roots, but which, in order to climb upwards, employ a most remarkable method. They coil themselves, serpentwise, round the first support that comes to hand. They are known as *volubile* stems, and they include the Hop, the Bean and the Convolvulus. In any given species of volubile plant the stem invariably twines itself always in the same direction. Let us suppose that we have before us such a plant, twined about its support, and let us take a portion of one of its spirals where it crosses the support up which it is climbing.   If the stem, up which it climbs, runs from right to left, we say that the rotation of the stem is from right to left ; while if, as it climbs, it crosses the stem from left to right, we say that the

rotation is from left to right. The Kidney-Bean and the Bindweed rotate always from left to right ; while the Hop and the Honeysuckle rotate from right to left.   While the great majority of plants employ the most varied means to lift themselves up to the light, some, known as running plants, creep over the ground, like the Strawberry.   From the mother-plant a number of shoots are given off, long and slender, which creep over the ground.   They are known as

FIG. 54.—Hop (volubile stem).

stolons or *runners*.   Having travelled a certain distance they expand at the tip into a small cluster of leaves, which strikes roots into the ground and presently becomes self-sufficient.   The new plant, when sufficiently developed, puts forth, in its turn, long runners that behave like the original runners ; that is, they creep over the ground, put forth clusters of leaves, and take root.   The figure shown on opposite page depicts a cluster of this kind, more advanced than its successors. From the axil of one of its leaves grows a runner, whose terminal bud has reached the stage of a sprout already provided with fairly well-developed roots.   A second runner, issuing from this sprout, has produced a third tuft, whose leaves are beginning to unfold. After an indeterminate number of such runners have been put forth, the mother-plant will be surrounded by young shoots, like so many vegetable .colonists, established wherever the weather and the nature of the soil have permitted. We may justly call them colonists, for they are actually buds which have emigrated from the parent plant to establish themselves elsewhere, just as the inhabitants of an over-populated country will expatriate themselves in the hope of an easier livelihood. In the

FIG. 55.—A Runner from a Strawberry-plant.

beginning the sprouts thus established round the parent plant are connected to the latter by the stolons. There are still communications between the colonists and the fatherland ; there is a flow of sap from the older colonists to the young ones, but sooner or later these relations are discontinued ; the runners, henceforth unnecessary, wither away and die, and each young sprout, sufficiently equipped with roots, becomes an individual Strawberry-plant. Here, entirely without human intervention, we have the operation of layering in all its stages ; the artificial procedure finds its equivalent and probably its model in the natural process. A long bough, lying on the ground, strikes root, and finally becomes detached from the parent plant by the destruction of the runner ; and so the gardener, burying a long shoot in the soil, waits until it has taken root, and finally isolates it by a snip of the scissors.

The Violet, that modest lover of brake and underwood, establishes colonies, like the Strawberry-plant, by means of runners ; its long shoots spread over the ground in all directions, striking root where they may.

There are other plants known as ground-creepers, which crawl along the ground, like those already described, and there strike root, but they do not make use of the long stolons so remarkable in the Violet and the Strawberry. Sometimes the offshoots, having struck root, do not become separate plants by the natural destruction of the ties that attach them to the parent stock ; apart from accident, the community is undivided, and the adventive roots contribute to the vigour of the whole organism, not to the mutual independence of the buds. Sometimes, however—and in the majority of cases—the old roots die away after giving rise to a younger generation. Such is the case with the Moneywort, a pretty flowering plant that grows beside drains and ditches, with yellow blossoms and round leaves, which have been compared to golden coins ; hence the name of the plant. Its stalks are long and cling close to the ground. Numbers of adventive roots are given off by the various tufts of leaves, holding the runners to the ground as they creep forward. But while the plant sends forth its new ramifications in all directions, the original stem withers away and dies. Thenceforth the runners sent out by the parent stem live a life of their own. They, in their turn, give life to other root-producing runners, which runners, when their work is done, put forth roots and wither away. Accordingly, year by year, the Moneywort forges ahead in one direction, while in the other direction

it dies out, so that in quite a short time no trace is left
of the original offshoot.   It is still a Moneywort, but it
is no longer the plant that was raised from seed.   By
this natural process of layering, which multiplies the
plants by geometrical progression, a single plant of
Moneywort may, in the course of a few years, cover a
considerable tract of soil with individual plants.   A
similar means of multiplication is exemplified by Thyme
and Veronica, which spread their lovely carpet on the
droughty slopes of our hills.

As a general thing, plants whose vertical growth is
impeded by unfavourable atmospheric conditions spread
themselves over the ground, sending forth ramifications
which attach them more firmly to the soil.   Such are
certain plants which are scourged by the bitter gales of
winter, and such, above all, are the plants of the Polar
regions.   Monotonous tracts of turf, containing only a
small number of vegetable species, cover the frozen soil
of Iceland, Lapland, Spitzbergen and Greenland.   Lashed
by the harsh winter winds, which prevent their growth
in an upward direction, the plants that grow in such
regions remain small in stature, twining themselves
together for the sake of the mutual support thus afforded,
until they become matted together into a sort of close-
grained felt, in order that they may contend, side by
side, with the inclemencies of the climate.   Their ramifications, pressed down upon the peaty soil by the incessant
winds, bind themselves down to it by means of strong
adventive roots.

There are numerous plants, and above all the monocotyledonous species, whose stems run hither and thither
beneath the surface of the soil instead of creeping over it.
These subterranean, creeping stems have roughly the
appearance of roots, for which they might well be mistaken were we to allow ourselves to be guided by super-

ficial appearances. These stems are known as *rhizomes*. Such are the subterranean stems of the Iris, the Asparagus and the Couch-grass. Rhizomes may be distinguished from roots by certain perfectly definite external characteristics. Never, at any point along its length, does a root bear leaves carrying a bud in the axilla ; not does it display scales, no matter how minute, because such scales are merely rudimentary leaves. But the rhizome, which in reality is a true stem, despite its resemblance to a root, displays all the organs of the stem proper : it will be found to exhibit leaves, or rather scales, bearing a bud in the axil. Be appearances what they may, we know that we have before us a stem, a rhizome, wherever scales and buds are to be found. Of these buds, some develop into ramifications which remain underground, adding to the length of the rhizome ; others put forth shoots which emerge into the open air, there to unfold their leaves and flowers. With the advent of winter the aerial branches die ; but the stem survives underground, being there sheltered from the frost. In this way the plant leads a double life ; one part remains underground, there to preserve a centre or focus of life, while the other makes its appearance each year above the soil in time to produce its flowers and fruits, and to die. Lastly, the lower face of the underground part of the plant gives off numbers of adventive roots.

The buds of the rhizome, when the moment has come for them to make their way upwards into the light of day, are obliged to penetrate a layer of soil, which will vary in thickness. For the purposes of this underground journey they are protected by short, thick scales, and do not develop into the ordinary mature foliage of the plant until they have been finally liberated from the embraces of the soil. Asparagus, as we see it in the shops, consists of sprouts from subterranean root-stocks.

FIG CACTUS OR PRICKLY PEAR

To face p. 128.

When completely developed these sprouts become tall,
feathery stems, with all but filamentous leaves, bearing
a crop of small scarlet berries.

There are two families of plants belonging to the
monocotyledons—the Gramineous and the Cyperaceous
—which are remarkable for the development sometimes
attained by their rhizomes. Who is there, for example,
unacquainted with the weed known as Couch-grass which

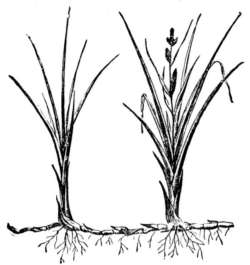

FIG. 56.—One of the Sedges.

so often invades our cultivated fields ? Its underground
stems, continually increasing in length and putting forth
ramifications, defy the hoe and the ploughshare, if we
attempt to extirpate them. In the marshy soil along
the banks of rivers, in semi-liquid mire, another Gramineous plant, the Rush, with which the gipsies used to
make their brooms, sends forth rhizomes, of the thickness
of a stout cord, which, sometimes on the surface of the
soil, sometimes plunging into the mire, will often cover
a distance of 50 to 60 feet. In the spongy soil of bogs

10

and marshes and on shifting quicksands certain Cyperaceous plants, certain Sedges, sometimes exceed even this
remarkable growth. Forming a confused tangle, crossing
and recrossing in an inextricable network, these underground ramifications form the best of all possible anchors
to hold a shifting soil in its place. In Holland a species
of Sedge is employed in order to anchor the dykes of
the low-lying pastures and to preserve the country from
the inroads of the sea. With its tough rhizomes it renders
permanent the treacherous tracts about the mouths of
the great rivers. A Gramineous plant, a *Psamma*, in
collaboration with the Scotch Fir, has solved the problem
of the sand-hills.

In some neighbourhoods the sea flings up upon the
shore enormous quantities of sand, which the wind
heaps up into the long wave-like hillocks known as
dunes. The Atlantic coast of France is bordered by
dunes ; in the English Channel they occur to the west-
ward of Boulogne ; in Brittany we find them running
southward from the neighbourhood of Nantes, along that
part of the coast known as Les Sables d'Olonnes ; and in
the department of Les Landes they run from Bordeaux
to the line of the Pyrenees, a distance of nearly 200
miles ; in this department of Les Landes alone the dunes
cover an area of 70,000 acres. This area is a vast desert,
a waste of innumerable shifting sand-hills, without so
much as a bush or a blade of grass to break the surface.
From the summit of one of these hills, in reaching which
one sinks up to the knees in sand, the eye follows, as
though fascinated, the graceful undulations of the ground,
the dazzling, rounded crests of the innumerable waves
that stretch away to the utmost limits of the golden-
grey horizon ; the gaze wanders across this chaos of
dazzling white crests and ridges, which, when swept by
the wind, is covered by a mist of driving sand until it

smokes like a foaming sea lashed by a tempest. Here is all the mirrored undulation, the infinite width of a sea whose waves rise or are stilled at the will of the wind ; but here the waves are of sand and motionless. Nothing disturbs the silence of these mournful solitudes, save now and again the hoarse cry of a passing gull, and at regular intervals the muffled roar of the Atlantic, concealed from sight by the curving flanks of the outlying dunes. Woe to the imprudent wanderer who should enter this wild desert on a stormy day ! At every squall clouds of sand are hurled into the air with irresistible force, while furious whirlwinds tear at the dunes and send their wreckage eddying through the air. When the storm is over the lie of the land is no longer the same ; what was hill is now a valley and what was valley is now a hill.

Whenever a gale springs up the dunes move inland. The wind blowing from the sea slowly rolls the dunes over into the hollows before them, and the hollows, having been filled up, becomes dunes in their turn ; and so it goes, until the dunes of the vanguard crumble and cover up the cultivated soil at the edge of the dune-land. At the same time the sea piles up fresh material on the beach, and this goes to form yet another sand-hill, which advances on the heels of the rest. In this manner the dunes gradually invade the cultivated areas and bury them under a vast layer of sterile sand. Nothing can check their progress. If a forest stands in their way it is buried, so that none but the loftiest tree-tops look down, like a sparsely grown thicket, on the terrible moving hills. Whole villages have been swallowed up : dwelling-houses, church and all have disappeared under the sand. What is to be done in the face of such an adversary, one whose advance is irresistible, pitiless in its regularity, winning some twenty paces yearly from the cultivated soil inland ? The scourge that human endeavour was powerless to prevent is opposed by a Gramineous plant, the Psamma, the Marram-grass of the sand-hills. With the meshes of its tough rhizomes the plant lays hold upon the shifting soil ; but as its action is wholly superficial it is helped in its work by a tree, the Maritime Pine, which drives its roots deep into the sand, eventually turning the sand-hill into an immovable complex. The grass begins the task of immobilization and enables the tree to grow ; while the Pine, having attained to a sturdy maturity, completes the task. So it was that an end was made of the ravages of the sand-hills ; and so, in saving a whole province from destruction, great forests were created, which yield an appreciable revenue.

The most fantastic stems are those of the Cacti. Strange and amazing shapes, fleshy tissues swollen with sap, bunches of terrible thorns, leaves reduced to the form of all but invisible scales or lacking altogether, and flowers remarkable for their size and abundance : such are the general features of these singular plants, lovers of the most infertile soils, of the sun-scorched wildernesses of Mexico and Brazil. The stem or trunk, always bristling with bundles of thorns, assumes in one variety the form of a lofty column fluted by deep longitudinal grooves, in another that of a sphere adorned by broad projecting ribs, like the meridian lines of a globe, and in yet another it consists of a mass of flat disks or " paddles " growing out of one another. The first of these forms is that of the Candle-tree, the second that of the Mammillaria, and the third that of the Opuntiae, one of which, the Nopal, provides pasture, on its paddle-shaped leaves, for the cochineal insect, from which we obtain a crimson dye ; while another, naturalized in Algeria, forms impenetrable thickets, covered with the watery, sweetish fruits commonly known as the Prickly Pear.[1] The fleshy tissue of the stem of the Cactus is, in time of excessive drought, the sole source of water to be found in the deserts of the more southern of the United States.

Enveloped in dense clouds of dust, according to Humboldt, tormented by hunger and a devouring thirst, horses and cattle stray into the desert. The cattle utter low, bellowing cries, while the horses, with necks outstretched and nostrils that snuff up the wind, endeavour to detect, by the moisture in the air, the presence of some pool or rivulet that as yet has not wholly evaporated. More happily inspired and

FIG. 57.—Echinocactus.

more cunning, the mule resorts to another method of quenching its thirst. There is in these deserts a plant of globular formation, covered with grooves and projecting ridges, the *Melocactus*, which contains, under its outer skin, bristling with thorns, a watery pulp or

[1] Known in France as the Barbary Fig (*Translator*).

marrow. With its fore-feet the mule crushes the spines, and then, cautiously protruding its lips, it ventures to drink the refreshing sap. But this method of quenching the thirst at a living, vegetable spring is not always free from danger ; for one often sees mules whose fore-feet have been lamed by the terrible thorns of the Cactus.

BUDS

THE stem, with its dependencies, is none other than the vegetable community, the common support of the individual organs whose association makes the plant. But what of these individual components ? What are they ? We have already seen what they are : they are the buds, whose structure we must now investigate.

A bud is a branch in the nascent state ; it is the infancy of the vegetable individual. It appears first of all in the shape of a small sphere of cellular tissue, which, piercing the bark, clothes itself in rudimentary leaves. Vessels take on an organized existence, communicating with those of the twig or stem, and the young nursling is rooted to the mother plant.

Buds are produced at certain fixed points ; as a rule the bud forms in the axilla of each leaf : that is, immediately above the point where the leaf is attached to the twig ; and again, as a rule the tip of every twig bears a bud. Those buds that are situated in the axillae of the leaves are known as *axillary buds* ; those that grow on the tip of the twig are known as *terminal buds*. Not all are equally vigorous : the stronger occupy the end of the twig, and the weaker the thicker portion. Those leaves that occupy the lower part of the twig—the part nearer the trunk—conceal, in their axillae, buds so minute that only a careful inspection will reveal them. These small and weakly buds often die without developing further. On the branch of a Lilac-tree you can plainly distinguish the difference of size between one bud and the next.

Whether terminal buds or axillary, they will be required to fulfil two fundamental functions which they divide between them. Some labour to achieve a prosperous present : they elaborate the sap and feed the community ; others work for a prosperous future : they produce and ripen seeds, whose destiny it is to multiply the species, to scatter it over the face of the earth and hand it down to future ages. The first category of buds produces only leaves when they develop ; the second category yields only flowers, or flowers and leaves simultaneously. Buds of the first kind are known as leaf-buds ; the others are known as flower-buds. On our fruit-trees the leaf-buds are slender and pointed ; the flower-buds are rounded in form and bulkier.

The axillary and terminal buds make their appearance in a regular and orderly fashion ; they constitute the normal population of the community ; they are found upon every plant destined to live at least a few years, unless accidental causes prevent their birth. But when the plant is in danger, and the ordinary buds, for this reason or that, are absent or deficient in number, other buds make their appearance, here, there and everywhere, even on the roots if need be, in order to stimulate a failing vitality and restore the plant to a more prosperous condition. These accidental buds are to the aerial portion of the plant what adventive roots are to the underground portion ; the dangers of the moment call them into being at any threatened point. The

places where they show themselves by preference are
the edges of a wound produced by cutting off a bough,
or places where the stem is constricted by ligatures, or
where the bark has been damaged by contusion. These
are known as *adventive* buds, but as their structure is
the same as the normal bud we will return to the latter.
During the spring and summer the buds increase in size
in the axillae of the leaves ; they are gathering strength
to help them through the winter ; the frosts come and
the leaves fall, but the buds remain in place,
firmly anchored on a little ledge of bark, just
above the scar left by the fall of the adjacent
leaf. In order that the bud shall be able to
survive the assaults of the frost and rain of
winter, which would otherwise be fatal to
them, a special provision becomes a necessity :
it consists of a thick outer sheath of varnished
scales, lined with a warm wrapping of down.
Let us take as an example the bud of a

FIG. 58.
Bud of
Chestnut-
tree.

Chestnut-tree. At the heart of the bud we find
the frail tiny leaves swaddled in a sort of cotton-
wool. Outside this a robust coat of scales, arranged
with the symmetry of the tiles upon a roof, closely
embraces it. Moreover, in order to prevent the heart
of the bud from the damp of winter, the various pieces
of this scaly armour are coated and caulked with a
resinous cement, which, though now it resembles a dry
coat of varnish, will grow soft and sticky in the spring
in order that the bud may expand and open. Then the
scales, no longer glued one to another, give way, enabling
the first young leaves to expand in the centre of their
open cradle. Nearly all buds, when the spring is in
travail, present, in varying degrees, a stickiness resulting
from the softening of their coat of varnish. In particular
I might mention the buds of the Poplar, which, if

squeezed between the fingers, yield an abundant flow of a yellow, bitter-tasting glue. This glue is assiduously collected by the bees, who turn it into *propolis*—that is, the cement or mortar with which they fill up the crevices and plaster the walls of the hive before building their combs. Despite its unobtrusive appearance, you will agree that the bud is a masterpiece : the outer coat of varnish repels all moisture, while its lining of cotton-wool or rusty red down keeps out the cold.

The scales form the essential factors of the bud's winter outfit. What are these scales, and whence do they come ? Observation and comparison will answer these questions. Armed with a needle, let us remove, one by one, the scales surrounding the bud from a Currant-bush or Rose-tree : we shall see that their shape is gradually modified as we work inwards, passing from the plainly recognizable leaf to the scale in its simplest form. The scales of the bud are merely leaves, modified with a view to special employment. In order to provide itself with a defence against the vicissitudes of winter, the growing bud transforms its lower leaves into scales. Some buds employ the whole leaf in this transformation : for example, the bud of the Lilac-tree ; others employ only the base of the leaf, as do the buds of the Currant-bush and the Rose-tree.

The subsequent leaves, which make up the heart of the bud, are of normal shape. They are tiny leaves, pale in colour, fragile in texture, and arranged with the most wonderful method, so that they may occupy the smallest possible space, without which it would have been impossible to pack them all into their narrow cradle. It will surprise you to see how much can be packed away under the scaly sheath of a bud, in a space often so small, that we should find it difficult to pack a single hemp-seed into it. There, in the bud, are dozens

BUD OF CHESTNUT.

First stage—The scales—Interior of bud—Sprouting of leaves—
 Opening of a flower bud—Expansion of leaves—Leaves on
 liberation from bud.

(From Pézard and Laporte-Blairsy's *L'Histoire naturelle par l'Observation directe.*
 Delagrave.)

To face p. 138.

of leaves, and whole clusters of flowers. The head of
blossom contained in the bud of a Lilac-tree will number
a hundred flowers or more. Yet everything is in its
place ; nothing is torn, nothing bruised. If all the
separate pieces of a bud were one by one unpacked, if
their natural arrangement were once deranged, whose
fingers would possess the skill to return them to their
place ? Only Nature's, that incomparable artist, whose
patience and skill are alike unmatched. Nature alone
has the power to make zero contain infinity.

The leaves in particular contort themselves in a
thousand ways in order to occupy as little space as
possible. You will find them, in the bud, rolled into a
slender cone or curling into a spiral, now at one side
only and now on both ; or they may be folded in two,
whether lengthwise or horizontal ; or they may be rolled
into pellets, or crumpled up at random, or folded fanwise.
The arrangement of the leaves in the bud is known as
prefoliation.

The buds that make their appearance in the spring
gather strength through the summer, subsequently
remaining stationary, we might almost say sleeping,
through the winter. The following spring they awake
and grow into twigs. It is obvious that these dormant
buds, which have to endure the heats of summer and the
frosts of winter, must be arrayed in such a fashion as
will protect them from the blazing sun and the winter's
cold. And in fact, all are clad in a coat of scales, for
which reason they are known as scaly buds. Such buds
will be found on the Lilac, the Chestnut, the Pear-tree,
the Apple-tree, the Cherry-tree, the Poplar, and indeed,
on nearly all our European trees.

But although the tree can afford to wait, and to devote
a whole year to the ripening of its buds, which are
accordingly clad in a scaly sheath, there is a host of

plants whose term of life is strictly limited. These live only a year and are therefore known as *annuals*. Such are the Potato, the Carrot, the Pumpkin, and many more. These must produce their buds in the space of a few months, or sometimes a few days. As these buds are not obliged to survive the winter they have no protective covering of scales, and are therefore known as naked buds. No sooner do they appear than they set to work, developing into shoots, unfolding their leaves and becoming branches that take their part in the work of the community. Presently, in the axillae of their leaves, other buds make their appearance, behaving in the same fashion : that is, they proceed at once to develop into twigs, which in turn will produce yet further buds. And so it goes on, until winter puts an end to this pageant of generations by killing the whole plant. Annuals, as we see, develop with great rapidity. In a single year they produce many generations of shoot growing from shoot, their number varying in accordance with their species and their degree of hardiness. Their buds, designed for immediate development, are always naked. On the other hand, such vegetable species as enjoy long life send forth their branches slowly, producing only one generation of shoots per annum ; and their buds, which have to survive the winter, are scaly.

There are certain species which combine the two categories of bud : the scaly buds, which enable the community to live on from year to year despite the inclemencies of winter, and naked buds, which quickly take part in the general labours. Such, for example, are the Peach-tree and the Vine. When the winter is over the Vine bears scaly buds padded with down, while the green shoots of the Peach-tree display scaly buds coated with varnish. Both these kinds of bud may be classified as dormant buds ; all through the winter they have been slumbering in their scaly, warmly-lined covering.   In the spring they develop into shoots, as is the general rule ; at the same time, in the axillae of their leaves other buds appear, which do not possess a scaly covering but promptly develop into fruits.   Thus, the Vine and the Peach-tree produce two generations in a single year : the first of these proceeds from scaly buds which have survived the winter ; the second, from naked buds which have first appeared that very spring, which are known, among foresters, by the name of *immediate* buds.   The twigs proceeding from these latter buds eventually give birth to scaly buds, which sleep through the winter and in the following year pass through the same stages.

Having glanced at the general history of buds, let us for a moment consider certain data of horticultural practice.   With very rare exceptions, as I have told you, every leaf bears a bud in its axilla, and in some cases several.   Now, in the case of these various axillary buds, their vigour rapidly decreases as they go from the tip of a branch to its root.   The buds near the tip of the bough are vigorous, while those nearer the root are sickly and feeble.   The buds growing in the axillae of the lower leaves show hardly any sign of growth, and more often than not they die before they are able to open.   In certain cases, however—for example, in order to keep within strictly defined limits the growth of branches of a fruit-tree, thereby favouring the growth of fruit at the expense of the branches—it may be profitable to stimulate the growth of the buds on the lower part of the twig rather than of those growing about the tip.   This result is obtained by means of pruning.   The twig is cut through close to its point of attachment, so that the portion left upon the tree contains only two or three buds. Henceforth the tree's full powers of growth are concentrated on the feeble survivors, which, but for the amputation effected, would have died of starvation, unable to compete with the more vigorous buds near the tip of the twig ; and the alimentary substances imbibed by the roots profit them only, instead of being distributed in very unequal rations amongst the whole of the buds growing on the unpruned bough. Recalled to life by the pruning-knife which destroyed their competitors, the two or three buds that are spared awake from their sickly somnolence ; gaining energy, they increase in size and finally become vigorous and productive shoots. Every stem of corn bears in the axillae of its lower leaves buds which, according to circumstances, die, to the detriment of the harvest, or develop, multiplying the number of ears. Let us first of all suppose that the corn has been sown in autumn. In this cold and rainy season vegetable growth is slow ; the stem does not rise far from the surface of the ground and the various buds, set close to one another, are almost level with the soil. Favoured by the nearness of the damp soil, these buds give off adventive roots, which nourish them directly, supplying them with an abundance of food which the ordinary root, left to itself, could never have provided. Thus stimulated by nourishment, they become so many stalks, each of which will, later on, be crowned with an ear of corn. But if the corn is sown in the spring, its rapid growth, under the influence of a mild climate, carries the buds upwards, too far from the ground to give them any chance of striking root. In such cases the stalk remains uncompanioned. In the first case one single grain of corn results in a whole tuft of stalks, bearing as many ears ; in the second case the crop is reduced to its simplest expression ; one grain of corn produces one stalk, one ear. Accordingly, the development of the lower buds is, in the production of cereals, a matter of the greatest importance. In order to make sure of it—or, as the farmer would say, in order to obtain *suckers*—the buds, or, at least, those that are lowest on the stem, must be in contact with the soil, which will provoke the output of adventive roots. Accordingly, shortly after the germination of the seed, the sown fields are rolled with a wooden roller, which, without breaking the young plants, buries them more deeply.

Such fortuitous buds as may make their appearance at indeterminate points, in order to repair the damage suffered by a plant imperilled, and also adventive buds, may likewise be subjected to such profitable treatment. Let us suppose that a number of saplings are planted at convenient intervals. If they are then left to themselves these saplings will grow upwards, each having a single trunk, and the wood obtained under such conditions is known as forest timber. But it may be of advantage to replace this single trunk by a group of several trunks. The plantation is then cut back or coppiced : that is, the trees are cut down level with the soil. Along the edge of the great amputation-wound thus produced, adventive buds make their appearance, sending up so many shoots ; so that the sapling, which would have consisted of a single trunk, is transformed into a stock, from which proceed many ramifications, all of the same age and of equal growth. The wood is then known as a *copse* or *coppice*. When the shoots have attained the size desired they are once more cut back, this process giving rise to a still greater number of shoots by multiplying a still greater number of open wounds. In this way the woodsman succeeds in producing a stock which is constantly cut back, recovering its vigour by putting forth adventive buds, and which yields a quantity of wood far greater than that which would have been obtained from a single tree-trunk allowed to grow without interference.

Respected by the woodsman's axe, the Poplar lifts above the earth its majestic and monumental mass of verdure ; the Willow, leaning its untidy and misshapen bulk, bristling with divergent shoots, over the slow-moving streams that traverse our pastures, is, in its natural state, distinguished for its beauty of form, for its pliant boughs and delicately pointed leaves. As ornamental trees they most certainly have nothing to gain by man's interference with their manner of growth. But alas ! profit and beauty do not always grow hand in hand, and if we wish to make such trees produce an abundant supply of logs and brushwood, decapitation, repeated at regular intervals, will transform them into ugly pollards, big-headed as tadpoles, hatched with scars, covered with oozing wounds, mutilated and mis-shapen, but repairing these mutilations by means of adventive buds, which renew, always more abundantly, the severed boughs.

Before leaving these adventive buds, which multiply their numbers as the plant's misfortunes are increased, contending against destruction to the verge of utter exhaustion, I may remind the reader of those trouble-some weeds—Couch-grass and other Gramineous plants —of which it is so difficult to rid our garden paths if we merely rake the surface. You may wear yourself out weeding your paths, until every weed has disappeared ; your task is completed, or, at least, so you believe ; you are wrong—in a few days' time the weeds have reappeared, more vigorous than ever. Now the explana-tion is obvious. In raking the paths you have merely " cut back " the weeds ; you have cut down the stems, but the wounds have covered themselves with adventive buds which promptly send up other stems. Instead of destroying the weeds you have multiplied them. There is only one way of really ridding your paths of such weeds : you must uproot them. Then, and only then, your task will be completed.

CHAPTER XIV

MIGRATORY BUDS

Fixed buds and deciduous buds—The Bulbiferous Lily—The Celandine— Bulbils—The structure of a head of Garlic—Bulbs—The structure of the Onion and of the Leek—Tunicated bulbs—The Hyacinth-glass— Fleshy scales—Tubercles—The Potato and the Jerusalem Artichoke— The Potato is a branch—Saffron—Solid bulbs—The tubercles of Orchids—Tubers—The Dahlia.

You will remember that the Hydra covers itself with buds, which become young Hydras, implanted upon the mother and living at her expense. Having reached maturity these young Hydras break loose and proceed to establish themselves elsewhere, where they live an independent life and become the basis of a new generation. A similar habit of migration is found in various polyps: the young polyps abandon the community and set forth in all directions to establish themselves as and where they please, themselves producing, by means of budding, fresh societies of polyps. In other polyparies, on the contrary, the community remains undivided; the animalcules produced by budding never leave the spot on which they are born. Plants, which are true vegetable polyparies, reproduce, feature for feature, these two modes of existence. In the one case the buds continue on the limb that has produced them, striking root at the point where they were born. This is the case with the great majority of plants, and it is with this mode of existence that we are most familiar. These buds, which are never spontaneously detached from the

146

mother plant, are known as *fixed* buds. To this category belong the naked or scaly buds, normal or adventive, of which I spoke in the last chapter. But in other cases, having attained a certain stage of development, the buds leave the mother plant ; they become emigrants, so to speak ; that is, they detach themselves and strike root into the earth, thenceforth to draw their nourishment directly from the soil. These latter buds we shall call *migratory* or *deciduous* buds, with reference to their desertion of the natal branch and their fall to earth when they have made their appearance on aerial roots. Now it is obvious that a bud intended to unfold in isolation by virtue of its own energies, cannot be organized like the bud that never leaves its fostering bough. In order to satisfy its first essential requirements, before roots capable of nourishing it have struck into the soil, it must of necessity possess a store of food ; so that every migratory bud accordingly bears with it a store of provisions.

Fig. 59.—Stem of the Bulbiferous Lily.

Lovers of flowers often grow in their gardens a beautiful little Lily, with flame-coloured blossoms : an Alpine plant. It is known as the Bulbiferous Lily. Here is a fragment of the stem, with buds in the axillae of the leaves. These buds have to live through the winter and unfold in the following spring. They have not, however, the winter garment, the coat of tough, leathery scales ; on the contrary, they are covered with very thick and succulent scales, tender and fleshy, calculated to feed the bud as well as to protect it. This abundant store of nourishment, which makes all the scales quite round and plump, marks them as being deciduous. And

indeed, towards the end of the summer they desert the
mother plant ; at the least breath of wind they fall, and
are scattered upon the ground, henceforth left to their
own resources.   If the summer has been wet, many of
them, without leaving their place on the axillae of the
leaves, throw out one or two tiny roots, which hang in
the air as though trying to meet the ground half-way.
By October all the buds have fallen ; lastly, the mother
stem perishes.   Presently the wind and rain of autumn
will cover them with dead leaves and leaf-mould.   Under
this protective covering they feed all through the winter
on the sap contained in their scales, gradually thrusting
their roots into the soil, until, when the spring comes
round, each of them unfolds its first green leaf in order
to continue its development, finally becoming a plant like
the original Lily.

The Celandine is a handsome plant which flowers in
the early spring.   Its flowers are golden yellow in colour ;
its glossy leaves are shaped somewhat like those of the
Fig-tree.   It prefers a damp soil.   Having flowered, the
stem puts forth buds in the axillae of its leaves ; but
these buds, instead of straightway becoming shoots, form
a globular, fleshy body, bursting with nourishing juices.
Presently the stem withers and dies, but the buds persist,
developing in the following spring, thanks to the food
stored in them.

Bulbils is the name given to such fleshy buds, destined
to grow to maturity independently of the mother stem,
as are those of the Celandine and the Bulbiferous Lily.
Garlic offers us another example, and one far more
familiar.   Let us take a whole head of Garlic.   Externally
there is nothing to be seen but the dry, white envelope.
Let us remove this : we shall find beneath it a number
of offspring which can easily be removed in a single
mass.   We then come upon more white envelopes, and

more cloves of Garlic, the whole head being a bundle of cloves and intercalated wrappings. These wrappings are the withered bases of the old leaves of the Garlic plant ; white in their subterranean parts, which still exist, and green in their open-air portions, which are now lacking. In the axillae of these leaves buds formed in accordance with the general rule, but as they are destined to develop in a state of isolation they have hoarded food in the thickness of their scales, and it is this which is responsible for their unusual size. Let us split one open lengthwise. Under a tough leathery covering you will find an enormous fleshy mass, which in itself makes up almost the whole embryo plant. This is the storehouse, the larder. With such a provision of food the bud can very well suffice to itself. Accordingly, when they wish to grow Garlic the gardeners do not resort to the seed ; this would take far too long. They employ the buds—that is, they plant, one by one, the cloves which make up the " head " of Garlic. Each of these cloves, feeding at first on its reserve of nutriment, puts forth roots and leaves and becomes a complete plant.

Before we proceed one thing may be noted. I have shown the reader that the " head " of Garlic consists of inverted leaves ; but where is the stem that should go with these buds and leaves ? Well, the stem is there, but is strangely compressed, to the point of being unrecognizable. If you remove all the cloves you will have before your eyes a hard, flattened object, marked with a number of scars equal to the number of embryo plants removed. Along its edges you will find traces of dead leaves or white wrappings, and at its base the vestiges of old roots. This curious object is the stem, which in this case, by reason of its extreme compression, is known as the *plate*.

From the bulbil to the bulb, from Garlic to the Onion,

is only a step. Split an Onion in two, from crest to
base : you will see that it consists of a series of fleshy
scales, closely fitted one within another and carried on
a very short stem, or rather on a plate like that of the
Garlic. In the centre of these succulent scales, which
are leaves transformed into storehouses of food, other
leaves make their appearance, whose shape and colour
are normal. An Onion is therefore yet another bud
equipped for an independent life by virtue of its outer

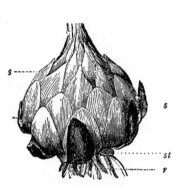

Fig. 60.—Bulb of White Lily.
    r, roots ; *s, s, s*, scales ;
    st, base of stem.

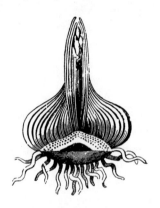

Fig. 61.—Bulb of Hyacinth.

leaves, which are converted into fleshy scales ; but the
Onion, on account of its size, is known as a bulb, the
term *bulbil* being a diminutive.

Bulb and bulbil differ only in bulk : the bulb is large
and the bulbil small ; that is all the difference. You
have doubtless noticed that the Onion, suspended from
the rafters of the kitchen ceiling, is awakened, during the
winter, by the heat of the room, so that it puts forth,
from the heart of its tawny scales, a fresh green shoot,
which seems to protest against the inclemencies of winter
and recall the delights of spring. As it grows its fleshy

laces become wrinkled and flaccid, falling at last into decay, when they serve to manure the growing plant. Sooner or later, however, its provisions being exhausted, the shoot will die, unless planted in the earth. We have here a most striking example of a bud living entirely on its own store of food. The Leek likewise is a bulb, but slenderer in shape. Like the Onion, it consists of a series of leaf-bases fitting one into another. A bulb of this structure is known as a tunicated bulb, because its fleshy leaves envelope the heart of the bud like so many coats or tunics.

In other instances the leaf-scales, too narrow to go right round the bulb, are arranged like the tiles of a roof. The bulb is then known as a scaly bulb. The common white Lily has such a bulb.

A large number of bulbs produce magnificent flowers, yet in many cases nothing could be easier to grow. We may take, as an example, the Hyacinth. Here is a section of a Hyacinth. You will see here all the constituent parts of a bulb : a short stem or plate, putting forth roots, and fleshy scales, fitting one inside another. Leaves of the ordinary kind are already sprouting from the heart of these scales, with a head of blossom in the bud. Hyacinth bulbs may be grown in the ordinary way —that is, may be planted in the ground ; and if so planted they bloom in spring. But they can also be grown on the mantelpiece or the window-sill, when they will flower in winter. The bulb is placed in the neck of a jar or bottle filled with water, or in a bowl containing damp moss. Stimulated by the warmth of the room, the bulb sprouts without further attention. It puts forth fine white roots that plunge into the water or the wet moss, unfolding its leaves, and, eventually, its beautiful heads of blossom. Do not imagine that a little fresh water has of itself worked a little miracle such as causing a delicate plant to flower amidst the rigours of winter. The bulb contains its own stores of food; stimulated by the warmth of the house, it flowers before its time, nourished on its own substance.

There are buds that affront the dangers of independent life which, before leaving the mother plant, amass no store of nutriment by distending their scales; but in such cases either the roots or the branches—according to the species of vegetable—are entrusted with the task of supplying food. Let us first consider the bud which will look to its branches for nourishment.

When it is destined to provide future nourishment for the buds which it bears, the branch, instead of seeking the open air, where it would be covered with leaves and flowers, remains underground, where nothing can interrupt its labours. There, shabbily clad in sorry brown scales, the last vestiges of the leaves which it has renounced, it obstinately gathers and stores up nutriment, hoarding up food on which the future of its buds will depend. It becomes corpulent and so misshapen that the botanists, no longer having the courage to call it branch, have given it the name of *tuber* or *tubercle*. Once it has amassed a sufficient store of food the tuber detaches itself from the mother plant and henceforth the buds which it bears obtain from it an abundance of food against their day of migration. A tuber is thus a subterranean branch; swollen with nourishment, having thin scales in the place of leaves and being covered with buds which it is compelled to feed.

The Potato is a tuber. We shall show that, despite its uncomely shape and its continuance underground, this tuber is really a branch, not a root, as is commonly supposed. A root never bears leaves, nor anything derived from the leaf, such as scales. It does not put forth buds save under exceptional circumstances; for

THE POTATO.

Spiral arrangement of buds—Eye, magnified—Eyes sprouting—
Transverse and longitudinal sections of potato—An eye—A
bud—Grains of starch—Pulp cells—Buds (lateral shoots)—
Peel and pulp—Vascular bundle—Surface of bud.

(From Pézard and Laporte-Blairsy's *L'Histoire naturelle par l'Observation directe.*
Delagrave.)

To face p. 152.

example, when the welfare of the plant is threatened ; but even in the face of the extremest danger it is, more often than otherwise, quite unable to bud. The production of leaves and buds is not among its functions. But what do we see on the surface of a Potato ? We perceive certain indentations, known as eyes, which are so many buds, for these eyes grow to be branches if the Potato is placed under favourable conditions. On old Potatoes we may find them, in the autumn, sprouting from the tuber, transformed into young plants, which need only a little sunlight to turn them green and enable them to grow stems. The gardener profits by this peculiarity. The tuber is cut into pieces, and each piece, planted in the ground, will produce a fresh plant, provided each portion con-

FIG. 62.—Potato with eyes or buds.

tains at least one eye ; if no eye is present it rots unproductively in the ground. However, before exhumation the eyes are concealed in the axillae of the small scales, which, later on, readily become detached, so that they may escape notice, unless we look for them on young tubers lifted from the ground with a special care. These scales are leaves adapted to an underground existence—leaves, just as the tough wrappings of a scaly bud are leaves.

Since it possesses leaves and buds the Potato must be a branch. Should the reader still feel doubtful of this fact I may add that on banking the plant—that is, on heaping up the earth about its roots—the young shoots buried thereby are converted into tubers ; I may add, too, that in dull, rainy seasons, some of the ordinary branches, being uncovered, become distended and transform themselves into more or less perfect tubers.

The tuber of the Jerusalem Artichoke does not conceal its character of branch so completely. Its buds are arranged upon it in pairs, on small protuberances, facing one another, counting from above downwards and from right to left, just as the leaves and their axillary buds are arranged on the stem.

FIG. 63.
Meadow Saffron
or Autumn
Crocus.

Saffron gives us yet another form of organization, half-way between the bulb and the tuber. The lower part of the stem becomes distended with a compact starchy mass, a tuber covered with fibrous and close-fitting bases of the leaves. In shape it is a slightly flattened sphere. In the axillae of its thin wrappings buds are found, of which the upper ones are the more vigorous, as is the habitual rule. The alimentary reserve allotted to these bulbs is in this case to be found in the stem itself, which becomes a storehouse of starchy food, full to overflowing, in place of the leaves, which remain in the shape of thin, withered wrappings ; and regarded from this point of view the organ that nourishes the buds is a tuber. But this organ, on the other hand, is tightly wrapped up in the still existent bases of the old leaves, just as it is in the Onion and all the tunicated bulbs. Regarded from this point of view, the underground portion of the Saffron is a bulb. In order to remind us of this it is called a *solid bulb*. It is a bulb by virtue of its " tunics," or concentric sheaths, the latter being the withered bases of old leaves ; but instead of being subdivided into a number of fleshy scales, this bulb is solid and compact, the store of nutriment existing in the very axis of the plant, in the stem transformed into a tuber. Planted in the earth, the solid bulb of the Meadow Saffron puts forth from its base a bundle of roots, while the terminal bulb, unfolding itself, produces leaves and flowers. At the same time each of the axillary buds gives rise to a bundle of leaves, dilating itself at the base until it forms a new bulb implanted on the first one. In order to feed its progeny the mother bulb gradually dwindles, becoming wrinkled, and withering away, until by the time the plant is fully developed nothing is left of it but a lifeless husk. By this time the young bulbs, enriched by the substance of the mother bulb, have attained their full growth ; and, breaking away from one another, each of them repeats, in the following year, the same stages of development.

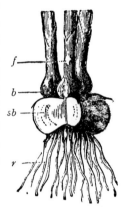

FIG. 64.—Bulb of Meadow Saffron. *r*, roots ; *sb*, solid bulb ; *b*, buds which have developed into new bulbs ; *f*, foliage.

The substance hoarded up in the fleshy scales of the bulb, or the starchy axis of the tuber, serves not merely to feed the young plant, but also to form fresh bulbs, fresh tubers, that assure the future of the species. I might compare it with an inheritance bequeathed by the past to the present, which the present in turn will bequeath to the future, enriched by all the labours of the generations which it has benefited. The bulb of the Meadow Saffron obtained its stores of food from the bulb that preceded it ; it will now transfer them to the bulbs that succeed it, which in turn will hand them down to others, enriched from generation to generation by the labours of the roots.

In certain cases, however, this inheritance retains an almost unchanging value ; so that it might be likened to a capital sum which the plant does not exploit, doing no more than faithfully handing it down. We see this in a number of the Orchids, the curious formation of whose flowers makes them of such unusual interest. Uprooted just as it is flowering, we may note, at the base of the stem of the common Purple Orchis, surrounded by roots, two egg-shaped tubercles, sometimes as large as a walnut. One is firm and fully distended ; the other is flaccid and wrinkled, yielding more or less to the pressure of the fingers. Between the two we may sometimes find certain withered husks or skins, those in the best state of preservation still retaining, though badly crumpled, the shape of a small empty sac ; by blowing into the open mouth we can make this assume the shape and size of the two tubers. Here we have the three ages represented : the past, the present and the future. This little crumpled sac, if time and the moisture of the soil have not destroyed it, represents the past. Last year it was a tuber, packed with food ; it emptied itself, reducing itself to a thin pellicle, in order to nourish the stem and bequeath its substance to the present tuber. The present is represented by the withered tuber, whose flesh is becoming flabby, slowly liquefying and transfusing itself into the newly formed

Fig. 65.—Orchis.

portions of the plant. The young shoot, before it had roots, was nourished upon its substance, and, still at the expense of its substance, the new tuber is growing full and fat. This new tuber, fresh, firm and full of life, represents the future, containing the germ of next year's plant. When summer is over the Orchis dies ; the stem will wither and rot, and the roots likewise ; the tuber which has fed it will be merely a worthless husk ; but the second tuber, which alone will survive the death of the plant, will live on underground, waiting for the warm sunny days of spring, before unfolding its single bud and producing a plant in all things like its predecessor.

Thus, it is by means of its twofold store of provisions, its pair of tubers, one of which empties while the other fills itself, that the Orchis hands down, from year to year, a bud equipped with provisions and perpetuating itself indefinitely on the same spot, provided that nothing

Fig. 66.—Tubers of the Orchis.

appears to interrupt this remarkable line of descent. The successive tubers follow an alternate order : that is to say, they appear now on the right-hand side of the stem and now on the left ; so that the plant does not actually move away from the spot on which it was born, but year after year shifts its position, to the extent of an inch or so, away from the common centre. The chance Orchis which you may find flowering in solitude in some lonely spot may be the descendant of hundreds of generations, which have followed one another on precisely the same spot and transmitted intact the tuberous inheritance, constantly consumed to meet present necessities, but as constantly fully restored to meet the needs of the future.

The nature of the Orchis' tubers is still in dispute ;
some insist that they are roots, while others regard them
as underground branches. Root or branch, it matters
little ; the twin tubers, the older of which transfuses
its substance into the younger tuber before it finally
perishes, none the less afford a remarkable example of
the methods employed by the plant to assure the future
of its descendants. In a large number of plants the
root is entrusted with the important function of hoarding

up foodstuffs and keeping them
in reserve for the next generation,
just as the branch may swell into
a tuber or thicken its scales to
form a bulb. A root distended
to provide a store of nutriment
for the benefit of the buds is
known as a *tuberous root*. As
examples, we have the Dahlia,
the Carrot, the Beetroot and the
Turnip.

Fig. 67.—Tuberous root
of the Dahlia.

Let us in particular consider
the root of the Dahlia. At first
sight this bundle of tuberous roots resembles nothing
so much as a bunch of Potatoes. But we shall discover that these tuberous organs bear neither scales
nor eyes. These distensions, therefore, are not tubercles ;
they are tuberous roots. All through the summer and
the autumn the Dahlia is covered with large and magnificent flowers. On the advent of frosty weather the aerial
part of the plant withers and dies ; but a few buds
persist, right at the bottom of the stem, together with
the bundle of tuberous roots which are destined to feed
them in the following year. The roots are unearthed and
stored in a dry place, where the frosts cannot injure
them. In the spring, the cluster of tubers is divided

into as many sections as there are buds in the truncated stem surmounting it ; when each section, provided with a bud and at least one fostering root, will produce a complete plant.

The part played by tuberous roots is in any plant what it is in the Dahlia : thanks to the store of food which their fleshy substance holds in reserve, they come to the rescue of the buds that have survived the death of the stem. Man, in providing for his own nourishment, profits by many of these reservoirs of food ; he is even able, by his ingenious methods, to stimulate their formation in plants which would not produce them if left to their own devices, or at all events would not produce them in anything approaching such abundance.

CHAPTER XV

GRAFTING

Grafting—First condition of success—Mistaken ideas of grafting—Grafting by approach—Cleft grafting—Crown grafting—Shield grafting—Tube grafting—The origin of cultivated vegetables—The Wild Potato— Seakale—The Wild Leek—The Wild Vine—Reversion to the wild state —The importance of propagation by grafts, cuttings and layering—The value of propagation by seedlings.

A BUD, or the twig or branch which it produces as it develops, is a unit, a self-contained entity, an individual member of a vegetable community ; it has a vitality of its own, and constitutes a separate plant, which takes root, not in the ground, but upon the branch which has produced it. This fundamental principle helps us to explain the migration of certain buds, such as the bulbils of Garlic, Saffron and the Tiger Lily, which detach themselves from the mother plant and, thanks to their adventive roots, become so many mutually independent plants. The same principle will be found to underlie the propagation of plants by slips or cuttings, and by layering : operations which remove the twig from the branch which supplied it with sap, and transplant it in the ground, whence it must henceforth imbibe its liquid nutriment. Lastly, it explains the process of grafting, which consists of transplanting the bud or the twig from its branch to another branch, from its tree to another tree.

The plant which is to supply the bud with nourishment in future is known as the *stock* ; while the bud or twig implanted in this stock is known as the *graft*. It is an indispensable condition of successful grafting that the transplanted bud must find, in its new position, food in accordance with its taste : that is, a sap constituted like its own. It is therefore necessary that the two plants—the graft, and stock that has supplied the scion— must be of the same species, or must, at least, belong to species very closely related, for similarity of the sap and its products can only result from similarity of organization. It would be waste of time were we to attempt to graft the Lilac on the Rose, or the Rose on the Orange. There is nothing in common between these three vegetable species, neither in the leaves, nor in the flowers, nor in the fruit. This difference of structure is infallibly accompanied by a profound difference in the constitution of the nutritive juices. The bud taken from the Rose-tree would die of starvation on a Lilac ; a scion taken from the Lilac would meet the same end on the branch of a Rose-tree. But we can easily graft Lilac upon Lilac, Rose upon Rose, and Orange upon Orange. We can even go further than this. We can transfer a bud from an Orange-tree to a Lemon-tree, from a Peach-tree to an Apricot-tree, from a Cherry-tree to a Plum-tree, and vice versa. For there is, between these pairs of species, a close relationship, as you may already divine, but will understand more clearly when your knowledge is a little greater. In short, if a graft is to succeed, there must be the greatest possible similarity between the two plants. The writers of antiquity were by no means clear in their minds as to the absolute necessity of this similarity of organization ; they tell us of Roses grafted on Holly in order to obtain green Roses ; of Vines grafted on Walnut-trees, in order to obtain clusters of grapes as large as walnuts. Such grafts as these, or any other between absolutely dissimilar species, have

12

never existed except in the imagination of those who have dreamed of them. Finally, it is indispensable that the area of graft and stock brought into contact should be as large as possible, and this contact should be effected between those tissues that possess the greatest vitality, and will, in consequence, be most likely to grow together. This contact, therefore, should take place between the cellular tissues of the two barks, and more particularly between the two layers of cambium, for it is there, above all, that we shall find the vital activities of the plant : in the new tissues forming between the wood and the bark. It is there that the sap circulates ; it is there that new cells are formed, and new fibres, producing on one hand a layer of bark, and on the other a layer of woody tissue. It is, consequently, there and only there that amalgamation between the scion and the stock is possible.

There are three principle methods of grafting : grafting by approach or inarching, grafting by cleft or tongue, and budding. The shape given to the recess or incision, and the arrangement of the portions brought into contact, give place in practice to numerous subdivisions which we cannot now consider in detail. We will here confine ourselves to essentials.

The process of *inarching* may be compared with layering, with this difference, that the soil is replaced by the plant which is destined to serve as stock. In layering we provoke the formation of adventive roots, either by burying a twig which is still connected with the branch or stem that feeds it, or by leading it through a broken flower-pot, or a piece of sheet-lead twisted into a cone, and filled with wet moss. When, called forth by this prospering environment, roots have been evoked in sufficient numbers the twig or shoot is gradually severed, by means of small notches, from the mother plant, and is finally detached from the latter. In grafting by approach, we propose to make a twig, a branch, or a whole tree-top strike root, not in the earth, but in a neighbouring tree, while it is still connected with the plant of which it forms a part. Let us suppose that two saplings are growing in close proximity, and that we wish to implant upon the first a twig or branch of the second. We make similar incisions in the parts which are to be brought into contact ; we ensure a precise coincidence between the young, living tissues, the cambium, and the cellular tissue of the bark ; and having applied ligatures to keep everything in place we leave the two wounds in contact to the slow chemistry of life. Fed by its own stem, from which it has not been divided, the graft to be transplanted mingles its sap with the sap of the new stock ; on both sides there is an organization of tissue for the purpose of cicatrizing the

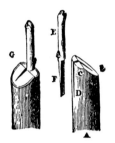

FIG. 68.—Cleft grafting.

wounds ; and these new tissues, being in close contact, undergo a kind of amalgamation, so that sooner or later the twig or branch forms part of the alien stem. It is now time to wean the graft, by depriving it, little by little, of the nourishment furnished by its own stem, and accustom it to the diet provided by its foster-mother, which we have forced upon it by artificial means. This result is obtained, as in a simple case of layering, by means of a gradual series of incisions or ligatures, made or applied below the plane of cohesion. When it is judged that the cutting is deriving all its food from the new stock it is finally separated from the mother plant.

The grafting of shoots corresponds with propagation by planting slips or cuttings. It consists of transplanting upon a new stock a twig or branch detached from the mother plant. The method most generally employed is that of *cleft grafting*. We will suppose that your orchard contains a Pear-tree of little value, raised from seed or brought from its native forest. You want to make it produce pears of good quality. The method employed is as follows : the trunk of the inferior tree is cut clean across and a deep incision is made in the stock. A twig bearing a few buds is cut from a Pear-tree of really good quality ; the butt of the scion is cut

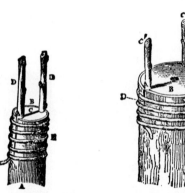

FIG. 69.—Cleft grafting.   FIG. 70.—Crown grafting.

at an acute angle and the graft is implanted in the cleft made in the stock, so that bark coincides with bark and wood with wood. The surfaces are brought into closer contact by means of ligatures, and the bare surfaces of the wounds are covered with grafting-wax or with clay held in place by a bandage. Thus bound up the stump is protected from contact with the air, which would dry it up. In the course of time the wound becomes cicatrized, and the bark and wood of the scion become welded to the bark and wood of the stock. Finally, the buds of the graft, fed by the stock, are transformed into branches, and in the course of a few years the inferior tree is replaced, above the level of the graft, by a tree of superior quality, yielding pears like those of the tree that furnished the graft. If we wish to obtain a tree with a large number of branches, and if the size of the stock will allow of it, there is nothing to prevent us from inserting two grafts in the cleft, one at either side. We could hardly place more than two scions in the same cleft, as it is essential that the bark of the graft should make contact with that of the stock, so that communication is established between the nascent tissues of the cambium of stock and scion. If the stock of the amputated tree is sufficiently vigorous we can even insert a whole circle of grafts along the circumference of the section, as shown in Fig. 70. This is known as *crown grafting*.

The grafting of buds consists in transferring to the stock an ordinary bud with the slip of bark supporting it This is the mode of grafting in most frequent use. According to the time of year when the operation was effected, the graft is said to be *sprouting* or *dormant*. In the first case the graft is made in spring, when the vegetable world is waking from its sleep, so that the bud or " eye " inserted under the bark of the stock " takes " almost immediately and shortly afterwards begins to sprout ; in the second case the bud is transferred in July or August, during the autumnal flow of sap, so that it " sleeps "—that is, remains stationary— all through the autumn and winter, once adherence to the stock has been effected.

You may have given asylum in your flower-garden to a wild Rose-bush, the common Dog-rose, that grows in wayside hedges in company with the Bramble. It is not a handsome bush. Its stems, its thorns, its leaves and its fruit are certainly like those of the cultivated Rose —but its blossoms are nothing to boast of. Five modest

petals, symmetrical in form, but scentless, and barely
flushed with crimson. We now wish to make the bush
produce the magnificent garden flower with its hundred
petals. While the autumn sap is flowing in July, August
and September, we make a T-shaped incision in the
bark of the wild Rose-tree, penetrating to the wood,
but without damaging the latter ; the edges of the
incision are lifted slightly, and we then remove from a
cultivated Rose-bush a strip of bark furnished with a
bud—known as a shield—taking care to remove any
wood which may adhere to the inner face of the shield,

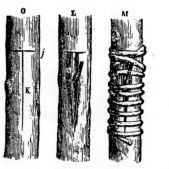

FIG. 71.—Shield grafting.   FIG. 72.—Fluke grafting.

while taking care not to injure the bark, and above all
the greenish tissue forming the innermost layer of the
bark. Lastly, the shield is inserted between the bark
and the wood of the stock, and the edges of the wound
are brought together by means of a ligature, so that
the shield is held firmly against the wood of the stock.
In the following spring the transplanted bud will be
found adhering to its foster-parent, whose stem is then
amputated above the level of the graft. Before long the
wild Rose-tree will be covered with cultivated Roses.

In *fluke* grafting a transversal cut is made in the bark
above and below the bark, a longitudinal incision being
made between the two circular cuts. If the operation

is performed while the sap is flowing the complete cylindrical section of bark may readily be removed. A cylindrical section of bark of the same dimensions is removed from the stock, whose stem must be equal in diameter to that of the scion, and is replaced by the section bearing the bud which we wish to transplant. The edges of the cylinder are held together and any defects of the joints are covered with ligatures and grafting-wax.

You are now familiar with the essential principles of the three methods of propagation employed in cultivation : propagation by slips or cuttings, layering and grafting. In order to realize the full value of these operations, let us for a moment consider the origin of our garden vegetables. You may perhaps have imagined that from all time, in order to provide us with food, the Pear-tree has diligently produced large pears melting with juice ; that the Potato, wishing to please us, has packed its thick underground branches with starchy pulp ; that the Cauliflower, merely with the idea of being pleasant, has of its own accord evolved its creamy-white head of modified floral leaves. You may have thought that Corn, Pumpkins, Carrots, Vines, Turnips and all the rest of them, being keenly interested in human affairs, have always of their own motion done their best for man. You may have supposed that the Grape is to-day just like that from which Noah obtained the juice that intoxicated him ; that Wheat, ever since it first appeared upon the earth, has unfailingly produced its harvest of grain ; that the Beet and the Pumpkin, when the world was still young, enjoyed the same corpulence that makes them of value to us now. In fact, you have had a sort of idea that our food-plants came to us in the beginning just as they are to-day. Alas, I must shatter your illusions ! The wild fruit or vegetable would, as a rule,

provide us with the pattern ; any value it may have is
the result of our painstaking care. Only our labours,
our cultivation of the plant, have enabled us to profit
by its qualities, by modifying them in one direction or
another.

In its native countries, on the mountains of Chili and
Peru, the Potato, in its wild state, is a meagre tubercle,
about the size of a Hazel-nut. Man extends the hospi-
tality of his garden to this sorry weed ; he plants it in
a nourishing soil, tends it, waters it and makes it fruitful
with the sweat of his brow. And there, from year to
year, the Potato thrives and prospers ; it gains in size
and in nourishing properties, finally becoming a farinaceous tuber the size of our two fists.

On cliffs overlooking the ocean, exposed to all the
winds of heaven, there grows a wild Cabbage, a long-
stemmed, untidy plant, scant of leaf, in colour a crude
unpleasing green, strong-smelling and with an acrid
flavour. Beneath these unpromising qualities it may
perhaps possess valuable potentialities. Such must
apparently have been the thought of the man who
first, in days whose very memory is lost, gave the wild
Cabbage of the cliff a place in his garden. His expecta-
tions were well founded. The wild Cabbage was continually improved by human care ; its stem grew stouter,
and its leaves, becoming more numerous, were compressed
in concentric fashion, into a close-packed head, white
and succulent, the final result of this wonderful metamorphosis being the heavy, spherical vegetable of to-day.
There, on the rocky cliff, we have the point of departure
of this precious vegetable. Here, in our kitchen-gardens,
we have its final achievements. But where are the
intermediate forms which, throughout the centuries, have
gradually endowed the species with its present characteristics ? These forms were improvements ; they had

to be preserved, and multiplied, and made the subject of yet further attempts at improvement. Who knows what accumulated labours have given us the modern cabbage ?

And the wild Pear-tree—have you ever seen one ? It is a somewhat alarming-looking bush, bristling with ferocious thorns. 'Its pears, a detestable fruit, which constricts your throat and sets your teeth on edge, are quite small, sour and astringent, and hard as so many pebbles. The first man to have so much faith in this refractory bush as to foresee the remote future when it should have become the luscious fruit that we enjoy to-day was indeed happily inspired.

In much the same fashion, starting with the grape of the wild Vine, no larger than an Elder-berry, man, by the sweat of his brow, has obtained the juicy grape of our modern Vines ; some sorry grass, to-day unknown, gave him Wheat ; in short, a few wretched bushes, a few weeds of unattractive appearance have, by his pains, been transformed into our garden vegetables and our orchard trees. The earth, in order that she might urge us to labour, the supreme law of life, has been but a harsh stepmother. For the nestling bird she provides abundant food ; to us she offers only the fruit of the Bramble and the Blackthorn. Let us not pity ourselves, for it is precisely our war upon dearth that has made us great. It is our business to do the best for ourselves by employing our intelligence ; our part is to put into practice the noble motto : Heaven helps him that helps himself.

From the earliest ages man has endeavoured to select, from the innumerable species of the vegetable world, those that seemed likely to lend themselves to his improvements. The majority have been of no service to us ; but others, doubtless predestinate, more specially created for the use of man, have profited by our care, and under cultivation have acquired qualities of the greatest importance, since we depend on them for our nourishment. The improvement obtained is not, however, so radical that we could count on its permanence were we to cease our care for it. The plant is constantly tending to return to its primitive condition, as though it had repented of its alliance with man. For example, let the gardener leave his Cabbages to themselves, without manuring and watering them ; let him leave their seed to sprout at random wherever the wind may blow it, and the Cabbage will quickly revert from its close-packed sphere of pale, fleshy leaves to the green, loosely-hanging leaves of its ancestors. The Vine, too, without our care, will return to the wild creeper of the hedge or thicket, a whole cluster of whose grapes is barely equal in volume to a single grape of the cultivated Vine. The wild Pear-tree too, on the verge of the woods, will revert to its long thorns and its unpalatable fruit ; while the fruit of the wild Plum and Cherry will be reduced to little more than stones covered with an acrid skin. In short, all the wealth of our orchards would be brought to nought.

This return to the wild state takes place even in our fields and gardens, despite all our care, if we attempt to reproduce the plant from its seed. Let us, for example, sow a few pips taken from a most excellent pear. Well ! the Pear-trees resulting from these pips will produce, for the most part, only middling, or bad, or shocking bad pears. Some of them will merely reproduce the mother-tree. Another series of pips is sown—those of the second generation. The quality of the pears is worse than ever. If we continue this process of sowing, employing always the pips of the previous generation, the fruit, steadily becoming smaller and harder and more acrid, will finally revert to the uneatable fruit of the hedgerow. Here is another example. What flower can surpass the Rose, with its noble bearing, its exquisite odour, its wealth of colour ? Let us sow the seed of this proud inmate of our gardens, and its descendants are no more than so much miserable brushwood, mere bushes of Dog-rose like those in our hedgerows. There is nothing surprising in this : the pride of our gardens had the wild Rose as its point of departure ; and by the sudden return to propagation by seed it has resumed the characteristic qualities of its race. There are some plants in which the improvements acquired by cultivation are more stable, persisting in spite of the tests of sowing, but only on the express condition that the gardener does not relax his care. All of them, left to themselves and propagated by seed, revert, in a few generations, to the primitive state, having gradually lost the qualities impressed on them by human intervention.

Since our fruit-trees and ornamental plants relapse more or less rapidly to the wild state if propagated by seed, how can we propagate them without risk of their degeneration ? We must resort to grafting, layering and propagation by cuttings—resources of inestimable value which enable us to give stability to the improvements won by long years of labour, and to profit by the qualities already achieved by our predecessors, instead of ourselves beginning a course of cultivation for which one human lifetime would hardly suffice. By the transplantation of buds or shoots we add to our individual achievements the accumulated results obtained by our forbears. Layering, propagation by slips and grafting faithfully reproduce all the characteristics of the plant involved. The fruit, flower and leaves of the plants derived from transplanted buds are precisely similar to those of the plant from which the bud is taken. Nothing has been

added to the qualities which we seek to propagate, but
neither has anything been subtracted from them. If the
plant providing the slip or graft produces double blossoms,
the plants resulting from this slip or graft will also be
double blossoms ; the very tint of the flowers is precisely
reproduced, and the full, sweet and fragrant fruits of the
parent plant are reproduced in all their fullness and
sweetness and fragrance by the scion. The slightest
peculiarity which, for some unknown reason, has made
its appearance in a plant raised for seed—sometimes
affecting only a single branch—such as the outline of
the leaves, or the local coloration of the flowers, is reproduced with the most meticulous exactness if the graft
or the slip is taken from the branch affected by this
modification. In this manner horticulture is daily
enriched by double blossoms or flowers of unusual colour,
or by fruit remarkable for its size, for late or early
ripening, for more than commonly luscious pulp or a
stronger flavour. Without the aid of grafting or propagation by cuttings, these precious accidents, having once
made their appearance, for what reason no one knows,
would be lost for ever on the death of a plant thus
favoured by chance ; and the gardener would have no
resource but to repeat, again and again, his attempts to
provoke improvements which, almost as soon as obtained,
would escape him for ever, owing to the lack of means
of stabilizing them and rendering them perfect.

Propagation by seed—and we must not forget this—is
quite unable to perpetuate such qualities as are, to us,
of the greatest value, but, to the plant, are of no importance and may even be a harmful drain on its vitality.
It gives us the vegetable as created by Nature, stripped
of those accessory qualities which man has contrived to
impress upon it. The seed of double blossoms will
produce single flowers ; the pips of improved fruits will

give us degenerate fruits : if not always after a single sowing, at least after several generations ; and the wild type reappears in all its rustic strength, to which we are obliged from time to time to resort, in order to renew the vitality of species enfeebled by an unduly protracted course of artificial propagation.   Every seed is the point of departure of a fresh association with tendencies and qualities of its own ; while propagation from slips and grafts is none other than the dismemberment of an association whose least characteristics it will faithfully reproduce.   And we have here the sum of the advantages offered by the two methods of propagation.   If we wish to obtain varieties of colour, foliage, size or shape, we must resort to propagation by seed.   Amongst the plants thus obtained some will vary from the parent plant, and may perhaps display peculiarities worth preserving. When this occurs—and only propagation by seed can give such a result—propagation by grafts and slips must of necessity be resorted to in order to perpetuate it. From seed we obtain new characteristics ; by grafting and the cultivation of slips we perpetuate them.

If only history had preserved the record, what a tale might we not read of long and laborious endeavours to obtain our various cultivated plants from a few worthless weeds.   Think of all the fortunate inspirations that resulted in the selection of species which could profitably be modified ; the patient attempts to subject them to cultivation, and, year after year, to improve them in this way or that ; of the care that prevented their degeneration, handing them down to us in a state of perfection ; think of all these things, and you will understand that in the least of our fruits or vegetables there is more, very much more, than the labour of the gardener who provides them.   There is in them the accumulated labour of perhaps a hundred generations—the labour required to transform the weed into the vegetable. We live on the fruits and vegetables created by our predecessors : we live by the toil, the energy, the ideas of the past. If the future world, in its turn, is able to live by our efforts—by the might of our arms, as well as the power of our thoughts—our mission on earth will have been worthily fulfilled.

CHAPTER XVI

THE LEAVES

*Plate or Lamina—Nervures and systems of innervation—The entire Leaf—
Denticulation, Lobes and Partitions—Laciniate Leaves—Composite
Leaves : Palmate and Pennate—Seed-Leaves—Bracts—Aquatic
Leaves—Sessile and Embracing Leaves—The fall of Leaves—The
Separating Layer—Persistent Leaves—The Sheath—The Stipules—
The co-ordination of Leaves to allow access of the maximum amount
of light—Arrangement of the Leaves of the Pear-tree—The Quincunx
—Alternate Leaves of the Elm—Tristichous Leaves of the Galingale—
Verticillate Leaves—The alternation of Verticles.*

PLANTS draw their nourishment both from the air and
from the soil. Their connections with the soil are
established by means of roots ; their intercourse with
the air is effected by means of leaves. A leaf, if we
reduce it to its lowest form, is made up of three parts :
the *plate* or *lamina*, the *petiole* or leaf-stalk, and the
stipules. The petiole is what we commonly call the tail
of the leaf ; it ends in the lamina ; the stipules are
foliaceous expansions situated at the base of the petiole.

The plate or lamina of a leaf has two surfaces ; the
upper surface, smoother and greener, is that which faces
toward the heavens, while the under surface, paler and
rougher, is that which faces toward the ground. It is
traversed, in its thickness, by bundles of *nervures* which
form the scaffolding or skeleton of the leaf. These
nervures consist almost entirely of fine bundles of woody
fibres, tracheal tubes and veins. The intervals of this
framework are filled in with green cells. When a leaf
falls to the ground the cellular portions quickly decay,

while the nervures, more refractory, persist and form a
sort of fine lacework.   Already we have noted the two
principal arrangements of this leafy framework.   Sometimes the nervures lie parallel with one another through
the whole length of the leaf ; sometimes they put forth
ramifications which often come together again, thus
forming a network.   Apart from a few exceptions, the
leaves with parallel nervures belong to the monocotyledons,

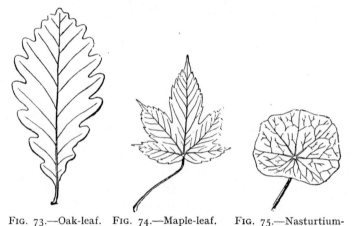

FIG. 73.—Oak-leaf.   FIG. 74.—Maple-leaf.   FIG. 75.—Nasturtium-
leaf.

while the leaves whose nervures are reticulated belong to
the dicotyledons.

The *innervation* or arrangement of the nervures is of
three principal types in the leaves of dicotyledonous
plants.   The most important of all the nervures—the
primary—continues the leaf-stalk, following the midrib
of the leaf, and subdividing itself to the right and the
left, into *secondary* nervures, distributed on either side
of the primary nervure just as the barbs of a feather are
arranged on either side of the shaft.   Such innervation is
said to be of the *pennate* type.   The Oak-leaf (Fig. 73)
is an example of this type.

Secondly, precisely where the petiole enters upon the lamina, a number of nervures branch out from it, of approximately equal size, radiating from their common point of origin much as the fingers radiate from the palm of the hand. This *palmate* innervation (Fig. 74) may be seen in the Maple.

In the third case the petiole terminates, not near the border of the leaf, but at a more or less central point, whence the principal nervures radiate in all directions, as though from the centre of a buckler, whence this type of innervation is known as *peltate*. We have an example in the leaf of the Nasturtium (Fig. 75).

If the margin of the leaf is continuous, without denticulations or indentations, like the leaves of the Box, the Olive, the Lilac, the Laurel, etc., the leaf is said to be

Fig. 76.—Hemlock-parsley.

entire. But in general the margin of the leaf is more or less extensively indented. The shallower indentations give us denticulated or crenelated leaves. Incisions that reach half-way to the centre of the leaf divide the leaf into *lobes* ; those that reach the nervure at the centre of the leaf divide the latter into *partitions*. Lastly, the divisions and subdivisions of the border may be so numerous that the leaf consists of little more than nervures with only the narrowest margin of cellular tissue. Leaves whose subdivisions are multiplied indefinitely— such as

13

those of the Carrot, Fennel or Hemlock-parsley (Fig. 76)
—are known as *laciniate*.

When the lamina is single and undivided, as in the
Pear, the Vine and the Lilac-tree, the leaf is known as
single, but the same leaf often comprises several distinct
laminae. For example, consider the Rose. We shall find
that one leaf comprises from three to seven laminae,

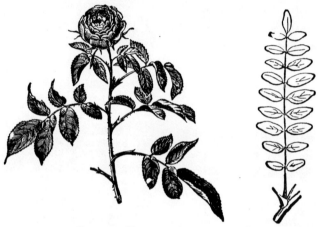

FIG. 77.—Rose.

FIG. 78.—Leaf of
Robinia or Acacia.

connected by a common leaf-stalk, which represents the
median nervure of an ordinary leaf. Each of these
subdivisions of the complete leaf, subdivisions which at
first sight we might be inclined to regard as so many
distinct leaves, is known as a *foliole*, and the leaf in its
entirety is known as a *composite leaf*. The leaf of the
Rose is thus a *composite leaf*, comprising one, two, or three
pairs of folioles, and one terminal foliole in addition.
We find the same structure, with a larger number of
folioles, in the Robinia, or common Acacia. On the
common petiole, sometimes called the spine of the leaf,
are inserted secondary petioles, each of which is continued

by the central nervure of the corresponding foliole (Fig. 78).

The symmetrical arrangement of the folioles, right and left of the common petiole, once more reminds us of the arrangement of the barbs of a feather on either side of the shaft, for which reason the Rose-tree and the Acacia are said to have *composite pennate leaves*. In other instances the folioles radiate from the end of the common petiole, constituting a leaf of the palmate type. The leaf is then said to be a *composite palmate leaf*. We shall find examples of this in the Horse Chestnut and the Virginia Creeper (Fig. 79).

FIG. 79.—Leaf of Virginia Creeper.

In the case of a given plant or tree the immense majority of the leaves are constant in type, but this fixity of formation is not absolute. At the principal stages of its development the plant modifies its foliage more or less ; the leaves that grow at the very base of the stem often differ in form from those that appear farther up the stem, while these may differ from the leaves adjacent to the flower.

The first two leaves put forth by the young shoot, the leaves that consist of the cotyledons, or, as they are called, the *seed-leaves*, do not often assume the shape of the leaves that follow them. They are nearly always entire, no matter how far the rest of the leaves may be sub-divided. As examples, we may note the heart-shaped seed-leaves of the Radish, and the tongue-shaped seed-leaves of the Carrot and of Parsley. Moreover, at the base of the stem, the leaves often display a special formation, deriving from the general form by gradual

modifications, or even without transition. Thus, a
pretty meadow flower, known as Lady-smock, displays
leaves growing from the base of the
stem consisting of broad denticulated
folioles, while the leaves growing higher
up the stem consist of narrow tongue-
shaped folioles (Fig. 80).

In other species we find leaves of
different form quite irrespective of
their height from the ground, and
occurring on the same branch. Thus,
the Paper Mulberry (Fig. 81) displays
entire leaves and leaves of two or
three lobes growing side by side. The
Paper Mulberry was originally a native
of Japan. It thrives in our climate
and is not unknown in our public
parks and avenues. The Chinese make
paper from the fibres of the bast layer
of the bark, and the Polynesians employ this layer as the ordinary material
of their garments.

Lastly, in the neighbourhood of
the flowers the leaves become smaller,
simpler and less subdivided, sometimes
losing their green colour and assuming
a tint like that of the flowers. They
then differ so greatly from ordinary
leaves that the botanists have given
them a special name : that of *bracts*.

FIG. 80.—Lady-
smock.

When the plant is aquatic its aerial leaves are often
different from those that are submerged. We have a
remarkable example in certain Ranunculi, with small
white flowers, which may be seen in ponds in the early
spring. The topmost leaves, which emerge above the

water, are simply lobulated ; the lower leaves, entirely immersed, are subdivided into delicate green tufts. The leaves, as we shall learn later on, are the respiratory organs of the plant. In the water, where the gases which the plant must breathe are less abundant than in the open air, the leaf is subdivided into tufts of green threads, so that it may expose a more extensive surface for absorption. In like fashion the gills, which are the respiratory organs of the fish, consist of a great number of minute laminations, which are exposed, in the cavity behind the gill-covers, to the life-giving contact of the oxygenated water. The Arrowhead, or Adder's-tongue, is found by the water's edge, and is sometimes actually immersed. When it grows out of the water its leaves are shaped like an arrow-head, and are borne on a long leafstalk, whence the name of the plant is derived ; but when the leaves are immersed in the stream they assume the form of narrow ribbons, a yard, or even more, in length.

FIG. 81.—Paper Mulberry.

The " tail " of the leaf is known as the petiole. It is a narrow bundle of vessels and fibres, which expands into the lamina or blade of the leaf, where it ramifies, producing the nervures of the leaf. In form it is usually cylindrical, with a narrow groove along its upper face. Sometimes,

however, it is flattened in the horizontal plane, and sometimes in the vertical plane. In the latter case the weight
of the leaf is in unstable equilibrium on the petiole that
supports it, the latter being turned edge upwards, and the
leaf is constantly shaken by the least breath of wind.
This may be observed in Poplar-trees and in the Aspen,
which for this reason is called the Quivering Aspen,
because of the constant quivering of its foliage.

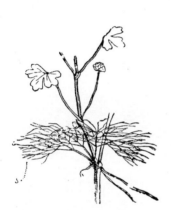 

FIG. 82.—Pond Crowfoot.
a, aerial leaves ; s, submerged leaves.

FIG. 83.—Arrowhead or
Adder's-tongue.

There are certain leaves whose petiole measures many
times the length of the blade of the leaf ; there are others
in which it is extremely short, and others from which it
is entirely absent. Leaves without petioles are known
as *sessile*. As a rule, the sessile leaf is attached to its
support by the whole of its base, so that it surrounds
the supporting twig or stem along a more or less
extensive proportion of its circumference : in other
words, it embraces it, and is therefore known as an
embracing leaf (Fig. 84).

When they are arranged in pairs along the stem, face
to face, embracing leaves often come joined together at
the base, forming a whole which
seems a single leaf, with two symmetrical halves, pierced at the
centre by the supporting stems.
Some of the Honeysuckles display
this curious arrangement, which is
especially pronounced in the neighbourhood of the blossoms.   When
the red berries of the Honeysuckle
are ripe, piled up as they are
in the hollow of the two combined leaves, they have the look

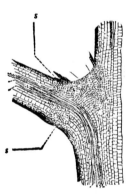

FIG. 85.—Point of attachment of a leaf
with its stem.

FIG. 84.—Sow-Thistle.   s, s, separating layer.

of a heap of fruit artificially arranged in a green
saucer.

At its point of attachment to the stalk the petiole is
commonly somewhat swollen, its increased diameter
giving the leaf a firmer foundation ; it is attached, moreover, to a slight lateral excrescence of the stem, a sort of
little bracket.   The manner in which the leaf is connected

with its support is not by any means a mere juxtaposition ;
there is an actual continuity between the leaf-stalk and
the twig or branch ; the fibres, tracheae and vessels of the
first are continued, without interruption, into the second.
In autumn, when its days are done, the dying leaf,
none the less, falls cleanly from the twig without effort,
and without fractured tissues, leaving a regular cicatrix
in which we may perceive, in the midst of the cellular
tissue forming the outer envelope, a certain number
of dark specks, which are the broken fibro-vascular
bundles.

The mechanism of the fall of an autumn leaf is note-
worthy for its beautiful simplicity. When the leaf
begins to lose its normal green coloration and assumes a
yellow or scarlet hue—the sign of decay—the last of its
diminishing vitality is employed in preparing the way
for an easy separation. In the little swelling beside the
axil a transversal stratum of very small cells is formed, of
transparent cells, full of starch, which does not occur
elsewhere in the leaf. This is known as the *separating
layer*. These starchy cells, which are not especially solid,
and are, moreover, without cohesion among themselves,
give way before the tugging and jerking of the leaf,
which flutters in the slightest breeze ; and a narrow crack
appears, which surrounds the whole prominence. The
bundles of fibres and vessels alone are not involved in
this disaggregation ; but they are too fragile to support
very long the pull of the leaf ; they, too, give way, and
the leaf parts from the twig. This gradual separation
may be observed in the majority of our trees : for
example, in the Walnut, Poplar, Elm, Lime, Lilac and
Pear, to name a few.

More rarely this layer of small starchy cells—the
separating layer—is not formed in the thickness of the
" bracket." The dead leaf then hangs on the tree through

a great part of the winter, falling only when torn away by the gales. We see this in the Oak, whose dead, rusty-brown leaves linger long on the tree, giving way only little by little to the assaults of winter. It may even happen that withered leaves remain on the tree for several years, disappearing only when destroyed by the gales. Thus, the Date-palm displays at the top of its trunk the graceful bunch of its enormous green leaves. Externally dead leaves are visible, but they are more or less intact ; lower down are leaves reduced, by the protracted action of the atmosphere, to broken leaf-stalks ; further down still these relics disappear, corroded by time, and the trunk shows merely the vague scars of old, long-detached leaves.

In many plants, just above the point of detachment, the petiole increases its width and curls up at the edges, transforming itself into a sort of furrow or conduit, which surrounds or encloses the stem as with a sheath or scabbard ; whence this part of the leaf is known as the *sheath*. Beyond this the petiole resumes its habitual form. The scabbard is especially remarkable in certain plants of the Umbelliferous family, notably in the Angelica. It forms a long, strong sheath or casing, which increases the strength of the stem, which is itself hollow, containing a wide central bore. The hollow stems of the Gramineous plants—that is, their straw—are also provided with leaves that ensheath them to a great extent. In Angelica and many other umbelliferous plants the blade of the leaf progressively diminishes in size from the base of the stem to the summit ; while at the same time the sheath increases, so that the topmost leaves are merely wide membranes wrapped about the young twigs and the flower-clusters as yet in the bud.

If the expansion that produces the sheath, instead of adhering to the petiole throughout its length, detaches itself on either side, being partly or wholly isolated, the resulting structure is what we know as the *stipules*. The stipules are therefore foliaceous expansions attendant upon the base of the petiole.   They occur in a large number of plants, but not in all, for their function, like that of the petiole, is of quite secondary importance.   The really important and active portion of the leaf is the blade or lamina, which is almost always present, and whose functions, when it is absent, are performed by other organs which then assume its structure.   I will ask the reader to refer back to Fig. 77, which shows the composite pennate Rose-leaf.   Right at the base of the common petiole you will see, on either side, a green membranous border, the upper end of which terminates in a small, unsupported auricular point.   These are the stipules ; but the shape and width of these organs vary in an astonishing degree according to the species of plant. Sometimes the stipules are free and grow to such a size that one might well mistake them for leaves ; thus, the pennate leaves of the Pea (Fig. 86) are provided with two enormous stipules, much larger than the folioles, but they may be distinguished from the latter by the fact that they are located at the very base of the petiole instead of being strung out along its length.   Sometimes they are welded to the petiole, as in the Roses, or to one another, as in the Astragali ; sometimes they surround the stem, forming a sheath that sometimes ends in a graceful little collar.

In many plants—as the Hawthorn, the Pear-tree, the Apricot-tree—the stipules are highly ephemeral ; they fall when the leaf which they accompany is unfolded. Their chief purpose is to serve as a protecting envelope for very young leaves.   Let us examine the tip of a Geranium-stem ; you will see that the nascent leaf is protected on either side by wide stipules, like the curtains ot a cradle. When the leaf is unfolded and strong enough to fend for itself the stipules wither and fall.

Some of the Figs, and in particular the tree that furnishes india-rubber, are still more remarkable in this

Fig. 86.—Leaf, flower and fruit of the Pea.
The leaf bears wide stipules at its base, while its terminal folioles are transformed into tendrils.

respect. Their young leaves are rolled up together in cone-shaped packets, each being covered with a long hood, formed by the stipules. When the time has come the hood falls away and the leaf which it shelters expands.

It may be that you have never particularly noticed

the order in which leaves are arranged as regards their succession from end to end of their supporting twig. You may have accorded them merely that vague, unreflecting glance which one gives to matters of no intrinsic importance ; and if anyone had asked you how the leaves grew along their supporting axis, you would probably have replied : " Oh, more or less anyhow ! "   But they are not by any means arranged just " anyhow " ; everything in this world obeys the harmonious laws of number, weight and order.   Everything has weight, everything has size, everything can be numbered.   The humblest weed arranges its leaves in accordance with the rules of an exquisite geometry, whose elements I will explain.

The first need of a leaf is to expand itself in the open air, to seek the light ; you need be in no doubt as to its motives.   If leaves were superimposed too closely they would get in one another's way ; they would overshadow one another and hide the sunlight from one another ; yet the sunlight is absolutely necessary to their task.   To avoid, or rather to extend, this harmful superimposition, the plant strings out its leaves along a spiral line which ascends with geometrical uniformity ; it is like the spiral staircase of a lofty tower.   At the bottom of this spiral ascent it places a first leaf ; a little higher up, but not in a vertical line with the first bud, the second finds place ; still higher, and still to one side, is situated the third leaf ; and so forth, so that the points of attachment of the various leaves rotate as they ascend, but are never superimposed.   Sooner or later, inevitably, when all the possible situations of the leaf are occupied, it will happen that some one leaf will be found vertically above another leaf ; the spiral, in its rotation, has superimposed two points of attachment, but with such a distance between that the rays of the sun fall upon the lower leaf practically without interruption by the upper leaf in the same position

on the spiral. From the points where these two leaves
are remotely superimposed the original order recom-
mences, in such fashion that the subsequent leaves
correspond, one by one, with the leaves on the lower
part of the spiral.

Here we must resort to a pictorial representation.

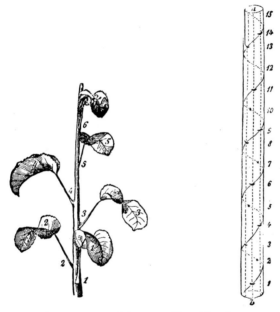

FIG. 87.—Arrangement of leaves   FIG. 88.—Arrangement of leaves
        of Pear-tree.   of Pear-tree.

Fig. 87 represents part of a branch of a Pear-tree. Let
us start from the first leaf we come upon, which we will
call leaf No. 1.   In passing from this leaf to the next—
in ascending, so to speak, to the next story—we shall
follow the imaginary spiral which we can picture as
winding round the branch, passing the different leaves in
their order of succession. We now come to leaf No. 2.
You will see that in order to avoid incommoding leaf No. 1

by its shadow it has taken up its position to one side of
the former. Continuing, we come to leaf No. 3, which
is superimposed on neither of the first two leaves. Leaf
No. 4, again, does not correspond with any of its predecessors. One more stage of the spiral stair leads us to
leaf No. 5, which, once more, is so placed that it cannot
overshadow those below it. Lastly, leaf No. 6 is placed
precisely above leaf No. 1, and forms, we might say,
the roof of the five-storied structure.

Above leaf No. 6 the spiral still ascends with the same
distribution of the leaves. Leaf No. 6, superimposed on
No. 1, is followed by No. 7, superimposed on No. 2 ;
after which we have these Nos. 8, 9, 10, 11 superimposed
on leaves Nos. 3, 4, 5, 6. On reaching leaf No. 11, we
find that this leaf lies on the line which has already
passed through leaves Nos. 1 and 6 ; and we once come to
this line on reaching leaves Nos. 16, 21, 26, etc.—that is,
whenever we ascend the spiral by an additional space of
five leaves. Thus, the leaves of the Pear-tree are arranged
in successive sequences of five. In any one series of five
consecutive leaves there is no leaf so situated as to cast
its shadow upon any other leaf. There is superimposition,
but it is of series upon series ; the leaves as a whole are
aligned on five straight rows, running from end to end
of the branch. One of these rows includes the leaves
1, 6, 11, 16, etc. ; the second, the leaves 2, 7, 12, 17,
etc. ; the third, the leaves 3, 8, 13, 18, etc. ; the fourth,
the leaves 4, 9, 14, 19, etc. ; and the fifth, 5, 10, 15,
20, etc. Note that each of these series is composed of a
sequence of numbers of which each consecutive term is
increased by five ; let us also note, in Fig. 88, that
in passing from leaf No. 1 to the corresponding No. 6,
or, generally speaking, from any one leaf to that immediately above it, the imaginary spiral which passes through
all the leaves will have travelled twice round the branch.

This arrangement of leaves, superimposed in lots of five, each series of five making two revolutions of the spiral, is known as a *quincunx,* and is very often seen in dicotyledonous plants.

There are other and more complicated arrangements ; for example, that in which the leaves are superimposed in series of eight, each series making three turns of the spiral ; or that in which they are superimposed in series of

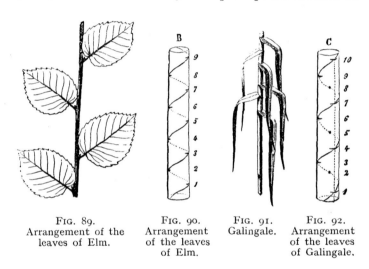

FIG. 89.
Arrangement of the
leaves of Elm.

FIG. 90.
Arrangement
of the leaves
of Elm.

FIG. 91.
Galingale.

FIG. 92.
Arrangement
of the leaves
of Galingale.

thirteen, which include five turns ; and there are yet others. But these arrangements are unusual in proportion to their complication, and we need not linger over them. Let us return to simpler examples. In the Elm (Fig. 89) the leaves are strung out along two straight lines, one including the odd numbers, 1, 3, 5, 7, etc., and the other the even numbers, 2, 4, 6, 8, etc. Here, accordingly, every other leaf is superimposed. With this arrangement the leaves are known as *alternate,* since they are alternately arranged along two straight lines, on the right or the left of the branch.

In the Galingale (Fig. 91) leaf No. 4 is superimposed on leaf No. 1, leaf No. 5 on No. 2, leaf No. 6 on No. 3, etc. Here we have the superimposition of series of three leaves, and each series of three includes one turn of the spiral. This arrangement is known as *tristichous*, because the leaves are arranged upon three straight lines. It is seen in many monocotyledonous plants.

Leaves arranged one by one along a spiral, in accordance with one of the laws of which I have given you some examples, are known as alternate leaves. The point of

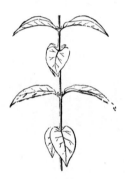

FIG. 93.—Opposed or opposite leaves.

FIG. 94.—Three-leaved whorls of Oleander.

their growth upon the plant is called the *node*, and the space between two consecutive nodes is known as the *internode*.

In other cases the leaves are grouped in pairs, or in threes or fours, or even larger groups, about the same node. These groups are known as *verticils* or *whorls*, and the leaves are *verticillate*. When there are only two leaves they are more frequently spoken of as *opposed* or *opposite* (Fig. 93). In such arrangements each pair of leaves is set at right angles to that below it, always with the evident purpose of casting as little shadow as possible. For that matter, this is a general law, and whatever their number, the leaves of a whorl are not superimposed on those of the whorl beneath it, but are opposite the intervals which divide them. This arrangement is denoted by the statement that two consecutive whorls alternate their leaves. We have a good example of this in the Oleander, whose whorls consist of three leaves apiece (Fig. 94).

CHAPTER XVII

THE MOVEMENTS OF LEAVES

The gyration of leaves—Experiments of C. Bonnet—The Sophora or Japanese Pagoda-tree—Alstroemeria—Quivering Sainfoin—The Dionaea or Venus' Fly-trap—Carnivorous vegetables—The Sensitive Plant—Effects of shock, heat, light, electricity and corrosive chemicals —Influence of habit—The action of ether and chloroform on animals— Their effect on the Sensitive Plant.

IN the animal we find voluntary movement; in the plant, immobility. The animal moves from place to place, at the bidding of its instinct; the plant persists in a continual repose. This contrast between activity on the one hand and inertia on the other is apparently so definite that it has been proposed as the differential quality between the animal and the plant. If we take a general view of the matter this difference appears to be authentic; but if we examine the matter in detail there are many striking exceptions which betray a close analogy between animal and vegetable life as regards their general properties. The sister of the animal, and older than the latter, the plant has sometimes, like the animal, the power of spontaneous movement; and there are certain facts which make us wonder whether it is not perhaps to a certain extent capable of feeling : that vague, unconscious sensibility which occurs in the lower strata of animal life. This chapter will be devoted to rehearsing the principal data bearing upon this difficult and important problem.

A leaf has two surfaces ; the upper surface is smoother

and greener ; the under surface is paler, and rougher on account of the prominence of the nervures. Their anatomical structure is not precisely the same, nor is their part in the cycle of plant life ; the surface fronting the light of heaven has functions differing from those of that looking on the shady soil. What will happen, then, if the leaf is artificially turned upside down, the under side facing the light and the upper surface the shade ? Thus turned about, so that the side made for the light is in shadow and the side made for the shadow braves the light, the leaf cannot perform its customary task.

With a very gradual but persistent and continuous movement, the leaf, of its own accord, turns itself over, twisting its leaf-stalk until its upper and under surfaces have returned to their normal position. If, from time to time, the gardener should intervene to restore the leaf to its topsy-turvy condition, the leaf, by further twisting of the leaf-stalk, restores matters to their normal condition. Bonnet, the botanist-philosopher of Geneva, describes this action of the plant : " I have turned over or bent the twigs of more than twenty species of plants, herbaceous as well as lignous, and have kept them fixed in this position. The leaves of these twigs having likewise been placed in a position the very reverse of that which is natural to them, I presently had the pleasure of seeing them return to and resume their usual position. I have repeated the experiment with the same shoot as many as fourteen consecutive times, and still this wonderful power of reversal showed no sign of failing." The persistence with which the leaf twists and untwists and twists itself in order to evade obstacles and return to the position demanded by its nature, reminds us of the invincible obstinacy of the germinating plant, which makes a sudden right-about turn when the position of the seed is altered, so that the root once more grows downwards

and the stem upwards.   But the leaf, as though subject
to fatigue, turns itself about less quickly each time the
experiment is repeated.   In Bonnet's experiments, a
Vine-leaf required twenty-four hours to return to its
natural position after the first reversal.   But after the
fourth reversal it needed four days, and after the sixth,
eight days.   The return to normality was made most
rapidly under the stimulus of sunlight.   The Genevan
scientist records that a leaf of Mountain Spinach returned
to the normal position in two hours, under the radiance
of a blazing sun.   This promptitude was not surpassed
by any other plant.

Apart from artificial reversals, the work of the human
experimenter, the plant is sometimes compelled to
turn over all its leaves.   There are some plants whose
ramifications point not upwards but downwards.   This
abnormality is sometimes the purely mechanical result
of the length and weakness of the branches, which hang
perpendicularly downwards, being devoid of the rigidity
which should support their weight ; the Weeping Willow
is a familiar example.   Sometimes it is due merely to
the natural propensities of the plant, whose vigorous
shoots bend downwards, not under their own weight, but
owing to their natural tendency.   Thus, the Japanese
Pagoda-tree, which is often to be seen in our gardens,
curves all its boughs crozier-wise downwards at their
base, its branches, stout or fragile, forming a green cage
of foliage at some distance from the trunk.   This reversal
of direction results in the reversal of all the leaves ; but
the leaves, as they grow, prove capable of taking up the
position most proper to them.   They are composite
pennate leaves, like those of the familiar Acacia.   The
common leaf-stalk displays at its base a considerable
dilatation which rotates upon itself, pulling after it the
whole leaf, despite the weight of the latter, and turning it

PAGODA-TREE.

J. Boyer.

To face p. 196.

back to the natural position. The Alstroemeria, commonly known as the Peruvian Lily, is a graceful amaryllidaceous plant, whose original home is the land of the Incas. In this country it is a greenhouse plant. Its foliage displays a most singular anomaly. The leaves consist of a long elliptical blade which contracts into a petiole in form like a narrow ribbon. Now, this ribbon-like petiole is always twisted on itself, so that the leaf is topsy-turvy. If we untwist the petiole, in order to return the leaf to what, it seems to us, must be its normal position, we shall discover, with profound astonishment, that the upper surface is pale and wrinkled, while the lower surface is smooth and green. Here, then, we have a plant which, by some inexplicable abnormality, has all its leaves upside down, although the stem rises perpendicularly and appears to be in no way exceptional. The ribbon-like petioles, in making a half-turn upon themselves, return the leaves to their proper position, the smooth, green under surface being now turned upwards and the pale, wrinkled upper surface downwards. If it were permissible to compare the work of creation with the work of man, should we not perceive, in the leaves of the Peruvian Lily, a malady of location, the result of a momentary absence of mind which turned upwards what should have been turned downwards ? But the error is at once realized, and the petioles set it right by means of the torsion which they exert.

To these movements, these expressions of a slow tenacity by which leaves whose normal position is reversed are restored to their normal position, we may add a few others, extensive and sudden, which are more like the motions of an animal. Three plants above all are famed for such movements : the Quivering Sainfoin, Venus' Fly-trap and the Sensitive Plant.

The Indian Sainfoin was first observed a century ago

in the scorching plains of the Ganges delta by Lady Monson, who travelled extensively in India in order to study the natural history of the country. Since then this singular vegetable has been introduced into the hot-houses of Europe, where it has been possible to confirm the description of the learned traveller. Its leaves, like those of our Clover, consist each of three folioles, with the difference, that the folioles of the Indian Sainfoin are very unequal in size, the central foliole being some-times as much as four inches in length, while the two lateral folioles are in proportion extremely small, seldom exceeding an inch in length.

The large foliole is subject to an alternate rise and fall, in accordance with the presence or absence of sunlight. During the night it hangs downwards, its under surface touching the twig or stem. At daybreak it begins slowly to move, erecting itself by degrees as the sun ascends. By noon on a really brilliant summer's day it is in a straight line with the petiole. Then, if the heat is sufficiently intense, it begins to quiver in a very percep-tible fashion. As the sun declines, so the foliole likewise subsides, resuming, for the night, its pendant position. In addition to this general oscillation, which depends upon the height of the sun, the plant is subject to an incidental oscillation which depends on the luminosity of the heavens. If a cloud casts its shadow on the landscape the foliole droops ; but if the day becomes fine again the foliole once more moves upwards. It is indeed so sensitive to the influence of the light that we may see it all day long changing its direction, rising and falling, accordingly as the sky becomes darker or brighter.

The movement of the two lateral folioles is really more remarkable, and is independent of the stimulus of light. In the darkness as in the light, in the night as in the day, provided the temperature is sufficiently high, these

two folioles fall and rise in continual alternation, like
two wings, slowly beating the air in reverse directions.
As soon as the right-hand foliole has reached the limit of
its ascent, the left-hand foliole falls, remaining for a
moment stationary at the lowest point of its course, and
then once more ascends, while the opposite foliole once
more moves downwards. Two minutes suffice for the
rise and fall. The ascent is slower than the descent, and
is sometimes effected by jerks, like those of the second
hand of a watch. The rate of these jerky little impulses
is about sixty to the minute. This perpetual oscillation
increases in its activity when the weather becomes moister
and warmer ; it is continued even by leaves detached
from the plant and ceases only when the folioles are
dead. In our greenhouses the Indian Sainfoin is less
rapid in its oscillations ; and at times it may even while
away its long hours of exile by prolonged immobility.

Similar movements, but far less noticeable, may be
observed in the leaves of the Pea and the Kidney-Bean.
There is reason to believe that many vegetables, even
those with which we are most familiar, would display
spontaneous movements like those of the Indian Sainfoin,
were we to examine them with sufficient care. As a
general thing they escape us, on account of their very
small range and their deliberation.

The Dionaea, or Venus' Fly-trap, is a small plant found
in the marshes of North Carolina. Its leaves consist
each of a petiole, expanded on either side into a wide
wing, and a rounded blade, whose two halves can rotate
about the median nervure as about a hinge, and press
against one another. This lamina is bordered by long,
stiff, pointed hairs or spines. If an insect alights upon the
blade the leaf quickly closes its two halves and imprisons
the insect in the net formed by its interlocking spines.
The more the insect struggles to release itself the more

forcibly the vegetable trap contracts. Then something happens that is even stranger, which we should be inclined to relegate to the category of fables, were it not confirmed by the most credible witnesses. The leaf proceeds to exude, around the victim, a fluid which converts the dead insect into a mass of liquid putrescence. The liquid elements of this animal pulp are finally absorbed by the leaf, which by thus imbibing them nourishes the plant. There are, then, carnivorous vegetables which trap their prey in order to feed upon it. The Dionaea,

FIG. 95.—Dionaea or Venus' Fly-trap.

amongst others, has turned its leaves into traps wherewith to capture game.

The Sensitive Plant is a herbaceous plant originally found in South America, much sought after on account of its extreme irritability, which has made it famous and earned it a name. It is grown in pots, under glass and in the garden. Its leaves are bi-pinnate, and the stem is armed with spines growing hookwise and its flowers are arranged in little globular clusters.—Let us suppose that the plant is standing in the sunlight, all its leaves fully displayed: one of the folioles—for example, one of the pair at the tip of the leaf—is lightly touched. This foliole at once moves obliquely upwards, its companion on the opposite side does the same, and the two bring their upper surfaces into contact above the petiole. The impulse thus given spreads farther. The second pair of folioles comports itself like the first, and the third does likewise, and the fourth, and the fifth, so that gradually all the folioles, in due succession, close upon one another.

The propagation of the stimulus may follow the reverse direction. If we touch a foliole at the base of the double row, the other folioles come together in order from the base of the leaf to the tip. We see, then, that the impulse is transmitted in either direction indifferently, communicated from the foliole first touched to those adjacent to it. If the foliole is only lightly touched the three or four pairs of folioles adjacent to the point stimulated will fold themselves together, but the others remain unaffected. If the stimulus is rather more violent the folioles close together from one end of the leaf to the other, the secondary petioles come together in a bundle, and the common petiole, pivoted upon its point of attachment, droops and points earthwards. Lastly, if the plant is roughly handled all the leaves hastily close up, assuming a withered appearance and hanging along the stem as though dead. In any case the trouble is but of short duration. When all is quiet the petioles turn slowly on their bases, the

FIG. 96.—Two leaves of the Sensitive Plant, one expanded and erect, the other flexed and contracted.

leaves erect themselves, and the folioles are once more expanded. On the scorching plains of Brazil, where the Sensitive Plant covers wide expanses of soil, a galloping horse, or the step of a passer-by, is often enough to provoke the extreme irritability of the plant. The slight vibration set up in the ground by the step of the traveller is often enough to make the nearer Sensitive Plants close their leaves ; the movement of the plants affected stimulates those adjacent to them, so that the impulse is propagated in all directions. Suddenly, without apparent cause, the expanse of foliage covering the ground is seen to be full of movement, and a few moments later it has assumed a faded aspect.

The Sensitive Plant is not affected merely by a touch, a mechanical shock ; it is sensitive to many stimuli which affect the nervous irritability of the animal, such as the electric spark, a sudden change of temperature, the action of heat and cold, or the corrosive effect of chemical reagents. With its leaves outspread in the warm air of a greenhouse, a Sensitive Plant suddenly closes up if we open a window in order to admit the cool air from without ; and it does the same if, having expanded its foliage in the shade, it suddenly encounters the burning rays of the sun. To make it furl its foliage it is enough that a cloud should cool the air by veiling the sun awhile. The discharge of an electric spark disturbs the plant profoundly ; but the most violent result is produced by corrosive chemicals or by heat. If we focus the rays of the sun with a lens on a foliole, or burn the foliole slightly with a slip of paper, the plant will within a few minutes close and let fall the whole of its leaves, starting from the injured point. We may obtain the same result by depositing on a foliole, with every possible precaution to avoid shaking it, a tiny drop of some corrosive liquid, such as sulphuric acid. Both these tests, although they affect only one single point on the Sensitive Plant, and even then do not cause any shock of impact, cause a very profound and lasting impression, for the plant subjected to this experiment will perhaps refuse to unfold itself for as long as eight or ten hours. If the ordeal is repeated several times in succession the most vigorous plant may languish and eventually die. Such facts remind us of the animal organism, which quickly recovers from a slight emotion, but, after acute pain or grief, may lie for some time in a state of collapse, dying if too violently assaulted by the repetition of the torture.

The analogy goes farther than this. In the animal any part is liable to the perception of pain and is able to transmit this perception to the whole organism, which suffers with the injured part and either comes to its relief, or at least shrinks away from the danger. There is a community of suffering between all the parts of the body ; let any point be injured, the irritation spreads in all directions, and sets up a general uneasiness. A similar solidarity of the organs and a like faculty of transmitting a local impression in all directions are found in the Sensitive Plant. We have just seen that the impression spreads from one foliole to the next, from the summit to the base, or from the base to the summit, indifferently ; and it spreads with the same facility from one end of the plant to the other. Let us lay bare, while guarding against any sudden jerk, some point on the roots of the Sensitive Plant ; and on the point in question let us place a drop of sulphuric acid. We shall see the plant hastily furling its leaves from base to summit, just as it would have furled them from summit to base if the acid had been applied to one of the uppermost folioles. Lastly, if the injured point is about midway up the stem, the disturbance will be propagated in both directions simultaneously, the folioles gradually closing up both above and below the point of injury.

In the animal habit deadens sensibility, and the slight

perturbation which at first might produce signs of uneasiness ceases to provoke such symptoms when long continued. The Sensitive Plant likewise allows habit to take the upper hand. In this connection the following experiment may be noted. A Sensitive Plant, fully expanded, is placed in a carriage. At the first jolting of the carriage, as it sets out, the leaves are shaken and close up. But as the journey is a long one, the plant gradually becomes more or less reassured, recovers from its perturbation, and finally expands its foliage as though it were in a state of complete repose. The jolting of the wheels over the stones, the sudden jerks, of which the smallest would, at the beginning, have thrown it into a state of commotion, no longer affect it ; the Sensitive Plant has now grown accustomed to them. The carriage stops, and the plant merely expands itself more fully. Now the journey is resumed ; and again there is a sudden contraction of the foliage, but of shorter duration than the first, as though the original ordeal had in some sort armed the plant against its present trials. Finally the carriage may start and stop, and the plant remains fully expanded.

Certain substances, such as ether and chloroform, possess the property of benumbing the perceptions, of suspending them for the time being, producing what we know as anaesthesia. This wonderful property is exploited in suppressing pain during major surgical operations. Rendered insensible for a few minutes, the patient is indifferent to the scalpel that cuts into his flesh. Let us place a bird under a glass bell-jar, together with a sponge soaked with ether. In this atmosphere, steeped in vaporized ether, the bird is quickly overcome by a profound state of torpor ; it falters, and falls to the ground, to all appearances dead. We will now withdraw it from the bell-jar, since if this condition were too far prolonged the bird would no longer return to life. We shall find that the heart is beating as usual, that the breathing is quiet and uniform. Consequently the bird is still alive ; yet one might pinch it, prick it, and even inflict a serious wound, without eliciting the slightest quiver or symptom of pain. We have before us life intact, but without its sensibility. The bird soon recovers from this condition, as though from a passing intoxication, recovering its senses and its capacity for suffering, and is finally just as it was before the experiment.

Let us subject the Sensitive Plant to a similar ordeal. After the lapse of a certain time, much longer than in the case of the bird, the irritability of the plant is blunted. The Sensitive Plant is withdrawn from the bell-jar full of ether vapour, with its foliage fully expanded, just as it was before the experiment ; but for some time the foliage remains insensible. You may shake the folioles, scorch them, treat them in any way you please, but you will not induce them to fold themselves up. As in the case of the bird, this insensitiveness is ephemeral ; provided it has not been kept too long under the bell-jar, in which case the plant, like the bird, would inevitably perish, the Sensitive Plant gradually becomes more capable of perception, and finally will once more furl its leaves at the lightest touch.

Having briefly considered these facts, what radical difference do we perceive between the sensibility of this curious plant and the sensibility of the animal ? I mean the animal to be found at the very foot of the ladder of evolution ; as, for example, the Polyp, which, affixed to its submarine rock, expands its tentacles as a flower its petals, or closes them, shrinking into itself. There is no perceptible difference. Between the animal and the plant there is no absolute line of demarcation ; all the attributes of the animal, even movement, and sensitiveness to impression, are found in the plant, at least in the condition of a vague rudiment or vestige.

CHAPTER XVIII

THE SLEEP OF PLANTS

Discovery of the sleep of plants—Bird's-foot Trefoil—What is meant by the sleep of plants—Nocturnal attitudes of various vegetable species—Return of leaves to the position which they occupied in the bud—The sleep of pinnate leaves—Various examples—Result of prolonged excitation— Altered aspect of the landscape during a long-continuing wind—Sleep of the Sensitive Plant—Influence of age—Action of light—Decandolle's experiments—The sleep of plants cannot be compared with that of animals.

LINNÆUS once received from Sauvage, the celebrated professor of Montpellier, a semi-tropical plant, the Bird's-foot Trefoil, whose flowers he wished to study. The delicate plant, which had been transported from the scorching coasts of the southern Mediterranean to the freezing fogs of Sweden, none the less contrived, with a good deal of assistance, to flower in the hothouses of Upsala. It was a red-letter day for the botanists when the first flowers appeared—tiny yellow flowers, grouped in threes, in the midst of a bundle of leaves; so that Linnæus suffered a most unpleasant surprise when, on returning, one evening, to inspect the plant, there was no longer any sign of the flowers which he had noted some hours beforehand. The opening of the flowers had escaped him; they had all disappeared, doubtless cut down by some jealous hand or destroyed by insects. The ill seemed to be without remedy, when, on the following day, Linnæus, once more inspecting the plant, found a display of blossoms as abundant as it had been before; the same flowers, perfectly fresh, were present in their original places. The mystery was soon explained. It was discovered that on the approach of night the Bird's-foot Trefoil folds up its expanded folioles, and erects them about each group of flowers, so that the latter become invisible even to the most attentive gaze. At the same time the flower-stalks droop slightly and the branches hang downwards. Such was the point of departure of the observer who discovered the nature of *the sleep of plants.*

This is the term by which we describe the arrangement which the foliage of many vegetable species displays during the night, and which is entirely different from that assumed during the day. For plants do sleep ; not all, and not those with tough, stringy leaves, such as the Oak, the Holly, and the Laurel ; but those with delicate, and, above all, composite leaves ; they sleep ; that is to say, during the night they assume a posture that differs from that of the daytime. Spinach, when night approaches, raises its drooping leaves toward the top of its stem, folding them up against the still tender tip of the shoot, while the frail, impatient Balsamin that grows by the running streams, does precisely the contrary ; it folds its leaves downwards towards the base of the stem. The Oenothera, which displays its great yellow, fragrant flowers by the riverside, turns its topmost leaves into a nocturnal shelter surrounding its corollae ; the Oxalis, whose leaves consist of three heart-shaped folioles, fold the latter in two along the median nervure, and allow them to hang, head downwards, from the end of the common leaf-stalk. The Clovers, like the Bird's-foot Trefoil, muster their leaves round about their flowers ; the Lupins, on the other hand, though members of the same family, leave their flowers bare at night, while their leaves point downwards. In the Pyrenees, where the white Lupin and red Clover are grown together, the same field, at different times of day, presents an absolutely different appearance. In the bright sunlight it is a rich carpet of verdure enamelled with the red blossoms of the Clover and the white bloom of the Lupin ; when the shadows of evening have fallen the Clover draws a curtain of leaves over its flowers, while the foliage of the Lupin droops downwards.   Half the plants in the field seem to have died.   The Clover seems to have lost its flowers and the Lupin its leaves.

The animal, according to its species, varies its preparations before going to sleep.   The hen ascends to her perch, tucking one foot in her down, and hides her head under her wing ; the cat seeks the hearthrug, where she curls herself up ; the sheep kneels before lying down with her legs drawn up beneath her ; cattle lie on their flanks ; the hedgehog rolls herself into a ball ; the adder coils himself in a spiral.   In the same way, each vegetable species has its own way of sleeping, which differs greatly in different species. Despite this great variety, the behaviour of plants at night is, nevertheless, subject to a general law, for we may note, in the leaf, a marked tendency to resume, in the night, the position which it occupied in the bud, when, still wrapped in downy scales, it slept the profound sleep of infancy.   Thus, one rolls itself roughly into the form of a cone, a spiral twist ; another folds up like a fan ; a third shuts up like a book ; a fourth crumples itself up in careless fashion ; in short, each leaf assumes more or less the same creases as those which it assumed in the bud.   The arrangement for nocturnal repose is most striking in the composite leaves. Examine, by daylight, an Acacia, a Mimosa, or any one of those trees with composite-pinnate leaves so often to be met with in our gardens.   Examine it again at nightfall.   What a curious change has come over the arrangement of the foliage !   The expression of the tree has

PERIWINKLE OPENING TO THE FIRST RAYS OF THE MORNING SUN.

To face p. 208.

entirely changed. In the day the folioles are outspread on either side of the common flower-stalk, giving the foliage a tufted appearance, and a look of vitality that is pleasant to behold ; but when evening comes, the folioles, as though overwhelmed by fatigue, lie prone in all directions. The foliage now looks as though stripped ; it has a sickly, dismal appearance. One might well conclude that it had been withered by drought, or stricken to death by the heat of the sun. But this condition is merely ephemeral : to-morrow, at sunrise, you will see the tree once more expanding its leaves as fresh and green as ever.

With the aid of a few examples we can describe this condition of sleep more exactly. In the Mimosa, the folioles, fully displayed in a state of vigilance, close themselves up from base to tip over the common petiole, partly overlapping one another like the tiles of a roof. In the Amorpha or False Indigo the folioles may be seen, horizontally outspread, by the light of the earliest dawn. As the sun rises, the folioles, too, erect themselves, and by noon will be pointing toward the zenith. They then begin once more to droop, and on the approach of night are limp and pendant, hanging back to back under the common petiole. The Bladder-Nut-tree, whose membranous and dilated pods are like so many little bladders, sends its folioles to sleep in quite a different position. They will be found under the petiole, pressed against it, in pairs, the back being outermost. The Cassia-tree of Maryland allows its folioles to droop at night, as does the False Indigo. In this fashion any given pair of folioles must, one would imagine, bring their under-surfaces together, and slumber back to back ; but by twisting themselves on their short base they contrive to press their upper surfaces together The Sensitive Plant folds up its folioles, and lowers them until they lie approximately

15

lengthwise along their common support, being arranged in two overlapping rows, reclining side by side.   Moreover, the secondary petioles are gathered together in a sort of bundle, the most important of all revolving on its point of attachment, and the whole leaf, uniformly folded, swings downwards like the arm of a semaphore.   This nocturnal position is precisely that assumed by the Sensitive Plant during the day on the application of a suitable stimulant.

The same remark may be applied to a number of plants in which certain movements may be excited.   We shall find that they all assume, during sleep, the attitude which they affect if the irritability of their foliage is exploited.   Thus, if the three folioles of a leaf of Yellow Wood-Sorrel are for some time lightly percussed they will fold up along the median nervure and hang downwards from the tip of the flower-stalk.   Now this is precisely the position which they spontaneously assume on the approach of night. Again, if a branch of Mimosa or Acacia is roughly shaken for some considerable time, it folds its leaves as it would have done under the influence of the darkness alone.   This is the cause of the change of aspect which a prolonged gale may cause in the landscape ; there are several trees whose foliage is by no means easily affected that eventually surrender to the continued assaults of the wind and assume their nocturnal posture in broad daylight.

This propensity to sleep is noted more particularly in

FIG. 97.—Yellow Wood-Sorrel.

youth ; but as the plant ages its waking periods become longer, and only with difficulty can it be lulled to sleep. We find the same thing in the young animal, which easily falls into a sound and protracted sleep, whereas when it is old its periods of sleep become short and irregular. Having reached a certain stage of maturity, some plants, which at first display a marked tendency to sleep, eventually lose the power of sleep altogether ; the leaves, as they grow stiff with age, no longer obey the all but imperceptible causes of their nocturnal attitude.

And what are these causes ? For what purpose do the leaves of the plant expand themselves by day and close again at night ? In short, what is it that causes plants to sleep or wake ? This is a highly obscure problem, to which are related some of the most difficult problems of light. We know that light plays a great part in these problems, though its action is by no means exclusive. All leaves capable of sleep open in the morning and close at night ; all expand themselves when the sunlight reappears and all close up when the sun departs. It is therefore evident that the light of the sun, whose influence on vegetable life is in all respects so great, is also a cause of the diurnal and nocturnal movements of leaves. This action of the light has been experimentally proven by Decandolle.

Some Sensitive Plants were placed in a closed room which was kept, all day long, in a state of absolute dark ness, but at night was lit by six powerful lamps. Upon this reversal of the normal order of things, which turned the day into night, and the night into day, the Sensitive Plants at first hesitated, sometimes opening and sometimes closing, without any fixed rule. Some slept while it was light and others kept awake in the darkness ; however, after some days of conflict between habit and the new conditions of existence, the plants submitted to the artificial alternation of light and darkness. In the evening, when their day began, they expanded ; in the morning, when their night began, they closed up.

The stimulus of light, which, applied in a manner contrary to the normal state of affairs, changes the hours of sleep into hours of waking and vice versa, is therefore one of the causes of the movements of leaves ; but it is not the only cause. Having subjected certain Sensitive Plants to the continued action of artificial light, and others to the continued action of darkness, Decandolle observed in both cases an alternation of sleeping and waking, but these alternate periods of sleeping and waking were shorter than under natural conditions and very irregular. Thus, an endless day does not prevent the plant from sleeping nor does an endless night prevent it from waking. On the other hand, while the Sensitive Plant will reverse its habits and adapt itself to the conditions of the experiment when light and darkness alternate in a manner contrary to their natural periodicity, there are plants which are less impressionable, which, if subjected to the same ordeal, refuse to make any change in their habits. Such are the Wood-Sorrels, which obstinately defied all Decandolle's attempts upon them. Continuous light, continuous darkness, and the alternation of light during the night and darkness during the day, produced no effect whatever ; the Wood-Sorrel slept and waked during the customary hours of sleep and waking, despite all the wiles of the experimenter.

By virtue of a mechanism necessary to the maintenance of life, a vegetable contains within itself the essential cause of the periodical movements of its leaves ; light, varying in intensity according to the sensitiveness of the plant, evokes these movements but does not produce them. Further than this we cannot go ; the sleep of the plant is inexplicable, as is that of the animal also. To

us it is all the more profoundly mysterious because
of its dissimilarity to our own sleep. Plants, indeed,
do not sleep in the ordinary acceptation of the term ;
we shall not observe in them any state of somnolence
comparable with the slumber of the sleeping animal,
but merely a return of the leaves to the order in which
they were in the bud. This return to the order of early
youth is apparently a sign of repose, of the temporary
suspension of the vital activities, although the plant's
way of life is quite the contrary of all that repose would
seem to demand of us. The slumbering leaves assume
forced postures, difficult to retain, but which they do
retain, by virtue of a rigidity which they do not exhibit
in the waking state. If we try to lift a leaf which is
hanging from its twig asleep, or to press downwards a
leaf which is sleeping in an erect position, the leaf will
break off at the point of attachment rather than give way.
Compare the rigidity of the slumbering Sensitive Plant
with the inert flaccidity of the sleeping animal, and you
will realize that between the sleep of the plant and that
of the animal there is perhaps nothing in common but
the name.

CHAPTER XIX

THE STRUCTURE OF LEAVES

*Epidermis—Epidermic cells—Functions of the epidermis—Aquatic leaves—
Hairs—Glandular hairs—The hairs of the Nettle—Their analogy to
the poisonous weapons of certain animals—Stomata—Their number—
Their functions—The breathing of vegetables—Consequences of
breathing—The nervures of leaves—Parenchyma—The intercellular
meatuses—Air-chambers—Contents of cells—Chlorophyll—The part
played by the cells containing chlorophyll—Chlorophyll is found only
where the light has access.*

By lightly scratching the surface of a leaf with a penknife
we shall find it easy to remove a shred of fine membranous tissue, extremely thin and transparent as glass.
Wherever we apply the sharp steel point, whether on the
upper or the under surface of the leaf, whether on the
blade of the leaf or the leaf-stalk, we shall find the same
fine pellicle. It is known as the *epidermis.* We have
already noted that a similar membrane occurs on young
twigs and shoots. Examined with the naked eye, the
epidermis appears to be in no way remarkable ; only
with the aid of the microscope can we detect its curious
and beautiful structure. Under the microscope the
shred of delicate membrane is seen to resemble a mosaic
of minute tesserae assembled side by side like the blocks
of a parquet flooring, its formation, according to the species
of vegetable, rectangular, or lozenge-shaped, or polygonal
and rectilinear, or sinuous. Here and there we shall see
apertures shaped like button-holes, with thick protruding
borders, while here and there a few of the blocks that
constitute the epidermic mosaic are distended like blisters,

or they protrude like horns, or expand into the shape of the conventional star. There are three things to be noted in the epidermis : the cells which, being assembled, form a mosaic, the extensions with which some of them are equipped, and the button-holes occurring here and there.

The elements of which the epidermis consists are cells. You are now fairly familiar with these tiny closed bags which we found in the bark and wood, and above all in the pith. As a rule they are round in form, or slightly misshapen by mutual pressure. They contain a great variety of substances : liquids, grains of starch, crystals, gums, sugar, oils and resins. In the epidermis of the leaf, on the other hand, the cells are commonly flattened ; they are fitted together with perfect exactness, however irregular their shape may be ; they are arranged in one single layer, and their cavities contain nothing like the varied materials to be found in the cells already described. The epidermis is thus a sort of cellular varnish which is spread all over the leaf.

Its immediate function is to form a check upon evaporation. All leaves, even those that in appearance are driest and most withered, contain more or less water, which is necessary to their vital functions. The roots draw water from the soil ; the young wood—the alburnum or sapwood—leads it to its destination ; the leaf receives it and employs it in ministering to the needs of the community. If there were nothing to protect the water contained in its tissues, the first warm rays of sunlight would leave it faded and soon to fall. Well ! it is the epidermis that prevents, or rather retards, evaporation as effectually as though it were a water-proof varnish. When the roots cannot find water in the soil with sufficient rapidity to replace that which has been consumed, evaporation, checked only by the epidermis, finally results

in withered leaves, and the stricken plant bows its head.
It is enough to have seen the piteous condition of a plant
which has not been watered in warm sunny weather, in
order to understand the disastrous results of evaporation
which has not been balanced in time by the water imbibed
by the roots. What would become of it were the plant
exposed without epidermis to the drying action of air
and sunlight ?

As for the aquatic plants, there is no need for them to
take precautions against undue drought, since they are
immersed in water. Their leaves are entirely without
epidermis, which enables them to imbibe all the water
they need. But once exposed to the air, these plants,
which grow so vigorously in the water, wither and shrivel
up with unusual rapidity owing to the lack of the epidermic
envelope which would guard them against evaporation.
Lastly, floating leaves, semi-aquatic, semi-aerial, adopt a
third method : they have no epidermis on the lower surface, in contact with the water, but the upper surface,
which is in contact with the air, is provided with a layer
of epidermis.

In order to demonstrate the efficacy of the epidermis
as a preventive of evaporation, which might, if too active,
endanger the life of the plant, I will remind you of something that you may have experienced, if you have ever
attempted to prepare, for your herbarium, any aquatic
plants, such as Pond-weed, Crowfoot, or the like. These
plants are placed in a press between sheets of brown paper,
dripping with moisture, just as they were taken from
their native pond or ditch ; yet before the day is over
they are dry ; while terrestrial plants, which often appear
to be quite devoid of sap, may require weeks to become
perfectly dry. Why does the moist plant dry so quickly
and the shrivelled one so slowly ? You should now
be able to answer this question without difficulty. The

aquatic plant, devoid of epidermis, quickly surrenders its moisture to the sheets of absorbent paper ; the terrestrial plant, covered with epidermis, is slow to give up the sap in its veins.

As a general thing the cells of the epidermis are flat and the membrane which is built of these flattened cells is commonly smooth and unbroken. But it is not unusual for certain cells, and sometimes for all, to swell up into small conical processes, or wart-like excrescences, or hollow spines, which are loosely described as hairs. The surface of the leaves, in such cases, may be entirely covered with small prominences, like the little globules of the Raspberry or Blackberry, or it may be covered with a fine velvety down, or a thick growth of stiff bristles, or protected by a sort of fur, according to the degree of elongation and the delicacy of the epidermic cells. The Ice-Plant erects its epidermis, on the twigs as often as on the leaves, into tiny blisters like beads of ice ; whence the familiar name which has been given to this curious vegetable which reflects the blaze of the summer sun as though from necklets and diadems of ice. The Cottony House-Leek transforms a few cells of its epidermis into long silky filaments that interlace and cover the star-shaped leaf-buds with a sort of gossamer like that of a cobweb. The hairy leaves of other plants form a kind of cotton-wool ; in others the elongated cells form a sort of velvet ; while others, like the Nettle, secrete poison into the hollow channel of the hairs and employ them as weapons of defence. Those plants that are covered with epidermic hairs are not the species most exposed to the frosts of winter ; but chiefly the species which are exposed to the untempered heat of the sun. The Primavera of the Glaciers has naked leaves ; the seaboard Athanasia, on the scorching shores of the Mediterranean, is muffled in a dense cotton-like down, as white as snow. In shady

places and moist soils we rarely find a leaf covered with
down or hair; but we often find such on dry soils
scorched by the sun and swept by the winds. It would
therefore seem that the plant, in muffling itself with down,
is guarding chiefly against evaporation; in order to
protect itself still more securely from the loss of the
water which keeps it moist, it adds, to the obstacle of
the épidermis, the further obstacle of a fleecy covering.

The simplest form of hair consists of a single epidermic
cell prolonged in the shape of a horn. This cell may

FIG. 98.—Star-shaped   FIG. 99.—Scale-like   FIG. 100.—Glandular
hair of Sweet   hair of the   hairs of the
Alyssum.   Bohemian Olive.   Snapdragon.

put forth ramifications, producing a hair with two or
more branches, with intercommunicating cavities. In
other cases a number of cells may be assembled end to
end, forming a hair divided into compartments. Among
these multi-cellular hairs there are single forms and
branching forms; and in some of these the branches
radiate from a common centre; there are others whose
short, rounded cells are strung together like a chaplet;
while others, formed by the assemblage of long radiating
cells, assume the form of a star-shaped scale, adhering
to the leaf by its central point. These scaly hairs have
usually a brilliant, almost metallic lustre, you might
almost take them for tiny fish-scales, or the silvery dust
left on the fingers after touching a butterfly's wings

It is these that give the foliage of the Olive its silvery tinge. They also are responsible for the silvery appearance of the under surface of the leaves of the Bohemian Olive and other trees.

There are certain hairs that are dilated at the tip, by the presence of one or more cells inside which are elaborated special substances, such as acids, resins, scents or viscous liquids. These are known as glandular hairs, the term *gland* being applied to the tiny cellular compound in which the work of elaboration takes place. The glandular hairs of the Hop prepare the substance known as Lupulin, which gives beer its flavour and its bitter taste ; while those on the pods of the Chick-pea produce a substance with a very tart flavour known as oxalic acid.

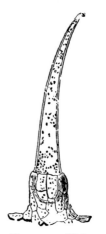

FIG. 101.—Hair of the Nettle.

Other hairs are filled with an irritant liquid, a sort of vegetable poison, which, if injected into the flesh, causes the keenest discomfort. Such are the bristling hairs of the Common Nettle. They consist of one single cell, swollen at the base into a capsule, which is drawn out into a long, tapering tube which ends in a little knob without an orifice. The capsule itself is partly enclosed in a short cylindrical support, which, in order to receive it, is hollowed out like a goblet. This support, consisting of a tissue of minute cells, appears to be the laboratory in which the poison is prepared, while the capsule is the reservoir in which it is collected and stored. When one of these hairs, a true poison-dagger, pierces the skin, the knob at the tip breaks, and the capsule of poison, thus opened, pours its contents into the wound, owing to the contraction of its elastic walls. The admixture of the acrid liquid with the blood causes the pain and redness at and around the wounded spot.

Which of us has not, once at least, unwittingly plunged his hand into a bed of Nettles, and well remembered the pain and smarting caused thereby? But these are nothing compared to the effects of certain Nettles found in tropical countries, where the climate results in the development of the simple hair of our Common Nettle into a really formidable weapon. The Crenellated Nettle of India stings so cruelly that the pain lasts for several days and may even cause convulsions. One traveller states that on visiting the botanical gardens of Calcutta he had three fingers stung by this terrible Nettle. For forty-eight hours he suffered the most excruciating pains, accompanied by slight tetanic contractions. The results of this sting continued for nine days after the accident. Lastly, the Burning Nettle of Java is known by the natives as the Devil's Leaf; the name is well deserved, for we are told that the sting of this plant will cause the keenest pain for a whole year, provoking attacks of tetanus and sometimes even causing death.

It is interesting to compare the structure and mechanism of the hair of the Stinging Nettle with those of the poisoned weapons of animals, and in particular with that of the Viper. Everybody must have seen a Snake darting from between its lips a black thread, forked, and exceedingly flexible, which flashes in and out with extreme rapidity. Many people imagine this to be the reptile's weapon, its " sting." This, however, is a vulgar delusion; the black, forked thread is nothing more than its tongue, an absolutely inoffensive tongue, which the animal uses in order to snap up insects, and to express, after its own fashion, the state of its emotions, by projecting it rapidly from between its lips. All Snakes without exception possess a tongue; but only a comparatively small number—the Viper, the Cobra, the Rattlesnake, etc.—possess the terrible poison-gland and envenomed fangs. This apparatus consists in the first place of the two fangs, which are two long, sharp teeth situated in the upper jaw. These fangs are movable; they may be erected at will for attack, or left lying in a groove in the gums, where they are harmless as a dagger in its sheath, so that the reptile runs no danger of wounding itself. In addition to these fangs, the Snake also possesses spare fangs, in an immature condition which are found in the jaw, behind the actual poison-fangs, ready to replace the latter should they be broken. For the time being the two older fangs suffice; and it is these two fangs that constitute the weapon of the Viper

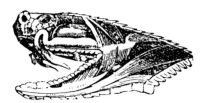

FIG. 102.—Fangs and poison glands of the Rattlesnake.

or Adder and other venomous Snakes. It is these two fangs that leave two red specks on the wounded part; two genuine hypordermic injections; and it is they that do all the harm, for the imprint of the rest of the jaw, when the wounded part reveals it, produces no effect whatever, beyond causing quite superficial bruises or punctures. But how is it that two little pricks can cause such serious organic disorder, and even death? It is because the reptile inoculates the wounds caused by its fangs with a terrible venom, just as the Nettle pours into the minute wound made by its hair the poisonous contents of the capsule at the base of the latter. This poison is a liquid humour of inoffensive appearance, tasteless and odourless, hardly to be told from water. If placed on the tongue, or even if swallowed, it produces no effect ; which is why a snake-bite may without fear be sucked, in order to extract the poison ; but once it finds its way into the blood its terrible powers are immediately apparent.

In order to inject the poison into the wound, the fangs are hollow and pierced, close to the point, by a minute orifice. A membranous duct leads the poison into the dental cavity ; a small capsule stores it up in reserve, and a special organ, a gland, secretes it. The same apparatus is found in all the venomous Serpents, from the European Viper to the hideous Asp of the Algerian Sahara, which kills in a few hours, and the Cobras, whose fangs will cause the almost instantaneous death of an Ox or Buffalo.

Even the insects, whose weapons display such artistic refinements, do not display any essential modification of this deadly appliance. There is always a gland which elaborates the venom, a capsule in which it is stored, and a perforated sting which injects it into the wound. Each species, however, carries its weapon after its own fashion. The Spider has two poisonous fangs folded back just within the mouth ; the Scorpion bears its sting upon the point of its tail ; the Wasp, to avoid blunting the fine point, carries its weapon in a scabbard contrived in the tip of the abdomen. If we now refer to the hair of the Nettle, we shall see how closely it resembles the poison-dagger of the animals. The cylindrical support which prepares the irritant fluid in its cellular tissue represents the gland in which the poison is elaborated. The base of the hair, dilated into a capsule, is the reservoir in which the fluid is collected, and represents the organ in which the animal stores its poison. Lastly, the hair itself is a sharp, hollow stiletto, analagous to the fangs of the reptile, and the sting of the Scorpion or the Wasp, save that its tip is closed by a little knob which breaks

in the wound, allowing the fluid to escape, while the fangs
or stings of the living creature are always open at the tip.

The third category of organ which a rapid examination
has shown us in the shred of the epidermis under the
microscope, consists of the minute openings whose shape
reminds us of a buttonhole. Each of these is a tiny
slot, bordered by two symmetrical cells, arching outwards,
and thicker in the middle than at the ends, much like
two lips, so that the hole somewhat resembles a little
mouth, sometimes closed,
sometimes open. From this
resemblance to a mouth, the
Greek for which is *stoma*,
we obtain the name *stomata*,
by which these apertures in
the epidermis are known.
They occur chiefly on the
lower surface of aerial leaves,
and on the upper surface in
the case of floating aquatic
leaves. It is useless to look
for them without a micro-

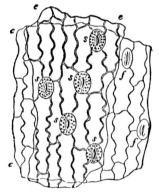

FIG. 103.—Stomata of the Lily.

scope, their dimensions being excessively minute. The
prick of the finest needle would make a very large
hole in comparison. Their number, too, is prodigious.
The lower surface of a leaf of the Common Mar-
guerite contains approximately 7,000 stomata to the
square centimetre ; the Vine contains some 12,000 or
13,000, and the Olive over 20,000, while the Pedun-
culated Oak contains 25,000. It has been calculated
that one leaf of ordinary size from a Lime-tree is
pierced by over 1,000,000 stomata. What inconceivable numbers should we not arrive at were we to
calculate the total for the whole Lime-tree, with its tens
of hundreds of thousands of leaves !

The stomata, like the hairs, are not exclusively confined to the leaves ; we find them in varying abundance on various parts of the plant which are exposed to the atmosphere, and chiefly on the green portions—the stipules and the bark of the young shoots. In general they are lacking in those organs that burrow into the ground or are immersed in water. The green surfaces outspread to the air are their especial habitat ; which is why I am telling you about them in the chapter dealing with the leaves, the most important green surfaces of the plant. Their functions are of the greatest importance, as I shall presently explain. For the moment I will merely observe that the stomata enable the atmosphere to attain the thickness of the tissue of which the leaf is composed. They are orifices of entry and exit which permit of a continual flow of gaseous material between the interior of the plant and the outer atmosphere. Thus, one of the functions of the stomata is to enable the leaf to exhale in vapour the water with which it is impregnated.

Plants are constantly exhaling gases ; especially in the sunshine do they emit invisible vapours into the air. To convince ourselves of the amount of moisture exhaled with our own breath, we breathe against a cold window. The invisible vapour in the breath condenses, clouding the glass, finally trickling down in tiny drops. The moist exhalation of the stomata may be detected in the same way. We thrust a living twig, showing no visible traces of moisture, into a dry flask. In a short time the inner surface of the flask is covered with tiny drops. The tiny mouths of the leaf, therefore, breathe out moisture just as a man does ; their breath is as moist as our own. The amount of vapour that escapes by each of these breathing-pores is too small to be measured, but on account of the enormous number of stomata the total quantity of water exhaled is considerable. A tree of average dimensions exhales into the air some 2½ gallons of water daily; while a single plant of the ordinary Sunflower will exhale in twelve hours, in dry, warm weather about two pounds' weight of water.

This exhalation fulfils a manifold function. To begin with, it prevents the temperature from rising to a height that might be dangerous to the flower. The evaporation of a liquid content or constituent cools the object at whose cost the evaporation takes place, the specific heat of vapour being so high that evaporation withdraws from the source of moisture a very large quantity of heat. Pour a few drops of some volatile liquid—say of ether— into the hollow of your hand, and as it evaporates you will be conscious of a sensation of intense cold. The ether, in evaporating, carries off a certain quantity of your bodily heat. I may also remind you of the shivering sensation which you experience on leaving your bath. The thin layer of water covering the body is the cause of this sensation; in evaporating it withdraws from us a little of our own heat. Once the skin is dry evaporation ceases, and the shivering stops as though by magic. These two examples are enough to give you some idea of the fall of temperature caused by evaporation. Consequently, when, owing to the heat of the sun, the plant is in danger of becoming too hot, a condition which might imperil its very life, the stomata exhale vapour in order to expel the danger. A thousand, ten thousand, twenty thousand little mouths, in an area no greater than that of a finger-nail, cool the leaves by evaporating the water contained in them. You will therefore perceive that the exhalation of the stomata is more active by day than by night, in the sunshine than in the shade, and in dry warm weather than on damp cold days.

At a time when the plant is no longer in any danger, even during the night, exhalation still takes place, though

16

it is then much less abundant. The drops of water which in the morning adhere like dew to the tips of the grass-blades, or roll down into the hollows of cabbage-leaves, are the result of this very nocturnal exhalation, condensed by the coolness of the night. Why do not the stomata cease to exhale vapour in the darkness, during the cool hours of the night, when the plant has no reason to fear an excess of warmth ? The reason is this : in order to nourish itself, the plant draws from the earth, by means of its roots, water holding in solution traces of every soluble constituent of the soil. This water is absolutely limpid, since it contains only the smallest traces of such nutritive substances. In order to obtain sufficient food the plant is obliged to absorb very large quantities of water. This meagre nutriment filters through the roots into the still young wood, and from the wood it rises to the leaves, which at once proceed to break it up. The alimentary particles are retained by the substance of the leaves, there to undergo profound chemical changes, combining with other materials, drawn from the atmosphere through the stomata, finally becoming, under the influence of the light, a nourishing fluid, which we might truly call the blood of the plant, since all its organs draw upon it for their formation, their maintenance and their growth. This nourishing liquid is known as the *descending sap*, since once it has been prepared in the leaves it percolates downwards from the leaves to the twigs, from the twigs to the branches, from the branches to the trunk, and from the trunk to the roots, distributing, wherever it flows, the material for fresh formations. The other fluid, which the roots draw from the ground, is known as the *ascending sap*, which ascends from the roots to the leaves, by way of the sap-wood. It consists chiefly of water, most of which the stomata will be obliged to exhale, in order to concentrate the nutritive substances dissolved in it. This task of concentrating the raw materials ascending to the leaves never ceases, for the absorption of moisture by the roots goes on continually ; which explains why the stomata are always exhaling vapour, even during the night. Unceasingly they expel into the atmosphere, in the form of vapour, the excess of water always absorbed by the roots, without which the nutrition furnished by the soil could not ascend to the leaves ; and it is the stomata that concentrate the excessively diluted ascending sap in order to transform it into the rich solution of the descending sap.

We will reserve our consideration of the sap for a later chapter, and continue to examine the structure of the leaves. We have studied the epidermis, with its flattened cells, forming a thin membrane which checks evaporation ; with its hairs, often thick enough to form a downy quilt which increases the obstacles that prevent a too rapid loss of moisture ; and its stomata, or exhaling mouths, which enable the plant to get rid of its excess of water at a suitable rate. But the content of the leaf that lies between the two plates of epidermis is still more important. In the first place, we shall find there a sort of girder which gives its strength and solidity to the leaf. It consists of fibres and bundles of vessels, the whole constituting the petiole or leaf-stalk. After it enters the blade of the leaf the bundle of fibres and vessels sometimes puts forth a number of ramifications of almost equal importance, as in the leaf of the Plane-tree, and sometimes continues, undivided, along the centre of the leaf, as in the Laurel. These direct pro-longations of the leaf-stalk, simple or multiple, are known as *primary nervures*. From these nervures spring yet others, still smaller, which are known as *secondary*. These give rise to *tertiary* nervures, and so forth, so that, proceeding from subdivision to subdivision, the single bundle of the leaf-stalk is finally divided into a number of extremely fine nervures, which, forming junctions with one another, make up a network of innumerable meshes. You will have seen the beautiful lacework to which leaves which have lain long rotting are reduced ; these are merely the fibro-vascular network deprived of the cellular tissue which filled the meshes while the leaf was alive. The function of this beautiful scaffolding is not confined to stiffening the blade of the leaf and keeping it outspread ; it has another function of very much greater importance. It is through the vessels of the leaf-stalk that the ascending sap is conveyed to the leaf ; it is through the vessels of the nervures and their ramifications—ever smaller and more numerous—that the sap is distributed all over the blade of the leaf in order that it may there be concentrated by evaporation by the stomata and the chemical action of light, finally becoming the nutritive fluid which we know as the descending sap ; moreover, it is through this identical network of vessels and fibres that the sap thus elaborated returns from the leaf to the branch, in order that it may find its way to the various organs which it is to nourish. The fibro-vascular network is thus the means of communication between the leaf and the plant. It conveys to the blade of the leaf the raw materials of the descending sap ; and it also conveys this nourishing sap back to the plant, once it has been prepared in the laboratory of the leaf, which we still have to examine.

This laboratory, in which the essential activity of the leaf resides, is known as the *parenchyma*. It consists of a tissue of cells filling up the meshes of the fibro-vascular network, including a certain number of the nervures in its thickness. The cells of the parenchyma are of a pale green, and are commonly irregular in form, grouped without any very well-determined order. Their shape and their arrangement will be found, in the great majority of cases, to differ on the two faces of the leaf. On the upper surface of the leaf the microscope shows us two or three layers of roughly elliptical cells, with their major axes perpendicular to the epidermis, and so closely packed that few or no unoccupied intervals occur. In the thickness of the leaf itself, and on the lower surface, the cells are highly irregular in arrangement, contact being only partial, so that many unoccupied spaces occur, which are known as *intercellular meatuses*, or *lacunae* when

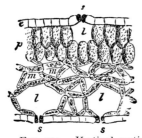

FIG. 104.—Vertical section through the leaf of a Sunflower.

e, Epidermis ; *s, s,* stomata ; *l, l,* lacunae or air-chambers ; *m, m,* intercellular meatuses ; *p,* parenchyma.

FIG. 105.—A portion of the lower surface of the same leaf.

c,c, epidermic cells ; *s,s,* stomata.

their dimensions are larger than usual. From this difference of texture results the difference of colouring on the two surfaces of the leaf. The upper surface shows, through the transparent and colourless epidermis, a deep green tint, because there the green cells are assembled in a firm, compact tissue, while the colouring of the under surface is pale because there the green cells form only a loosely packed tissue, riddled throughout with cavities, after the fashion of a sponge.

Lastly, each stoma communicates directly with an empty space, rather larger and more regular in shape than the others, known as an *air-chamber*. The various intercellular meatuses in the neighbourhood of these

air-chambers all communicate one with another, and
finally with the air-chamber, a sort of waiting-room,
where the gaseous products of the leaves are collected
before escaping into the atmosphere through the orifice
of the stoma ; and there, too, are collected, provisionally,
the gaseous substances derived from the atmosphere,
before they are distributed to the cells, where they
undergo the wonderful transformation of which I shall
tell you later.   The air-chamber is thus a sort of cross-
roads, a place of storage for the gaseous substances which
emerge from the cells,
or which are destined
to enter them ; the
stoma, opening in the
epidermic layer which
forms the ceiling of the
chamber, is the door of
exit and entry.   Various
corridors proceed from
the chamber, narrow and tortuous, taking advantage of
the smallest intervals between the cells ; while here and
there, along the course of these corridors, open the more
spacious cavities of the intercellular meatuses.

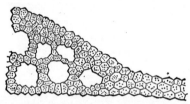

FIG. 106.—Section of a subaqueous leaf
of Common Pondweed, without epidermis and riddled with large lacunae.

This structure permits us already to realize how the
exhalation of leaves takes place.   Each of the cells in the
thickness of the parenchyma is filled with a fluid consisting
chiefly of water ; but it is surrounded by cavities filled
with air.   Through its thin membranous walls, permeable
to liquids, the cell evaporates its contents, saturating
with moisture the air contained in the surrounding
cavities ; and this moist air, slowly driven from one
meatus to another, sooner or later reaches some air-
chamber which exhales it between the lips of its stoma.
Thus, by means of the cavities by which the whole parenchyma is riddled, and the innumerable stomata opening

through the epidermis, every cell throughout the leaf, however remote its situation, is nevertheless kept in touch with the outer air by continual gaseous exchanges.

In the wonderful laboratory which we know by the name of leaf, the real workshop is the cell; the rest of the leaf consists merely of ways of communication. The vessels of the nervures convey the fluid containing the raw materials of the ascending sap and the nourishing products contained in the descending sap; the inter-cellular meatuses, the air-chambers and the stomata serve to circulate vapours and gases. This perpetual movement to and fro has for its point of departure and its goal the cell, in which the marvellous work of the plant is finally accomplished. Now, in order to accomplish this task, the cell possesses an equipment which I must now explain to you.

You already know that a cell is a little sac completely closed on every side, whose walls consist of a delicate colourless membrane. The green colouration is caused not by the wall but by the contents of the sac. Under the microscope a cell burst open by compression emits a tiny drop of transparent fluid in which are floating a number of extremely minute green granulations. The transparent fluid consists almost entirely of water; as for the green granulations, they consist of a special substance known as *chlorophyll*, a term derived from two Greek words signifying the green matter of leaves. Sometimes the chlorophyll appears as a green jelly without definite form, and sometimes—and indeed most frequently—as a heap of corpuscles of globular form, which may be distorted by mutual pressure, so minute that it would take about 130 placed in a row to make up $\frac{1}{25}$ of an inch. A cell whose capacity is one cubic milli-metre would thus contain two millions. It is the chloro-phyll that gives the leaf its green colour. It is also the cause of the green hue of the young bark, of unripe fruit, and, indeed, of all the green portions of the plant. Whatsoever organs of the plant are green, the cells of those organs are filled with chlorophyll, whence their colour is derived ; and it always occupies the surface areas of the plant, in order that it may receive the light of the sun. Its task is so delicate and so difficult that without the aid of the sun, the great source of motive power of the universal energy of the world, it would

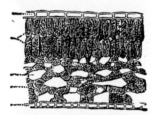

FIG. 107.—Section of a leaf of Balsamin.

never be accomplished. Consider how the cells containing chlorophyll seek the light : in the leaves, which are nearly always thin enough to allow the rays of the sun to reach their interior, the green cells make up their whole thickness ; but if there are deeprooted layers of cells in the leaf the green cells are always found at the surface, never in the interior, where the light could not reach them. Split a young twig : where are the really green strata ? Outside, on the surface. But I do not infer that the cells which are not green, being situated farther from the surface, are inactive. They, too, have work to do ; they perfect the already refined products in the sap, or at least store them up within their walls. But the first and essential task, the most arduous of all, is the sole and especial province of the grains of chlorophyll, which is why they all come to the surface, requiring the aid of the sun. And now that you know somewhat of the workshop and its equipment, I shall try to explain to you the sort of work that is accomplished there.

CHAPTER XX

ASCENDING SAP

Endosmosis—Absorption by the roots—Capillary action—Action of the foliage—Ascension of sap—Hale's experiment—Conservation of wood—Character of the ascending sap—Vauquelin's calculation—Mass of water evaporated by a tree—Modification of the sap during its movement—The Sugar Maple—Palm Wine.

WE shall now consider how the vegetable organism feeds itself, and how, with a few raw materials, such as water, a few gases, and a few salts, which for us are of no nutritive value whatever, they contrive to manufacture such a variety of substances, by which we are, all of us, nourished and kept alive. But in order to solve these difficult problems without going astray we might well call to our aid the most abstruse resources of physics and chemistry, and even then how many things would still remain impenetrable mysteries! I cannot call these resources to our aid ; my younger readers would scarcely understand me if I did. My explanation, therefore, must needs be brief and incomplete ; should my explanations puzzle them they must remember that the subject is a most difficult one ; at the same time, they should not forget that when they are older their wider knowledge will enable them fully to understand the points upon which I am trying, to-day, to throw a little light.

And now, to begin with, let us ask ourselves by what means the plants extract from the soil the substances which are necessary to them. An experiment in physics —quite a simple one, within your own power to perform,

the appliances for which you yourself can construct—
will answer this question. We will take a glass tube
open at both ends, about 3 feet in length and with a bore
equal to that of a goose-quill. We must also obtain the
bladder of a rabbit and tie it by its neck to one end of
the tube. Now we will fill the bladder with water
containing a little gum or sugar, and immerse it in pure
water, the glass tube being supported vertically above
the vessel containing the water. This apparatus is then
set aside, care being taken that the bladder is everywhere
covered by the water, and that it does not touch the
container. The membranous walls of the bladder will
thus be in contact with two fluids of different character,
one on either side. The outside of the bladder is bathed
by the thinner and lighter fluid—namely, by pure water ;
the inside of the bladder contains a denser fluid—namely,
a solution of gum or sugar. Well ! under these conditions
a most remarkable thing comes to pass : little by little,
as the hours go by, the pure water filters through the
membrane, making its way into the bladder and mingling
with the solution of gum or sugar. The contents of the
membranous sac are thus continually increased, a fact
betrayed by the rise of the fluid in the glass tube. If the
tube is not too long, the solution is thus increased in
volume, at the expense of the pure water which makes
its way through the walls of the bladder, until it finally
reaches the top of the tube and is spilt. The height
attained by the fluid will depend upon the area of the
membrane through which the infiltration takes place, the
calibre of the tube, the character of the two fluids, and
other conditions of the kind. The result which I have
briefly described is a constant one : whenever two
different liquids are divided by a membranous partition the lighter and more fluid liquid or solution
will filter through this partition, being attracted by

the heavier and denser fluid. This property is known as *endosmosis.*

Let us now go back to the roots of the plant. In their younger portions, and especially at the end of the finer ramifications, they consist of cells each of which, with inimitable perfection, represents the membranous sac of our experiment. These cells are full of a liquid which is the product of their vital functions, and analagous, in its density, to the solution which we employed in order to produce the phenomenon of endosmosis. Lastly, the soil is full of moisture, which holds in solution very minute quantities of foreign matter, so that it differs in its properties from pure water. All the conditions of endosmosis are therefore present : the membrane of the cell is bathed within by a dense and viscous liquid ; its outer walls are in contact with a more dilute liquid. The moisture of the soil therefore filters through the walls of the cells and makes its way into the roots. This first stage of nutrition in the plant is known as absorption. While the cells on the surface of the roots become dilated by absorbing the moisture in the soil, those lying at some distance from the surface fill themselves from the first, also by endosmosis, so that little by little the cellular tissue becomes fully gorged. We now come to very fine, long tubes or channels, which enable the fluid to ascend to such heights as may be necessary. These are the vessels or veins, profusely distributed throughout the lignous tissue and assembled end to end, reaching from the tips of the roots to the leaves. They represent, in the vegetable laboratory, the glass tube of our experiment in endosmosis. Just as this tube was filled by the overflow of the membranous bag, whose contents were continually being increased, similarly the liquid which overflows from the cells, owing to their constant absorption thereof, rises in the veins of the plant. It is difficult to

say just how high it would rise by virtue of endosmosis ;
at all events, with our appliances, so defective when we
compare them with those of the living organism, we
have found that endosmosis, taking place between water
and a solution of sugar, will develop a pressure capable
of raising a column of water to the height of one
hundred to one hundred and fifty feet.   The absorbent
power of the roots should therefore be sufficient to
force the water drawn from the soil to the top of quite
a tall tree.   However, other factors are at work in the
ascent of the sap.   One of them is *capillary action*.

A fresh digression into the domain of physics will here
be necessary.   The tube is called *capillary*, when its bore
is very narrow, so narrow as to be comparable to a hair,
the Latin name for which is *capillus*.   If you dip one
end of such a tube into a liquid, both ends being open,
you will perceive the following phenomena, which seemed
to contradict our everyday knowledge of the behaviour
of liquids :   If we dip one end of a tube of fairly large
diameter into water, the water will stand at the same
level inside the tube as outside ;   but with a capillary
tube the result is very different, the fluid within the tube
standing sometimes above and sometimes below the level
of the fluid outside.   It is lower if the fluid is of such a
character that it refuses to adhere to the walls of the
tube, and thus cannot moisten them.   We shall see this
happen if we immerse one end of a glass tube in a basin
of mercury.   It is higher if the liquid adheres to the
walls of the tube ;   and we shall see that it stands higher
in the case of a glass tube dipped into water.   Let us
confine our attention to the latter case ;   the other being
alien to the problem before us.   Once more, if we dip a
capillary tube into a fluid capable of moistening it, the
level of the fluid inside the tube will rise above the outside
level, and the height to which it will rise will be greater

in proportion as the calibre of the tube is finer. This is the fundamental fact of capillarity, a fact which you can very easily verify with tubes of varying calibres and some coloured water.

Let us now consider a porous body, riddled with small lacunae and narrow fissures. These lacunae and fissures, which in fineness may be compared with the bores of the tubes of which I have been speaking, in reality constitute so many capillary passages in which the liquid is able to rise. When, for example, you dip one corner of a lump of sugar in your coffee, you will see the brown liquid rise above the submerged corner, so that presently the whole lump is soaked. It is capillary action which has drawn the coffee up into the empty intervals of the sugar and lifted it above its own level. It is also by capillary action that the spongy tissue of a lamp-wick draws the oil from the reservoir of the lamp to the flame. And it is owing to capillary action that a heap of sand whose base is in the water becomes moist up to the summit. Now, where should we find better conditions of capillary action than in the tissues of the vegetable ? The cells of plant tissue are traversed by innumerable empty intervals. These veins or vessels are of an extreme fineness, such as could scarcely be rivalled by the finest of our tubes of glass. It is therefore obvious that the action of endosmosis is largely aided by capillary action, in the work of supplying the leaves with the fluid absorbed by the roots.

When vegetation reawakens in the spring the tree is still in the denuded state in which winter has left it, and at this period the flow of liquids to the topmost twigs of the tree is caused solely by the two forces which we have just been considering ; but from the moment when the buds have burst and the new foliage is outspread a third cause of ascension comes into play, even more

powerful than the other two.   Each leaf, as you know,
is the site of extremely active evaporation, which leaves
a vacuum in the organs which have furnished the water
evaporated.   But this vacuum is immediately filled by
the neighbouring organs, which give up their contents
and in their turn receive the contents of remoter layers of
cells.   From cell to cell, from fibre to fibre, from vessel
to vessel, the action is repeated at an ever-increasing
distance from the evaporating surface, and is thus propagated to the very tips of the roots, which, by continual
suction, replace the liquid which has disappeared.   This
action is something like that of a suction pump, whose
piston leaves behind it a vacuum which is instantly filled
by the water in the pipe beneath it, which in turn receives
more water from the bottom of the well.   Whether the
vacuum is caused by the movement of a piston, or the
evaporation by water from a mass of leaves, the result
is the same : we have the progressive ascent of a liquid
hastening, under the pressure of the atmosphere, to fill
an unoccupied space.

Endosmosis in the roots, capillary action in the roots,
and evaporation in the leaves, are the chief causes in the
ascent of sap.   The following experiment will enable you
to realize how great is the energy thus expended.—Very
much slower, indeed almost interrupted in winter, the
absorption of water during the first warm days of spring
attains a rate which makes up to the plant for the long
inertia of winter.   Fruit-trees which have been pruned
allow drops of sap to drip from the resected surfaces of
their amputated twigs, the ascending liquid overflowing
in the absence of its natural channels, which have been
removed by the pruner.   These drops of sap are especially
abundant on fresh wounds of the Grape-Vine.   In order
to measure the pressure of the sap, the physiologist Hales
amputated a Vine-stock and fitted upon the resected

surface a glass tube bent into the shape of a letter S.
The lower curve of the tube was then filled with mercury.
The sap, making its way into that part of the tube which
was fastened to the Vine, pressing upon the mercury,
pushed this before it into the empty portion.   The height
to which the mercury was thus raised was evidently the
measure of the ascending force of the sap.   Now, in his
first experiment, Hales found that the column of mercury
rose to the height of 0·87 metres ; in the second experiment the reading was 1·028 metres.   As mercury is
thirteen and a half times heavier than water the same
pressure would have raised a column of water through a
distance of some 39 feet in the first case and over 45 feet
in the second.   You will see that despite the exceeding
delicacy of its mechanism the plant, what with its cells
gorged by endosmosis and its vessels filled by capillary
action, is capable of exerting very great force.   A mere
Vine-stock, with nothing left but its roots, is able to lift
water to a greater height than could our suction-pumps.

This property of vegetable tissue, of readily imbibing
water and transporting it through considerable intervals,
is exploited in an operation of such importance that I
must not fail to mention it.   However dense it may be,
timber sooner or later undergoes certain profound changes
to the great prejudice of wooden structures.   Various
insects, in the larval stage, feed upon wood ; certain
cellular plants, such as fungi, mildews and dry-rot,
feed upon it.   Riddled in all directions by larvae and
insects which bore galleries through it, and sapped, fibre
by fibre, by vegetable parasites, the wood soon becomes
impregnated with air and moisture, and subject to a
gradual deterioration, the final result of which is humus
or vegetable mould, that brown dust which you so often
see in old, hollow tree-trunks.   Wood immersed in sea-
water is the prey of another agent of destruction, the

Teredo or Ship-Worm, a mollusc which perforates the wood, riddling it with passages until before long it is more like a sponge than a balk of timber. It is to prevent the ravages of the Teredo that wooden ships are often sheathed with copper below the water-line.

These causes of deterioration are powerless or at least far less destructive if the lignous tissue is artificially impregnated with certain substances that prevent the attacks of insects or the agents of dry-rot. Among these substances I may mention sulphate of copper, a poisonous salt, and the pyro-lignite of iron, which is obtained by dissolving old iron in the cheap vinegar produced by the distillation of wood. In order to introduce these preserving agents, the tree is made to absorb them in a

Fig. 108.—Injection of a preservative fluid into a tree still standing.

state of aqueous solution. At the base of the trunk, while the tree is still upright and covered with foliage, a few incisions are made, and around the trunk, at the level of these incisions, is fixed a wide band of waterproof fabric, tightly ligatured above and below, forming an annular tube which receives, through a pipe communicating with the tank, the preservative fluid employed. The evaporation from the foliage causes a powerful suction, which carries the fluid to the top of the tree, making it penetrate the minutest interstices of the wood. If the trunk is lying on the ground, sawn through at either end, the base of the trunk is enveloped by a waterproof bag, into which the fluid to be injected flows from a tank at a higher level. Here the suction of the foliage is replaced by capillary action, endosmosis between cell and cell, and the pressure of the fluid descending from the tank. It is also possible to make white woods absorb colouring matters which will give them this or that tint, as the cabinet-maker may desire. The method employed is similar to that described.

In performing the operations which I have indicated

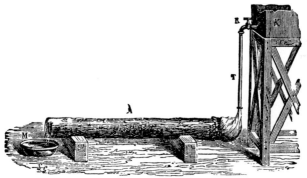

FIG. 108A.—The same operation in the case of a felled tree.

it is found that the preservative fluid readily penetrates the outer layers of wood or sap-wood, but enters the heart of the tree, or the true and mature wood, only with extreme difficulty. The reason for this will not escape you ; the outer layers of wood are the younger, consisting of fibres, and vessels whose cavities are unobstructed ; the inner layers of wood are older, and their fibres and vessels are encrusted with lignous matter, being choked by closely-packed ring upon ring of wood, broken down with age and no longer capable of serving their original purpose. The fluid consequently penetrates where circulation is possible, but where its course is too greatly obstructed it fails to do so. This is equivalent to saying that the ascent of the sap takes place through the sap-

17

wood, and chiefly through the outer layers, which are of more recent formation. Experiment leaves us in no doubt as to this fact ; if we fell a tree when the sap is flowing we find the sap-wood moist and the hard wood dry. Finally, in herbaceous plants, and all those vegetables in which the centre of the stem does not become indurated, the sap ascends by means of the whole mass of the lignous bundles.

If we wish to collect some sap in order to examine its character, the means of so doing is simplicity itself. With an auger we bore a hole, sloping upwards a little, into the sap-wood of a well-grown tree, fixing the end of a hollow reed in the orifice, to act as a draining tube. The sap, which will ooze out drop by drop, may be collected in a bottle. Now, what would you look to find in the contents of a bottle filled by such extravasated drops of sap ? There will no doubt be many things in it, for after all this precious liquid is the raw material from which the plant has to build up all the compounds contained within it : cellulose, sugar, starch, resins, oils, essences, perfumes and many other products. From the astonishing wealth of the results you might conclude that an enormous number of raw materials must be employed. But if that is your opinion you will soon be undeceived ; the ascending sap is little more than pure water, and the scientist often has the greatest difficulty in detecting the few substances dissolved in it, so minute are their quantities. Among these substances the most frequent are the salts of potash, calcium and carbonic acid. In short, the liquid from which the plant has to derive its nourishment is an exceedingly dilute solution consisting of an enormous mass of water and a few traces of substances in solution, which vary very considerably according to the species of vegetable. These scanty materials are almost the only ones utilized by the plant ;

and the water which has collected them by washing them out of the soil and has then borne them from the roots to the leaves by way of the sap-wood, and which makes up almost the whole of the sap, must, directly its course is completed, return, by way of evaporation, to the atmosphere, whence it fell in the form of rain. How many gallons of this very dilute solution must pass through the vessels of a tree—how much water must be evaporated by the leaves in order that the residue of utilizable substances shall represent the weight of the tree's annual increase ?   A calculation of Vauquelin's will give us the figures.

The composition of sap being what it is, the famous chemist calculated that in order to attain a weight of 1,000 lb., an Elm-tree must absorb from the soil and evaporate into the air 35,000 gallons of water, or some 34 gallons for a single pound of increase. Admitting that in the six or seven months during which the leaf is on the tree the weight of an Elm increases by 50 lb., the water absorbed and then evaporated in order to obtain this annual increase would fill a tank 10 cubic yards in volume ; that is, 30 feet long, 3 feet wide and 3 feet deep. Such a calculation fills us with amazement, if you think of the enormous amount of mechanical work performed by a whole forest in order to draw from the soil and raise to a height of 120 feet and finally pour into the air the torrents of water of which the sap of the forest in question in great measure consists. And this prodigious task is accomplished quietly, calmly, invisibly, and barely suspected ; from the tips of the topmost twigs of the tallest trees this terrific weight is cast to the four winds without straining the most delicate part of the vegetable mechanism. The cell, which a mere touch would crush, in association with other cells, performs the work of a Titan.

The sap, however, is not always the limpid water which Vauquelin made the basis of his calculations. Certainly the liquid which the vegetable organism absorbs from the soil is almost always extremely poor in solid contents, but, as it makes its way further and further into the tissues of the plant, it dissolves various substances which have been held in reserve in the cells, having been derived from the previous labours of the plant. By means of an incision made in the stem we very often obtain not the liquid which the roots absorbed, but a sap enriched by the products which it finds in its path, and notably sugar. Thus a North American Maple exudes, from incisions made in the trunk, a liquid with a very sweet flavour, whence sugar is obtained by evaporation. Again, a number of different species of Palm-trees, if the great terminal bud be amputated, exude a sugary sap, which, being fermented, becomes *palm wine*, and yields, if distilled after such fermentation, the spirit known as *arrack*.

The fluid drawn from the soil consequently reaches the leaves already modified; it contains, in addition to the elements furnished by the soil, those given up by the tissues traversed in its ascent. Nevertheless, it is not yet a liquid aliment; in order that it may become so, this crude or non-elaborated sap has to undergo, in the leaves, firstly, an evaporation which removes the excess of water, and secondly, a chemical reconstruction which gives it entirely new properties. I have already spoken of evaporation; there remains the chemical action of the leaves, the most remarkable task of all the many tasks accomplished by the chemistry of living things.

CHAPTER XXI

THE CHEMISTRY OF LIFE

A friend's misfortune—Elements or simple bodies—Analysis of bread—The elements are the same whether in organic or in mineral substances—The fundamental elements of living organisms—Directly or indirectly animals are nourished by plants—The plant builds up the elements into organic substances.

I SHALL never forget how rudely a friend of mine was treated by a famous cook. On a certain holiday he found the artist in sauces in a state of gastronomic meditation before his pots and ovens. You can picture the man : an enormous face, a series of chins, a groggy nose covered with warts, a majestic paunch, a napkin at his hip and a white cap on his head. The saucepans were gently bubbling on the range. Under their lids puffs escaped of delicious and appetizing odours. It was a feast merely to inhale them. An open fire was blazing before the truffled fowl and the turkey skewered all over with bacon. Beside it a plump ortolan, exhaling an aromatic odour of juniper, was smoking on a round of buttered toast.

" Well ! " said my friend, after the usual exchange of courtesies, " what masterpiece are you producing now ? "

" Jugged hare with plover garnish," replied the artist, sucking his finger, with signs of profound satisfaction, and he raised the lid of the saucepan. Immediately the kitchen was filled with a fragrance fit to awaken the demon of sensuality in the most ascetic of hearts.

My friend praised it highly, and then : " You are a

very able cook, as anyone would agree," he said ; " but it is easy for a cook to make tasty dishes out of good materials—to make a tasty dish with a plump fowl or with a garnish of plovers ! The ideal would be to produce the roast, or the contents of this saucepan, of which you are so justly proud, without a fowl, or a hare, or a garnish of plovers. The precept, ' To jug a hare, first catch your hare,' is too exacting. Do not catch the obliging hare. It would be better to take something else, quite ordinary, within everybody's means, and none the less to produce your jugged hare."

The cook was bewildered, my friend was speaking with such apparent sincerity.

" A real jugged hare without having a hare—a roast fowl without having a fowl ? Could *you* do it ? "

" No, I couldn't do it myself ; I haven't sufficient skill, more's the pity. But I do know someone who can do such things, besides whom you and your friends are so many clumsy dabblers."

The cook's eye flashed ; the pride of the artist was wounded to the quick : " And what would he use, if you please, this master among masters, for I suppose he doesn't make a roast fowl out of nothing at all ? "

" He uses the most ordinary ingredients. Would you like to see ? I have got them all here."

My friend took three bottles from his pocket. The cook took one from him ; it contained a fine black powder. The gastronomic artist felt, smelt, and tasted.

" It's charcoal," he said. " A nice thing to give me ! Your charcoal fowls ought to be magnificent ! Let's see the second bottle ; that's water, unless I'm very much mistaken."

" Yes, it is water."

" And the third bottle ? Why, there's nothing in it."

" Yes, there is something ; it's full of air."

" Get away with your air ! Well, they wouldn't lie heavy on the stomach, these roast fowls made of empty air. Are you serious ? "

" Quite serious."

" Do you mean it ? "

" I mean it most absolutely ! "

" This genius of yours makes his fowls out of charcoal, water, and air, and nothing else ? "

" He does."

The cook's nose turned blue.

" And with water, charcoal and air, he would make that *brochette* of ortolans ? "

" Yes."

The cook's nose turned from blue to violet.

" With charcoal, air and water, he would make that *paté de foie gras*, that *compôte* of pigeons ? "

" Yes, a thousand times yes ! "

The cook's nose went up into the air ; it was now crimson. There was a sudden explosion : the cook believed himself to be in the presence of a madman who was poking fun at him. He took my friend by the shoulders and put him out of the kitchen, casting at his feet the three bottles containing the ingredients that were supposed to make a fowl. The irascible nose gradually changed from crimson to violet, from violet to blue, and from blue to its normal colour, but the demonstration of how a fowl may be made of charcoal, air and water, was never completed. I will here explain the matter for the reader, since he may be as puzzled as the cook.

Chemistry reduces all terrestrial substances, whether of organic or mineral origin, to some eighty odd primordial substances, which are known as elements or *simple bodies*, by which we mean that the methods of decomposition employed by the chemist have no effect upon them. If, by a series of operations, proceeding from the complex to the simple, the chemist obtains sulphur or phosphorus or carbon, for example, from the sap of a plant or the flesh of an animal or a mineral extracted from the womb of the earth, he goes no further in his attempt at simplification, convinced, by long experience, that all the power of his acids and reagents, the violent heat of his furnaces, and all the forces, whether slow or sudden, gentle or violent in their action, which he might call upon to aid him, will henceforth be unable to affect the substance which he has just obtained. He admits his inability to split up the substance any further by calling phosphorus, sulphur, carbon, and so forth, *simple bodies* or *elements*. The elements now known to us are some eighty in number. Fifty or more possess a peculiar lustre, which we call metallic : they are the metals : iron, copper, lead, gold, silver, and many less well known. The other elements do not possess this lustre ; they are the metalloids, of which the more important are oxygen, nitrogen, hydrogen, which we know chiefly in the gaseous state, and carbon, sulphur, phosphorus, etc., which we know as solids.

In order to make up this list, the chemist has explored everything : the atmosphere with its gases and vapours, the seas and the saline compounds which they hold in solution, and the soil with its wealth of minerals—and even the inaccessible depths, the very bowels of the earth, spill their substance on the surface through the craters of volcanoes—down to plants and animal organisms, those wonderful laboratories in which life groups the elements in their more complex forms. Thus, as far as the Earth is concerned, matter has but few secrets from the chemist ; every terrestrial substance, no matter what its origin, function, properties and appearance, can always be resolved, by decomposition, into some of these eighty elements. Minerals, plants, animals, and indeed everything we know of, is composed of these elemental ingredients, and by analysis is resolved into these isolated substances.

Those who are not already familiar with these ideas are commonly profoundly astonished by the statement that everything can be reduced to a few of these eighty simple substances. It is not difficult to realize that a piece of stone, of any sort, may be reduced to certain metals or metalloids ; it is a mineral, made up of other minerals. But that bread, living flesh, fruits, and the thousand substances which the plant and animal worlds produce, may be reduced to the same simple bodies as the minerals is a fact accepted only after some hesitation. This is an important point ; and we may well linger for a moment in order to decide whether the chemist's assertion is well founded. For example : bread. What simple bodies does it contain ? Without entering into the more complex details of its composition we may assert that, at all events, it contains a great deal of carbon. Let us place a slice of bread over a red-hot stove. The bread is scorched and turns black. If we wait long enough we shall find that finally nothing is left of it but so much charcoal. This charcoal, or carbon, comes from the bread ; so much is plain ; and as we cannot give what we do not possess the bread that yields carbon must have contained carbon from the outset, but carbon combined with other substances, so that we could not detect it. These other substances have disappeared, driven off by the heat ; and the carbon, deprived of these other substances, makes its appearance, as most obviously carbon, black and friable. So that bread—white, appetizing, and nourishing—contains carbon, which is black, savourless, and uneatable. Let us hold a sheet of glass over the smoke that rises from the scorching bread ; it is rapidly covered with a fine dew, just as though one had breathed upon it. This moisture comes from the smoke and the latter comes from the bread. Bread, therefore, contains water—or rather oxygen and hydrogen, the elements that go to make up the water. The dough had salt mixed in it ; so the bread contains salt, which consists of a metal, sodium, in combination with a gaseous metalloid, chlorine, a gas highly dangerous to breathe. So that if we go no farther it is obvious that in a mouthful of bread we are eating at least one metal and four metalloids. Among these simple bodies some are quite harmless : the carbon, oxygen and hydrogen ; but the others, the sodium and the chlorine, are extremely formidable when isolated. From the fact that bread, the staff of life, contains two substances which in themselves are deadly, you will see how chemical association can modify the original properties of an element. In combination what was a poison often becomes a wholesome food ; while in other cases what is in itself harmless becomes a poison in combination with other bodies. We need not pursue the matter farther, for the reader will now begin to realize that everything in nature, organic as well as inorganic or mineral, is composed of the same elements.

In the animal and the plant, therefore, we shall not find any elements that do not belong to the mineral kingdom ; living matter and dead both contain the same metals and metalloids. Life borrows its materials from the mineral kingdom and sooner or later returns them thither, for all comes thence, by way of chemical association, and all is given back again. What is to-day a mineral substance may one day, through transformation by vegetable organisms, become a living substance, part of a leaf, a flower, a fruit, a seed ; just as all that goes to make up an animal or a plant will assuredly, before very long, be reduced to mineral substances, which Life will use again for fresh creations, forever destroyed, forever renewed. The chemical elements constitute the common base of all things, from which all is derived and to which all returns, without the loss or gain of a single atom of matter ; they are the primordial substance, on which both life and chemical energy act in accordance with their peculiar laws.

Carbon, which we know principally in the form of coal and charcoal, is found in all the compounds existing in living Nature ; it is essentially the element of organic life. Consequently, all animal or vegetable substances, subjected to the action of heat, become carbonized : that is, their other elements are driven off in its state of volatile compounds, the carbon being left as residue. A slice of bread which we toasted too long became carbon ; the same thing happens to meat, starch, sugar, cheese— in short, every substance furnished by plants or animals. Hydrogen combines with carbon to form the hydro- carbons—an enormous class of liquids including the alcohols, oils, inflammable spirits, and also india-rubber and other solid substances. To the combination of oxygen with carbon and hydrogen we owe the great majority of organic compounds, such as sugar, starch, wood, the vegetable acids and the fats. Lastly, nitrogen completes the series of the elements which play the greatest parts in the chemical products of life. We find it in fibrin, the basis of lean meat, or muscle, and of flour ; in casein, found in milk and a few vegetable seeds, such as peas ; and in white of egg or albumin, a sub- stance frequently found in vegetable fluids, especially in sap.

Carbon, hydrogen, oxygen and nitrogen, might well be called the *organic elements*, for we find them in every substance of animal or vegetable origin, two of them being combined, or three, even all four. The other elements may also occur in organic compounds, but in a far less general fashion ; they are, so to speak, accessory ingredients. Thus, sulphur, phosphorus, potassium, sodium, calcium, iron and other elements are found in small proportions in certain compounds. Phosphorus and calcium occur in the bones, iron in the blood, and sulphur in eggs ; but in a general manner we may regard the organic bodies as associations of some or all of the four basic elements : carbon, hydrogen, oxygen, and nitrogen.

Let us now return to my friend with his three bottles of stuff for making chickens. One contained carbon, one water and one air. Now, water is a compound of oxygen and hydrogen, and air is a mixture, not a compound, of oxygen and nitrogen. The three bottles together therefore contained the primordial elements of all living creatures, and all the dishes that the cook was preparing could be reduced to carbon and the elements of air and water. My friend really had in his three bottles the fundamental materials of the cook's chickens, and pigeons, and *paté de foie gras*, but the work of combining these materials so as to make flesh and flour, or any of the ingredients of the cook's delicious confections, was beyond the power of any but the great artist of whom my friend spoke. And whom do I mean by the artist ? No more and no less than the green cell of plants.

At the great banquet of Life three dishes only are served combined in an infinite number of ways. From the gourmet who dines on the gastronomic wealth of the four quarters of the globe, to the Oyster, that grows fat on a little slime borne upon the tide—from the Oak-tree whose roots drink the moisture contained in thousands of cubic yards of soil to the mildew that grows on a scrap of decaying matter, all things are derived from

the same basic materials : carbon, air and water. The
only thing that varies is the mode of preparation.

Animals—whether wolves or men, who are not wholly
unlike wolves, both as regards food and other things as
well—eat their carbon in combination, in the shape of
mutton ; while the sheep that gives us mutton absorbs
its carbon in the form of grass ; while grass . . . It is
this wonderful transformation which enthrones a vegetable cell as monarch of the world, with men and wolves
and sheep as its subjects. In flesh food the stomach of
man, like that of the wolf, finds carbon, air and water in
association, small in volume, in an aliment of high nutritive
value ; in grass the stomach of the sheep finds them quite
as wonderfully prepared, though less tasty and much
greater in bulk. But how does the plant that builds up
the flesh of the sheep, as the sheep goes to build up the
flesh of man, consume its portion of carbon, air and water?

It consumes them practically in the raw state. The
green cell, which is really a stomach of miraculous power,
digests carbon and drinks air and water, and of these
three things, selected from amidst all the substances
which it does not require, is constructed the blade of
grass, which provides the sheep with water, carbon and
air combined in a nutritious form. The sheep continues
the fundamental work performed by the plant, carrying it
just a little farther, and turning it into flesh and blood,
which flesh, by a very simple modification, becomes the
flesh of a man, or of a wolf, according to which consumes it.

Of this series of eaters and things eaten, whose labours
are most meritorious ? Man borrows the materials of
his body from the sheep, which provides them ready
prepared. The sheep extracts them from the plant, in
which they are already greatly concentrated ; only the
plant is able to absorb them from their original source.
The plant makes its meal of things uneatable ; it pastures

upon charcoal, air and water, and miraculously converts them into foodstuffs by which the animal benefits.   It is, therefore, in the last resort, the plant that builds up carbon, oxygen, hydrogen and nitrogen into organic substances, thereby offering a continual banquet to all creatures that people the earth.

CHAPTER XXII

DECOMPOSITION OF CARBON DIOXIDE BY VEGETATION

Combustion of Carbon—Carbon dioxide—Carbon dioxide in the exhaled breath of animals—The quantity of Carbon oxydized by human respiration—The production of Carbon dioxide by the decomposition of organic matter—The quantity of Carbon dioxide poured into the atmosphere—The purification of the atmosphere by plants—Some experiments—An experiment with jam—The part played by aquatic plants—The necessity of sunlight—Chlorophyll is essential—Vegetable parasites which are not green in colour—Parasitism of the Orobanche s or Broom-Rapes.

THE carbon intended for the food of plants must first be liquified, dissolved, in order to penetrate the most delicate tissues of the vegetable organism. Now the solvent of carbon is oxygen, one of the ingredients of the atmosphere. Let us look more closely into this matter, for our pains will be rewarded.

Let us apply a flame to a small piece of charcoal ; the carbon catches fire, becomes red-hot, and is consumed, giving off heat. Presently nothing is left but a pinch of ashes, whose weight is a mere nothing compared with the original weight of the carbon. These ashes are derived by mineral substances, in particular salts of potash and lime, drawn up from the soil with the water of the ascending sap. Being incombustible, they have resisted the action of fire, while the carbon, being a combustible material, has entirely disappeared. If the carbon derived from vegetables were not accompanied by these mineral substances it would not leave any residue of combustion whatsoever. It would totally disappear. To burn, is not, accordingly, to reduce to ashes, as is commonly said. The cinders that remain after combustion are merely a residue proceeding from the impurities of the fuel. No ashes are left if the carbon is absolutely pure.

What then has become of the carbon which we have burned ? It has been consumed, you will tell me ; it has burned away. Agreed ; but when a thing is " burned away," is it therefore burned away to nothing ? When the carbon has been burned, is there really nothing, absolutely nothing ? No ; for nothing in the world can really be annihilated. Try to annihilate a grain of sand. You may crush it, may reduce it to an impalpable powder, but as for destroying it, never ! The chemist, with all his panoply of drugs and apparatus, cannot destroy it any more than you can. He may fuse it in his furnaces, he may dissolve it in liquids, or reduce it to the state of invisible vapour ; by combining it with this or that other element or substance he will give it a certain definite appearance, or colour, or other properties ; but in spite of the violent treatment to which it may be subjected, the material of the grain of sand will always continue in existence. Annihilation and chance, two big-sounding words that are for ever on our lips, have really no meaning whatsoever. All things obey laws ; all things persist, matter being indestructible.

The carbon consumed is therefore not annihilated It is in the air, dissolved, in an invisible state. Drop a lump of sugar into water : the sugar dissolves, being disseminated in the liquid, and therefore ceases to be visible even to the keenest sight. None the less, this invisible sugar still exists. The proof is that it has communicated to the water a new property, a saccharine flavour. It is the same with the carbon : in the process of combustion it is dissolved in the oxygen of the air, and becomes invisible.

The dissolution which takes place in our fireplaces and stoves, in a violent fashion, with the production of intense heat, is not the only manner in which carbon can be consumed. A scrap of wood exposed to the wind and rain becomes finally black with age, gradually losing its hard texture and eventually falling into dust. Well! this decomposition is in all respects comparable to that which takes place in a furnace. It is still combustion, but is so gradual that there is no perceptible production of heat. Burned in this way, very slowly, by mere contact with the air, a whole tree-trunk will finally be reduced to a few handfuls of mould, just as coal or charcoal burned in a furnace is reduced to ashes. The same result is to be observed in the case of all decomposing vegetable or animal matter. All decaying matter is consumed— that is, its carbon is slowly dissolved by the atmosphere.

An animal organism, once it is dead, gradually dissolves and disappears into the atmosphere in the form of carbon in solution. All animals breathe: that is, they admit to the interior of their bodies a certain quantity of air, which is removed from moment to moment, whose mission is to maintain the vital heat by burning the carbon furnished by food. In order to produce heat, which becomes movement and mechanical work, the animal mechanism burns carbon just as does an industrial engine. Not a fibre of our being stirs without a proportional expenditure of combustible matter. To live is to burn, in the strictest acceptation of the word; to breathe is to burn. We find mention, in all ages, as a figure of speech, of the torch of life. But the figure of speech is an expression of actual fact. Air, because it contains oxygen, consumes the torch; it likewise consumes the animal. It makes the torch produce heat and light, it makes the animals produce warmth and work. Without air, the torch goes out; without air, the animal dies.

18

The animal is, from this point of view, comparable to an elaborate engine, actuated by a furnace. It feeds itself and breathes, in order to produce warmth and movement ; it consumes its fuel in the form of food, burning it in the depths of its body with the oxygen of the air supplied by respiration.

Once impregnated with dissolved carbon, the air is expelled from the body. Hence the double movement of respiration : inspiration, which draws pure air into the body, and expiration, which expels the air saturated with carbon. Thus, the combustion of a lump of coal in the fireplace, the putrefaction of a corpse, and animal respiration, are in the last resort phenomena of the same order. In all three cases we have a solution of carbon in the oxygen of the air, a solution accompanied by the liberation of more or less heat. Chemically speaking, to burn, to breathe, to decay, are synonymous.

When it is impregnated with carbon, oxygen, the respirable ingredient of air, acquires new properties. It then becomes an irrespirable gas, known to the chemists as carbon dioxide or carbonic acid. Subtle as the air itself, carbonic acid is invisible and impalpable. It cannot support life nor will it maintain combustion. Plunged into an atmosphere of carbonic acid gas, animal life is extinguished, and so likewise is the flame of a lamp. The reason is obvious. The heat-producing mechanism of the animal, the furnace of life, must be continually fed with pure air, which dissolved the carbon of the body and so produces heat. If respiration provides it only with air unsuitable, air already containing all the carbon that can be stored in it, the mechanism no longer works, the temperature falls, and life is extinguished. The flame of the lamp must be continually supplied with air, which maintains the heat of the flame by constantly dissolving carbon. If it cannot dissolve any more, if it becomes rich in carbonic acid, the air no longer maintains combustion, and the lamp is extinguished. The flame of a wick soaked in oil and the flame of life maintained by bread both burn in air, which dissolves their carbon, and are extinguished in carbon dioxide, which cannot do so.

On an average we burn about 120–150 grains of carbon hourly, so that the amount of carbonic acid gas exhaled by a human being in twenty-four hours is about 100 gallons. At this rate a man living for sixty years will burn, in round figures, about 10,000 lbs., or some 5 tons ; and the great human family, which is said to number, approximately, 1,500 millions, must burn at least 125,000,000 tons. Piled into a heap, this carbon would make a mountain whose base would be some 3 miles in circumference and 2,000 to 2,500 feet in height. Such is the quantity of carbon required to maintain merely the bodily heat of man. Between us all we eat the whole of the mountain, and by the end of a year we have exhaled it into the atmosphere in puff upon puff of carbonic acid gas, and have to start upon another mountain. What a quantity of carbon dioxide must not the human race alone have exhaled into the air if in a single year it can produce over 250,000,000,000 cubic yards !

The mind cannot grasp such figures ! And we have still to take into account the respiration of the lower animals, which, if we count those in the sea as well as those on the earth, must consume a very pretty heap of fuel ; for they are far more numerous than we are and populate the seas and the continents. What a mass of carbon is required to maintain the flame of life ! And it all goes into the atmosphere, which it vitiates.[1] And this

[1] Fabre says : " A deadly gas, of which a few breaths will kill you." It is carbon monoxide that is the deadly gas ; when dissolved in the blood it combines with the haemoglobin, rendering the latter permanently incapable of its function of carrying oxygen in unstable combination, and producing rapid asphyxiation. Authorities differ as to the toxic effect of the dioxide ; but a small percentage of this gas

is not all.   Substances which burn by decaying, such as
manure, are decomposed into carbon dioxide.   A cultivated field, even though it be not heavily manured, may
give off a daily volume of 50 to 100 cubic yards of carbonic
acid gas per acre.   The wood, charcoal and coal which
we burn in our houses, and above all in the powerful
furnaces of our factories, are also dissolved in the air,
in the form of deleterious gases.   Think of the quantity
of carbonic acid vomited into the air by the furnaces
of a factory into which coal is shot by the truckload !
Think of the volcanoes, those huge chimneys of the
subterranean fires, which in a single eruption eject
quantities of this gas, compared with which the amounts
produced by our industries are negligible !

Such figures may well make the reader apprehensive.
All things breathing, or burning, or fermenting, or
decaying, exhale carbonic acid, which is diffused throughout the atmosphere.   Will not the latter, since it receives
all these deadly emanations, eventually, in the course of
centuries, become unbreathable ?—Not a bit of it ; the
animal creation need have no fear of such a thing, either
now or in the future.   The atmosphere, though continually poisoned with carbonic acid, is continually purged
of the same.   And what is the providential purifying
agent entrusted with the general health of the world ?
It is the vegetable cell, which feeds upon carbonic acid
gas that it may save our lives and gives us the bread we
live by.   This deadly gas, into which the bodies of all
things dead are resolved, is the chief and essential food
of the plant.   The wonderful stomach of the plant-cell
can feed upon the products of putrefaction.   Life is
re-created from the poisonous relics of death.

in a room produces malaise and shortness of breath.   Deep inhalation
of the gas produces rapid insensibility, but recovery is frequent, whereas
the monoxide is extremely deadly, its compound with hæmoglobin
being stable.—*Translator.*

The leaf, as you know, is riddled like a sieve by an infinite number of orifices of microscopic mouths which we call stomata or breathing-pores. Through them the plant breathes, not pure air, as we do, but a poisonous gas, deadly to animal life, but wholesome to the plant. It breathes, through its myriad stomata, the carbonic acid gas contained in the atmosphere, absorbing it into the tissue of its leaves, and there, under the influence of the sunlight, a supreme transformation takes place, incomprehensible as life itself. The cells, being stimulated by light, decompose the carbon dioxide, *un*-burning or *de*-consuming the oxidized carbon (neither word is in the dictionary, which is a pity, since they express precisely what I wish to say), or de-oxidizing it, to employ the usual term. They undo what combustion has done : in other words, they separate the carbon from the oxygen combined with it. But you are not to suppose that it is an easy matter to divorce two substances wedded by the ordeal of fire, to un-burn a stuff once burned. The chemist, in order to extract the carbon in carbonic acid, would be forced to employ his most ingenious processes, his most energetic reagents, and this operation, which requires the most powerful means at the chemist's disposal, is performed quite quietly and easily by the green cell of the plant. It is done in a moment ; the carbon and the respirable gas, oxygen, are separated, and each resumes its original properties.

Deprived of its carbon, the oxygen is once more able to maintain life to feed a flame, as it was before it was associated with the other element. In this state the stomata reject it, and it is again available for combustion or respiration. It entered the tissues of the leaves as an unbreathable if not a poisonous gas : it leaves them as life-giving oxygen. Sooner or later it will return with a fresh cargo of carbon, of which it will divest itself in the storehouse of the cells, and being thus purged it will at once resume its aerial wanderings.

A hiveful of bees comes and goes between the hive and the meadows, alternately unladen and eager for booty, or bearing cargoes of honey, regaining their combs with heavier flight. Oxygen may be compared to a swarm returning to a vegetable hive ; it reaches the stomata with its load of carbon, looted from the veins of animal organisms, from putrefying leaf-mould and other matter ; and the oxygen gives it up to the cells and sets off again, indefatigable, to fetch another load.

As for the carbon thus obtained by the decomposition of carbonic acid, it remains in the tissue of the leaves and enters, as an ingredient, into the elaborated or descending sap, which becomes sugar, starch, wood, and other organic components of the plant. Sooner or later these materials are in turn decomposed—by slow combustion (decay) or rapid combustion (burning) or by the animal processes of alimentation and nutrition, and the carbon becomes carbon dioxide once more, which is returned to the atmosphere, whence other plants once more receive it, feeding upon it and then yielding to the animal world the alimentary substances which they have prepared. The same carbon comes and goes, following an invariable circle, from the air to the plant, from the plant to the animal, from the animal to the air, the common reservoir whence all living creatures derive, during their days of life, the greater part of the materials of which they are composed. Oxygen is the vehicle of carbon. The animal borrows its carbon from the plant in the form of food, making carbonic acid ; the plant draws from the air this deleterious gas, replacing it by oxygen, and, with its carbon, prepares the food of the animal world. The two organic kingdoms thus mutually help one another ; the animal manufactures carbonic acid, on which the plant feeds, while the plant, with the aid of this deleterious gas, makes respirable air and foodstuffs.

The simplest method of demonstrating the decomposition of carbonic acid by plants is to conduct a subaqueous experiment which will enable us to observe the exhalation of oxygen and to collect the gas given off. Ordinary fresh water always contains carbonic acid in solution, derived either from the soil or from the atmosphere, so that we need not trouble ourselves to provide the gas. Taking a wide-mouthed glass bottle filled with water, we immerse in it a freshly cut branch, covered with green leaves. An aquatic plant is to be preferred, as the demonstration will then be accomplished more rapidly, while the experiment can if desired be carried on for a greater length of time. The bottle is inverted in a bowl full of water, and is finally exposed to the direct rays of the sun. Presently the leaves are seen to be covered with tiny bubbles, which rise to the top of the con-

FIG. 109.

tainer (the inverted bottom of the bottle) and there form a stratum of gas. It will be found that a match will burn in the gas thus collected far more brilliantly than in the open air ; by which we may recognize the gas as oxygen. It is therefore evident that the carbon dioxide in the water must have been decomposed by the leaves into its two elements, oxygen and carbon. The oxygen is set free while the carbon remains in the tissues of the leaves.

The volume of oxygen thus liberated depends on the volume of carbonic acid gas dissolved in the water ; and when this small amount of gas is exhausted the experiment cannot, of course, be continued any longer. By this method we cannot collect more than a very small volume of oxygen ; it is sufficient, however, for us to recognize the nature of the gas. But the work of disintegration performed by the leaves is in reality far more active ; if nothing occurs to obstruct its functions a single Water-Lily pad will give off 500 pints of oxygen during a summer day. You will realize, then, that the few cubic centimetres obtained by our experiment are far from representing the full activity of the plant. If we gradually renew the carbon dioxide as it becomes exhausted, we shall obtain a much greater volume of oxygen. In this connection we may reproduce the curious experiment devised by Decandolle. We invert, in a basin full of water, two wide-mouthed bottles, side by side, one full of carbonic acid gas and the other of water in which an aquatic plant is floating. The whole is exposed to the rays of the sun. Through the medium of the water, which dissolves it, the carbonic acid gas in the first bottle gradually finds its way into the second, as the plant decomposes the carbonic acid in the surrounding liquid. The water bathing the leaves of the plant is thus able to renew its store of gas in solution, so that the chemical process continues for days on end. The progress of the decomposition effected can be followed by the eye. Every day the water rises a little higher in the jar containing the carbon dioxide, taking the place of the gas which has disappeared ; on the other hand, in the jar containing the aquatic plant we see the surface of the water sink as it is displaced by the oxygen released. If the experiment is conducted with care all the carbon dioxide in the one jar disappears, while in the jar containing the plant an almost equal volume of oxygen is collected.

These two methods of procedure are very unlike the process effected in the natural state. Instead of experimenting with whole plants, rooted in the ground and outspreading their foliage to the air, we experiment with fragments, with twigs or branches, which are no longer in touch with the soil, and are immersed in water, an environment alien to aerial vegetation. Can the results obtained under these artificial conditions really be applied to normal vegetation? Inquiries conducted by recent observers leave us in no doubt on this point. The first and most celebrated experiment conducted under natural conditions was M. Boussingault's experiment with the Vine.

The distinguished chemist introduced the branch of a Vine, covered with vegetation, into a large bulb of clear glass. The branch was still connected with the Vine-stock and bore some twenty leaves. The bulb was full of air, which was renewed at a moderate rate by means of an aspirating appliance. The atmosphere, you will remember, always contains a certain amount of carbonic acid gas, of which I have already explained the chief sources. Well!—analysis showed that the air leaving the bulb, after flowing between and over the Vine-leaves, contained only one-third as much carbon dioxide as the air entering the bulb. The carbon dioxide which had disappeared was replaced by an approximately equal volume of oxygen. It was therefore sufficient that the atmospheric air should drift through the foliage exposed to the rays of the sun for the leaves to deprive the air of three-quarters of its carbon dioxide, to decompose it, and substitute for it an equal bulk of oxygen.

I am afraid this laboratory equipment of glass globes and inverted jars and basins and aspirating apparatus may be a little confusing, so we will reduce experiment to its simplest possible terms. Let us repair to the nearest pond. There, in the stagnant water, is a prosperous population of tadpoles, which rest in the sunlight at the brink of the pond or, making for open water, frisk and wriggle about in shoals ; many varieties of snails may be observed, slowly crawling along under cover of their shells ; small crustaceans, swimming by fits and starts, striking the water with their tails ; larvae that make themselves sheaths of cemented grains of sand ; black leeches, that lie in wait to seize upon the passers-by ; and lastly, sticklebacks, pretty little fish that are armed with spines along their backbones. All these creatures breathe oxygen, but oxygen dissolved in water. If there were a lack of oxygen in the water of the pond the whole population would inevitably perish. Another danger likewise threatens them : the floor of the pond consists of black mud, a mass of decomposing substances ; dead leaves, the dejecta of its inhabitants, and dead animalculæ. This layer of putrefying matter is constantly giving off carbonic acid, which is as deadly to the tadpole and the stickleback as it is to us. How, then, is the water of the pond maintained in a respirable condition, and continually enriched with life-giving oxygen, so that the dwellers in the pond are able to live and prosper ?

The task of sanitation is performed by aquatic plants ; they feed on the carbon dioxide which they decompose with the aid of sunlight, replacing it by oxygen. Putrefaction furnishes the plant with its livelihood and the plant supports the animal organism. Now, amidst the species of water-weed that ensure the salubrity of stagnant water, there are certain Algae, the Confervae or Hairweeds, fine thread-like growths which cover the floor of the pond with a carpet of close, velvety texture, or float on the surface, or below it, in gelatinous masses. Place a tuft of such Hairweed in a jar filled with fresh water ; expose it to the rays of the sun, and after a few minutes you will see that the weed is covered with innumerable tiny bubbles of gas. These are bubbles of oxygen, derived from the carbonic acid gas dissolved in the water. Imprisoned by the slimy meshes of the water-weed, these bubbles increase in size until they buoy the plant up, giving it a frothy appearance, and eventually lift it to the surface. This experiment requires no special apparatus ; a little green, slimy-looking weed, dropped into a tumbler of water and set in the sunlight, will enable you to watch this natural oxygen-producing factory.

This Alga, producing a breathable gas in a glass jar full of water, demonstrates the work of sanitation which takes place in the depths of a pond, lake, river or sea. All the greenstuff in a tank or pond—Duckweed, Hairweed, certain growths of a slimy, felt-like texture, aquatic Mosses, and so forth, become covered, in the sunlight, with bubbles of oxygen which dissolve in the water and enable it to maintain animal as well as vegetable life. Thanks to these humble weeds, stagnant water, far from becoming pestilential, is enabled to support a variety of animal species. And we may learn from this fact a lesson by which we might have profited in our childhood. How often does not the schoolboy try to keep sticklebacks alive in a glass jam-pot ? He always fails ; the little fishes soon die if the water is not constantly renewed ; they die because the oxygen dissolved in the water has all been breathed. If, however, a good handful of Hairweed is placed in the jar the plant and the fishes will mutually benefit one another ; the Alga will provide the sticklebacks with oxygen while the sticklebacks will provide the plant with carbon dioxide, so that both will prosper, even though the water is not changed. When fish or molluscs are to be kept in an aquarium they must always be provided with their indispensable companions, water-weeds.

Two conditions are essential if the plant is to decompose

carbonic acid gas and liberate oxygen : the direct rays of the sun and chlorophyll. Carbonic acid cannot be decomposed, oxygen cannot be liberated under the influence of artificial light, however brilliant, or in darkness. You can prove this by placing a little Hairweed in a glass of water. Kept in the shade, the aquatic plant is unable to cover itself with bubbles of gas, no matter how long the experiment lasts ; but in the sun it quickly produces them.

When it is not subjected to the direct action of sunlight a plant cannot react upon carbonic acid gas, its principal food. It languishes ; it is starved ; it grows to abnormal heights as though seeking the light of which it is deprived ; its bark and leaves lose their green colour, and turn pale ; finally it dies. This morbid condition, due to the lack of sunlight, is known as *etiolation*. In the kitchen garden this condition is often provoked in order to obtain tenderer vegetables for the table, or to diminish, and even destroy, the strong and unpleasant flavour of certain vegetables. Thus, Lettuces are tied up with bast so that the heart, deprived of light, shall be white and succulent ; while Celery and Asparagus are often almost buried in the soil, as otherwise their flavour would be too strong. Cover a piece of turf with a tile or hide a plant under an inverted flower-pot ; in a few days' time you will find leaf and blade yellow and sickly.

Only the green portions of plants are able to decompose carbonic acid. Flowers, fruits and other organs which are not green are incapable of the task, even under the action of sunlight. All cells containing green granules of chlorophyll are able, with the assistance of the sun, to reduce carbonic acid into its two elements ; but cells that do not contain chlorophyll are quite powerless to effect this transformation. It is to these granules of chlorophyll that we must look for the chemical process which splits carbon dioxide into oxygen and carbon—a process which is still very imperfectly understood, though it is not without a certain similarity to the part played by the red corpuscles in the blood of animals. These corpuscles, whose dimensions are extremely minute, become impregnated with oxygen while traversing the respiratory organs ; they condense it in their porous substance, and in so doing increase its powers of combustion. Washed onwards by the circulation of the blood, they gradually give up their oxygen to the various organs which are bathed in blood, burning up used and waste materials, which are exhaled, with the breath, as carbonic acid gas and water vapour. In a like manner the granules of chlorophyll doubtless condense the carbonic acid and present it to the reaction of the sunlight under the conditions most favourable to its decomposition. The chemists, indeed, inform us that very finely-divided substances are apt to provoke, by their mere presence, delicate chemical reactions which it is extremely difficult or even impossible to provide without their aid ; so that it is highly probable that both the green chlorophyll of leaves and the red corpuscles of the blood owe their chemical efficiency to the fact that their substance is very finely divided.[1]

The principal element of the plant, namely, carbon, is

[1] Since the above was written much interesting and valuable research has taught us many new and surprising facts with regard to colloidal solutions—which are not true solutions at all, although they behave as such, the particles of the finely-divided solid being in a state of suspension : that is, they are too small and light to sink through the liquid. An industrial use has been found for these pseudo-solutions, and an expert has stated that the reason why the Israelites could not make bricks without straw was that without a colloidal solution of straw, or of the gluten of straw, the clay employed would not hold together. Whether an ordinary brick-mill for powdering dried clay could triturate straw to the necessary degree of fineness seems to me doubtful. We must not forget that the plasterer, from time immemorial, has used cowhair to bind his plaster—not a colloidal solution of hair ; and the West Country builder of " cob " cottages mixes straw with his moist loam or clay.—*Translator.*

furnished by carbonic acid gas, whose decomposition requires, as a necessary condition, the presence of chlorophyll in the superficial cells. Nevertheless, there are plants which are born, grow, and prosper without containing the smallest trace of chlorophyll in their tissues. Such are the Broom-Rapes or Strangle-weeds, very frequently encountered about our countryside, and occasionally a pestilential nuisance to the farmer. Picture to yourself a stem like a shoot of Asparagus, without branches, covered with thick scales, ending in a cluster of dingy-looking flowers. The colour of the plant as a whole is brown, inclining to a rusty-red or a yellow tinge. There, in a few words, you have the Broom-Rape. Now, how can these plants feed themselves in the absence of those granules of chlorophyll which are so indispensable for the preparation of sap ? Dig carefully down to the roots of the plant and you will find the answer to the riddle : the stem is welded to the roots of some neighbouring plant. The Broom-Rapes are parasites ; having no green granules, they cannot of themselves extract from carbonic acid the carbon which is their staff of life ; so they live at the expense of other plants, whose sap they divert to their own profit. Each species has its favourite victim ; one requires Thyme, another Hemp, and others Flax, Ivy, Clover, or what not. Deprived of its food-plant, it cannot unfold itself. For example, we will sow some seeds of the Broom-Rape in a flower-pot. All our care will be wasted ; not a single seedling will appear. Let us now sow a mixture of Broom-Rape seed and the seed of some plant for which the parasite shows a predilection, or some Clover-seed. Now everything will germinate ; the Broom-Rape will weld its stem to the roots of the Clover-plants and will live upon the carbonic acid decomposed by its green-leaved foster-mother, living prosperously while the latter dies of exhaustion.

Among the plants which, by reason of their lack of green pigment, are incapable of elaborating their sap and are thus reduced to living as parasites on other plants, I may mention the Dodder, whose red, thread-like tentacles fix themselves upon Hemp, Thyme, or Flax-plants, or upon the Furze-bush, or even the Grape-Vine; the Pine-sucker, a yellow parasite which establishes itself on the roots of forest trees, and on the Pine-tree in particular; the Motherwort, with its large purple flowers, whose pale subterranean stem sucks its sustenance at the water's edge from the roots of the Alder-tree; and the reddish-yellow parasite that affixes itself to the stem of the Rock-rose. In all these plants the leaves are reduced to mere scales, like those that envelope an unopened bud.

CHAPTER XXIII

THE DESCENDING SAP

The chemical action of the leaves—The descending sap—The blood of animals and the completed sap of vegetables—The downward flow of the completed sap—The effect of a ligature or the removal of a ring of bark—Some applications—The distribution of sap in the various portions of the plant—The formation of new tissues—Summary.

Let us now consider, as a whole, the details given in the foregoing chapters. The crude or ascending sap, a liquid containing a very small proportion of nutritive substances in a very large quantity of water, is absorbed from the soil by the roots and conveyed to the leaves by the sap-wood. There, filtering from cell to cell, it is distributed throughout the substance of the leaf-blade, and the superabundant water, necessary for the transport of the alimentary substances, is exhaled in the form of vapour from the stomata. At the same time, while evaporation concentrates their contents, the cells receive the carbon dioxide derived from the atmosphere. Under the influence of sunlight the granules of chlorophyll split the gas into its two elements. The oxygen makes its way through the membranous walls of the cells, enters the tortuous corridors of the cellular tissue, until it reaches the air-chambers, and finally the stomata, which reject it simultaneously with water vapour. The carbon remains in the leaf ; not isolated, nor yet in the form of an impalpable black powder, for it instantly combines with the ingredients contained in the ascending sap. The cavity of a cell is not merely a laboratory for decom-

posing carbon dioxide ; it is also, and in a far greater
degree, a laboratory in which new compounds are prepared ; wherein chlorophyll, aided by the sunlight,
arranges the elements in fresh formations. The carbon,
therefore, is immediately transformed ; it finds in the
cell, conveyed thither by the ascending sap, the three
other organic elements : the oxygen and hydrogen of
water, the nitrogen of certain nitrogenous or ammoniacal
salts ; and by combining with these it instantly becomes
the raw material of sugar, starch, wood, fruit, or flowers,
without ever passing for a moment into the state of
ordinary carbon.

What a wonderful and incomprehensible achievement
is this of the green leaf ! Amidst the serried ranks of the
cells, which you would think were existing in a state of
complete repose, what activity do we find, what miraculous transformations—transformations far beyond the
power of the scientist ! The cells are dilated with liquids
which ooze from one cell to another ; by means of trans-
piration, infiltration and circulation they exchange the
ingredients which they hold in solution, while vapours
are exhaled ; gases, too, are delivered, while others are
sped upon their way ; the sunlight awakens the chemical
energies of the cells, and the elements are grouped in
such a fashion that henceforth they are the raw material
of life. The result of all these labours is the *completed,
elaborated or descending sap.*

We cannot say that this sap is the material of wood,
bark, leaf, flowers or fruit ; it is none of these things and
yet it is in a sense all of them. The blood of an animal
is neither flesh nor bone nor hair ; yet hair, bone, and
muscle are built up by the blood. The sap of a tree is
analogous in its functions ; it is the raw material of fruit
and wood, of leaves and flowers, of bark and bud. It is
the life-blood of the plant ; for in it every organ of the

19

plant finds what it requires for nourishment and growth. The leaf organizes this indefinite liquid, gives it the vitality of life and makes more leaf-tissue out of it ; the flower derives from it the materials of its colour and its scent ; the fruit obtains the ingredients of starch, sugar and the gelatinous principle which enables us to make fruit jelly without the aid of gelatine, isinglass or the like ; the wood of the tree finds the raw material of its fibres ; the bark secures material for its outer sheath of cork, and for its lace-like sheets of liber. This liquid is quite unremarkable to the eye ; apparently so negligible, a mere nothing, it is in reality everything. It is the great breast of Nature. Plants directly, and animals indirectly —indeed, all living " creatures who on earth do dwell "— suck their aliment from this unfailing stream.

The enriched sap descends by way of the inner layers of the bark. Concentrated by the evaporation from the leaves, this nourishing sap cannot be obtained in large quantities, as in the case of the ascending sap, which consists principally of a large volume of water ; never-theless, we can easily demonstrate the fact of its descent through the bark. If we remove a ring of bark from the trunk of a tree the nourishing liquid will ooze forth and collect upon the upper edge of the wound, but nothing of this is observable at the lower edge. Thus checked by an insuperable obstacle, the sap accumulates along the upper edge of the denuded band and causes an abundant formation of tissues there, while below the bare portion the stem retains its original diameter. This lignous fillet or cushion, if we examine its internal structure, proves to be a confused mass of fibres and vessels, which show us that the sap sought a thoroughfare in all direc-tions, as though to find a way down and continue its journey below the obstacle.

A tight ligature, obstructing by its pressure the paths

which the nourishing sap ought to follow, provokes the formation of a similar fillet above the line of compression. You have doubtless seen a sapling or a young tree too closely tied to the stake or iron frame intended to give it support, strangling itself by its own growth unless some-one has remembered to loosen its bonds. Gradually the trunk swells above the ligature, which is finally over-lapped by the bark, and in some cases even buried in the substance of the fillet. Indeed, it is not unusual to find a tree whose trunk has thrust itself into a narrow crevice —as, for example, a rift in a rock—and has become so swollen above the obstacle as to present a shapeless excrescence. Such instances are due to holding up the sap in its downward flow.

If the whole circumference of the trunk is not subjected to strangulation, if there is anywhere a strip of living bark serving as a practicable isthmus, the nutritive fluid follows this path, leaving the obstacle on one side, and proceeds on its way to the roots. In such a case the tree continues to grow. But if the obstacle is an absolutely insuperable one—for example, when it is a firmly-bound ligature, or when a complete ring of bark is removed—the sap cannot make its way down to the roots, to feed them, so that the roots die, and soon afterwards the whole tree.

From these facts concerning the descending sap we may make the following deduction : Henceforth, in tying a plant to a supporting stake, be careful not to make the ligature too tight, or at all events loosen it before it is too late, or you will risk subjecting the trunk to a degree of strangulation that would prove fatal. We may draw yet another deduction in respect of budding and layering. There are certain vegetables which do not readily put forth adventive roots, so that they do not lend themselves to the methods of multiplication by slips or cuttings, or by layering.   If you wish to facilitate the production of such roots you can employ the following artifice : Remove a ring of bark from the branch which you want to put forth roots, or apply a tight ligature, and set the end of the branch thus treated in the ground.   The nutritive sap will collect upon the upper edge of the wound, or above the ligature, being unable to proceed any farther. This excess of nutritive matter will expend itself in creating fresh tissue, which, owing to the presence of cultivable soil, will assume the form of tufts of adventive roots instead of the usual fillet or cushion.

The edge of the bark where the sap is held up is so ready to produce roots that it may put them forth into the empty air if the atmosphere is sufficiently moist. Let us remove a ring of bark from a cutting, near the end ; and let us plant the severed cutting without burying the denuded portion in the earth.   Under these conditions the adventive roots do not appear in their habitual place, the severed end of the cutting, surrounded with moist earth ; they will be put forth into the open air, at the upper edge of the wound, and will grow downwards and bury themselves in the ground.

If the cutting is not completely " ringed "—if a longitudinal strip of bark is left, connecting the two edges of the wound—the sap will continue upon its downward course through this strip, and the adventive roots will form at the buried base of the cutting, just as if the latter had been left in its normal state.

The conveyance of nutritive sap takes place in a downward direction through the tissues of the bark, as we have just demonstrated ; nevertheless, the sap is also diverted from this general advance downwards into other secondary paths, which lead the sap to the various organs of the plant, sometimes crossing the general current and at other times actually ascending.   Buds, leaves young shoots, tissues in process of formation, all receive their share of food. A certain proportion of the sap exudes between the bark and the wood, and then, by a further elaboration, becomes that species of fluid wood, *cambium*, which every year produces a fresh layer of sap-wood and a fresh layer of liber ; while another portion is stored up in the laticiferous vessels, in the form of an opaque and coloured liquid, known as *latex* ; lastly, what remains reaches the roots, where a considerable expenditure of sap takes place in respect of the continual formation of fresh tissues whose function is to absorb by endosmosis. There the circulating movement is completed, only to begin again, without interruption, with the materials furnished by the soil. Starting from the roots in the form of the crude liquids sucked from the soil, the sap ascends by way of the sap-wood, reaches the leaves, which act upon it under the chemical influence of the sunlight, combining with the carbon derived from the atmosphere, and so becoming nutritive sap ; it then descends through the bark, being distributed to the various organs of the tree, and finally returns to its point of departure in the roots.

CHAPTER XXIV

THE RESPIRATION OF PLANTS

Life is maintained by a continual combustion—The twofold gaseous exchange between the plant and the atmosphere—The exchange in respect of respiration—The general result as regards the atmosphere—The seat of vegetable respiration—The quantity of oxygen consumed by flowers—The heat produced by the respiration of vegetables—The heat given off by certain Aroïdeae—Animal phosphorescence—Vegetable phosphorescence—The Agaric of the Olive-tree.

IN all organized beings, in plants as well as in animals, life is maintained by a continual destruction, by a gradual combustion, due to the presence of oxygen. In order to live, matter must be incessantly consumed and incessantly renewed. The reader will remember that we have already referred to that apt and beautiful expression— the flame of life. To give out light and heat, to be in any sense alive, the lamp must unremittingly consume its substance, its oil, and must as constantly supply its flame with fuel. So it is with life, that wonderful lamp which is lit at birth and extinguished at death. Nutrition renews the substance that has disappeared, respiration consumes the substance thus acquired, and from this perpetual conflict results the activity of the living being. To live is to burn, as I have explained, in respect of animal life ; and that to burn is to live is true likewise of vegetable life. Not a fibre performs its duty, not a cell accomplishes its purpose, without a loss of substance surrendered to the life-giving gas, oxygen. Plants breathe as do animals : the oxygen of the atmosphere penetrates their tissues and there maintains life by burning their carbon, becoming carbonic acid, which is exhaled into the atmosphere. There is thus, between the plant and the atmosphere, a twofold gaseous exchange, one relating to nutrition and the renewal of substance, and the other relating to respiration, which destroys the substance acquired.

In the course of the first exchange the air provides the plant with carbonic acid gas, which is decomposed into its two elements by the aid of the chemical action of sunlight ; and the plant restores to the atmosphere the oxygen set free by this decomposition. This exchange is periodic, not continuous ; it occurs only under the influence of sunlight, ceasing absolutely during the night, or even in shadow. And it takes place only in the green portions of the plant, only in the cells containing granules of chlorophyll ; the various organs otherwise coloured have no part in it, whether by day or by night. The important result of this organic process is the acquisition of carbon, which is necessary for the final elaboration of the sap. This exchange is therefore a process of nutrition ; that is, one of maintenance, not of expenditure ; nevertheless, we are accustomed to give the name of respiration to the function apportioned to the green parts of plants, and above all to the leaves, of absorbing carbonic acid gas and exhaling oxygen. The earlier observers of plant life, by failing to distinguish the two orders of ideas, have bequeathed to us this vicious expression, which, as a matter of fact, would be better avoided, lest it give rise to a regrettable confusion of thought.

Since to respire is to expend substance in order to maintain the process of vital combustion, I shall apply the term *the respiration of plants* to the second kind of gaseous exchange between the vegetable and the atmost phere. In this process the atmosphere provides the plant with oxygen, which slowly consumes the tissues and thus maintains their vitality ; the plant gives to the atmosphere the carbon dioxide which results from this combustion. The respiratory exchange is thus precisely the inverse of the nutritive exchange. It is, moreover, continuous and not periodic, and is not subordinated to the presence of sunlight. By night as well as by day, in the profoundest darkness as well as in the light, the plant respires ; it absorbs oxygen and rejects carbonic acid gas ; it behaves, in short, like the animal, whose respiration may be accelerated or retarded, but never ceases so long as life is present. All parts of the plant indistinctly, green or not green, aerial or subterranean, consume oxygen. Oxygen is necessary to the leaves, the roots, the germinating grain, the opening flower, the ripening seed, the unfolding bud, and the tuber feeding its shoots. In the absence of oxygen vegetable life is extinguished, just as is animal life. A plant will die in an atmosphere of carbonic acid gas, although this is its principal food ; it will die in any environment deprived of oxygen, or insufficiently rich in oxygen. Thus, in experiments relating to the chemical functions of leaves, we must, if we are conducting an experiment under water, make use of ordinary water containing both air and carbon dioxide in solution ; while if the experiment is conducted in a gaseous environment we must supply the leaves not with carbonic acid gas only, but with air containing minute traces of the gas. With insufficient oxygen and an excess of carbon dioxide the plant will die.

To sum up : the act of nutrition, whose result is the supply of carbon to the plant, consists in the absorption of carbon dioxide and the liberation of oxygen. This process is a function only of the green parts of the plant, and principally of the leaves, and is accomplished only under the direct rays of the sun. The act of respiration,

whose result is the maintenance of vegetable activity by
the slow and continual combustion of the tissues, consists
of the absorption of oxygen and the liberation of carbon
dioxide. This process is accomplished in all parts of the
plant, whatever their colour, in the darkness as well as in
the light of day. Its effect upon the atmosphere is
therefore precisely inverse to that of nutrition. In the
one case the air is purified by the removal of carbon
dioxide and enriched by the liberation of oxygen ; in the
other it is deprived of a certain amount of oxygen and
receives carbonic acid gas. But the work done by the
green parts of the plant under the action of sunlight is
beyond all comparison greater than that of vital combustion ; the quantity of carbon that enters into the
plant while bathed in sunlight is greater than that which
leaves it ; the plant exhales more oxygen than it absorbs ;
so that as regards the hours of daylight the effect of
vegetation on the atmosphere is to increase its content
of oxygen and to decrease its proportion of carbon
dioxide. During the night, when the chemical stimulus
of the light is absent, the action of the chlorophyll is
suspended, but respiration is continued, consuming oxygen
and giving off carbonic acid gas in exchange. As long as
it is dark the Earth's vegetation causes an increase in
the irrespirable constituents of the atmosphere and a
decrease of its respirable portion ; it vitiates the air
just as animals do. If we consider these gaseous exchanges
between the plant and the atmosphere, and if we define
their sum by the usual term, respiration, without taking
into account the really very different character of the two
functions, we may say that the diurnal respiration of
plants purifies the atmosphere, increasing the proportion
of oxygen, but diminishing that of carbon dioxide ; while
the nocturnal respiration vitiates the atmosphere by
diminishing the proportion of oxygen and increasing that

of carbon dioxide. But the balance is heavily in favour of the diurnal respiration ; the work of decomposition accomplished by the leaves predominates over that of the vital oxidization or oxygenation, although it occupies a shorter period. The leaf-surface and the time being equal, for example, the foliage of the Rose-Laurel decomposes, in the sunlight, sixteen times as much carbonic acid as it liberates at night. The main effect of vegetation is thus to increase the oxygen and decrease the carbon dioxide content of the air ; so that the wholesomeness of the air, always tainted by animal life, is always restored by plant life.

But we will now pass on, having sufficiently studied the great importance of the activities of chlorophyll in the harmony of organized life, and revert to the true process of respiration, which consists in the absorption of oxygen and the liberation of carbon dioxide. All parts of the plant, indistinctly, respire, since the life even of the smallest cell could not be maintained without incessant oxygenation ; nevertheless, the respiratory activity is as a general thing far more active in those organs that are not coloured green.[1] Fertile in the leaves, the bark, the roots and the lignous tissues, the absorption of oxygen acquires at certain points an intensity comparable to that essential to the maintenance of life in animals. Grain at the moment of germination ; the bud while it is swelling and casting off its envelopes ; the flower, above all when life is awakening in the fruit, rival the animal kingdom in respiratory activity. In

[1] Grant Allen, whose *Colour Sense in Insects* and *Physiological Aesthetics* are too much neglected, has an interesting passage on this subject. One may say, broadly, that plant tissues which are doing work are green ; while those which are absorbing or expending energy are other than green. Grant Allen instances the flower of the Coboea, which has three phases of colour. The reader may be referred to certain species of Clematis—there is a large collection of them to be seen at Kew—in which the showy pseudo-petals are in some stages of maturity partly purple, partly ordinary leaf-green.—*Translator.*

twenty-four hours a sunflower consumes 11 times its volume of oxygen, a flower 12 times and a passion-flower 18 times ; while during the same period a leaf of the latter plant will consume only 5 times its volume. This considerable expenditure of oxygen, replaced by an equal volume of non-respirable gas, accounts for the malaise experienced in a closed room containing large quantities of flowers.[1] An atmosphere vitiated by the active respiration of flowers, and further impregnated with their scent, may even have serious consequences. Lastly, vegetables that contain no chlorophyll—Broom-Rape, Cytinus, Dodder, and the Fungi, always, even in the sunlight, consume oxygen and consume carbonic acid gas.

Animal heat results from a chemical activity proceeding in all parts of the organism, and in particular from the combination of the carbon of the tissues with the oxygen respired. Similar combinations occur in the vegetable, though, it is true, with less intensity. And a concomitant of this chemical activity, however slow and feeble it may be, is a certain production of heat. This is confirmed by experiment. By means of highly sensitive apparatus it has been possible to detect, in young shoots, leaves, fruits, and flowers in the bud, an excess of temperature attaining, at most, to 1° Fahr. But in some plants, at the moment of flowering, the rise of temperature is sufficient to be appreciable by an ordinary thermometer, and even to the touch. The Arums are specially remark· able in this respect.

In France there are two Arums which grow properly in the hedgerows : one, the Common or Calf's-foot Arum,

---

[1] Suggestion probably plays its part here, as many persons, even when the windows are wide open, declare that Hawthorn and other scented flowers " smell faint," and at once persuade themselves that they feel ill. Probably this is why certain flowers are supposed to be " unlucky." —*Translator.*

frequent in the centre and the north of France, and the Italian Arum, confined to the south.   In both the flower consists of a large yellowish cone or *spathe*, like a conical paper bag, from the centre of which rises a fleshy stem bearing the floral organs, the stamens and pistils.   This stem ends in a dilated portion termed the *club*.   At the moment of flowering the heat of the club is perfectly perceptible to the hand.   A thermometer placed in the spathe rises to 15° or even 18° Fahr. above the temperature of the air.   Certain Arum Lilies of the Ile Bourbon, if a dozen or so be piled round a thermometer, will cause it to rise through 50° or 60° Fahr.   During this increased production of heat the inflorescence of the Arums is the seat of a chemical activity like that which produces animal heat.   A considerable volume of oxygen is absorbed, its equivalent in carbonic acid gas being exhaled.   The flower respires almost as actively as a warm-blooded animal, and like the animal it emanates heat as the consequence of combustion.

In a few rare instances respiration, at the height of its intensity, may render the vegetable phosphorescent, that is, may cause it to emit light without heat, like that of phosphorus seen in the darkness.   This curious property of the plant is found in a greater degree in animal life, and we will begin by considering it in the latter.   We all know the Glow-worm, the tiny star that is sometimes seen gleaming in the grass on peaceful summer nights.   She is a poor enough creature to look at, a creeping, wingless, short-legged insect, unable to disport herself in the air before the male, himself a winged beetle, is yet able to draw him to the ground, by lighting, at nightfall, the resplendent beacon formed by the hinder segments of the body.   Now in this living beacon there is actual combustion, but it is heatless ; oxygen is abundantly consumed and carbon dioxide exhaled ; moreover, the insect ceases to shine in a vacuum, or in a non-combustive atmosphere such as nitrogen. Phosphorus plays no part in this production of light ; the most delicate analysis fails to detect the smallest trace of this element in the phosphorescent substance of the insect ; it is the very substance of the Glow-worm itself that serves as fuel. In the South of France and in Italy we find the Fire-fly, which in its countless myriads threads the breeze in the evening twilight like a rain of living sparks. In Brazil and Cayenne there are the Pyrophorae, whose corselet bears two circular patches, two phosphorescent reservoirs of magnificent luminous intensity. During their nocturnal hunting expeditions the Indians attach one of these insects to each foot, in order to light up their path.

Phosphorescence is found also in a host of animals belonging to the lowest levels of the zoological scale ; annelidae, crustacea, molluscs, and radiolariae. In our climate there is a small earthworm that has the brilliance of a thread of phosphorus, while a millipede, the Electric Geophila, resembles, as its name tells us, a trail of electric sparks.

The sea, above all in the tropics, abounds in phosphorescent animal species. The most remarkable are the Noctiluci and the Pyrosomae. The Noctiluci are tiny gelatinous specks, transparent, and terminating in a moving filament. The Pyrosomae have the form of a hollow cylinder the size of a finger. They, too, are gelatinous and transparent. Where these phosphorescent populations are very abundant the ocean seems to consist of a rolling flood of molten incandescent metal. The vessel cleaving the waves thrusts from its prow two fountains of blue and red flame, as though it were ploughing a furrow in a bed of burning sulphur. Myriads of sparks ascend from the depths of the water ; phosphorescent clouds and luminous wreaths are seen drifting

amidst the waves.   The resplendently shining Pyrosomae
group themselves together in wreaths that are like
circular chains of white-hot metal.   Like steel cooling
after flowing from the furnace, they vary in shade from
one moment to the next ; from sparkling sapphire they
change to red, rosy pink, orange, green, and the blue
of the sky ; then suddenly they flash brighter and throw
off more brilliant sparks.   At intervals one of these
wreaths of light undulates to and fro like a firework
serpent, which coils and uncoils itself, rolls itself into a
sphere, and plunges into the waves like a red-hot cannon-
ball.   Oftener still the sea, as far as the eye can carry, is
like a plain of milk, steeped in a soft light, as though
phosphorus were dissolved in the water.

All these instances of animal phosphorescence, excepting
perhaps a few that are still imperfectly understood, appear
to be due to the same cause : the oxygenation of the
luminous substance with the formation of carbonic acid
gas.   We have here a peculiar kind of vital combustion,
producing light instead of heat.   Let us now return to
the plant.   Barely half a score of vegetables are endowed
with phosphorescence ; and it is worthy of note that this
property, the appanage of the lower forms of animal life,
is likewise observed only in those vegetables whose
organization is of the simplest, and especially in certain
fungi.   Agarics, Byssi, like so much cotton-wool, Rhizomorphs, like bundles of fine root-fibres,[1] which are
all formed exclusively of cellular tissue—these are the
plants which, in the darkness, emit a phosphorescent
aureole ; lovers of the shade, which spread their luminous
surfaces over some dingy and slowly rotting tree-trunk,
as the phosphorescent Earth-worm and the Electric
Geophile drag the segments of their bodies, like threads
of white-hot metal, through their dark burrows.

[1] The Byssi and Rhizomorphs, according to appearances, are fungi
in an incomplete state of development.

The Agaric of the Olive, a magnificent fungus of a bright orange-colour, frequently found in Provence, at the base of the Olive-trees, is, as regards phosphorescence, the most remarkable species in Europe, and in brilliance rivals the most noted tropical species. As in all the Agarics, the under surface of the " umbrella " is covered with thin radiating plates or gills, on which grow the corpuscles which propagate the fungus : that is, the seeds or *spores*. The whole assemblage of these luminations is known as the *hymenium*. The Agaric of the Olive is at first wholly dark in hue ; it consumes oxygen and gives off carbonic acid, as do all vegetables without any shade of green. Then, at the moment of the maximum vital activity, when the spores become fertile, the hymenium decks itself out as though for a festival and emits a soft white light, which recalls that of the moon, although it is visible only in the deepest darkness. During the whole period of this luminous emission the respiration of the plant is more active ; the absorption of oxygen and the exhalation of carbonic acid gas are increased by almost fifty per cent. Once the spores have ripened and have fallen from the gills in the form of a fine powder, the respiration diminishes and the phosphorescence ceases. We find here a fact of the same nature as that mentioned in respect of the Arums. In both cases the respiration is increased at the moment when the seeds wake to life, and the solemnity of the vital act is celebrated in the Arum by an emission of heat—in the Agaric by an emission of light.

PART II

CHAPTER I

THE CONSERVATION OF THE SPECIES

Multiplication by means of buds—It is not sufficient to ensure the prosperity of the species—A Spring Morning—Fish—The life-story of the Naiads—The conservation of the species—The Codfish—The egg—The life-story of the Medusae—Twiform Polyps.

WE have compared the plant to a community of polyps living in common on their stone support and increasing their numbers by budding. Each branch is an individual member of the plant as each polyp is an individual of the polypary. Now in either community two different functions go hand in hand.

The present is assured by *nutrition*; that is, the operation of the sap in the leaf-bearing branches of the tree and the operation of the alimentary juices in the stomachs of the polypary. The future is assured by *reproduction*; that is, the growth of buds that form fresh branches, and the formation of buds that become fresh polyps, which are based upon their forbears and continue them. Each individual of the community, whether polyp or branch, performs two simultaneous functions; it acts upon nutritive substances for the purposes of maintenance in the present, and produces buds, forming successors that perpetuate the race into the future. Thus the tree and the polypary go down the centuries, still prosperous, ever more populous.

But this procuration by budding, this procuration by fresh individuals superimposed one upon another and unchanging, fixed to the spot where they are born, does

291

not suffice for the prosperity of the species. With buds incapable of detaching themselves from the parent stem and of moving away in order to live an independent existence, with buds incapable of detaching themselves from the mother stem and founding new colonies elsewhere, the vegetable and the polypary increase without succeeding in peopling the sea with polyparies or the earth with vegetables. The dissemination of the species calls for mobile buds, which, on reaching maturity, abandon the spot where they were born, and establish themselves in isolation where chance leads them and become the origin of communities like those that produced them. Such is the function of the young Hydras, which, when sufficiently grown, detach themselves from the parent Hydra; and likewise that of the caduceous buds of plants, of bulbs, bulbils and tubercles, which separate themselves from the parent plant and survive its destruction, continuing the species while feeding their germs with the provisions stored in their tissues.

Now will these migratory buds, so large, because of their store of aliment, so costly to produce, and therefore few in number, suffice to maintain the animal or the plant in such numbers as will assure its future? Can the Hydra with its half-dozen of buds, the Orchids with their single tubercle, the Garlic with its few bulbils, evade the many chances of destruction that await them and perpetuate themselves in time?

Such is the problem which has now to be solved. And let me first of all remind you of a certain fishing expedition in which you, perhaps, took part, though you may have forgotten all about it. You were quite a little fellow then; but already you were turning over stones and picking bits of dead bark from the trees in the hope of finding those beetles whose resplendent wing-cases you still admire; but you would not have taken much interest in subjects of observation which were then beyond your comprehension. Now that you are older we may well return to a point which then escaped you.

Let me tell you all about it. We were a party of five or six, and I, the schoolmaster, was the oldest, but nevertheless I was more the companion and the friend of the rest than their master. They were impetuous, imaginative boys, full of the springtide sap of youth that makes us so expansive, so eager to learn. Talking of this or that, we were following a path bordered with Hyæbla and Hawthorn, where already the golden Rose-beetle was intoxicating himself with the sharp fragrance of the opening corymbs ; we were going to see whether the Sacred Scarabaeus [1] had yet put in his appearance on the sandy plateau of Les Angles,[2] and had begun to roll his ball of dung, which the ancient Egyptians regarded as a symbol, an image, of the world ; and we wanted to see whether in the fresh springs at the foot of the hill there were any young Newts, with gills like tiny branches of coral, concealed beneath the carpet of Duckweed ; whether the Stickleback, that graceful little inhabitant of the brooks, had donned his nuptial scarf of azure blue and purple ; whether the Swallow, newly come, was skimming the tips of the meadow-grass, hawking for midges, which sow their eggs as they dance in the air ; whether the Eyed Lizard, the Iguana of the olive-growing departments, was sunning himself on the threshold of his limestone burrow, displaying in the sun his grass-green flanks, sprinkled with spots of blue ; whether the Laughing Gulls, that come inland from the Mediterranean, following the shoals of fish that ascend the Rhône to spawn in its waters, were as yet hovering in flocks above the river, now and again giving a cry like a burst of insane

[1] *Cetonia aurea* (*Trans.*). See Fabre's essays on Beetles.
[2] A village in Le Gard, not far from Avignon.

laughter ; whether . . . but need I say more ?   Let me observe, in order to abridge the list, that, being simple-hearted creatures, deriving a keen delight from the feeling that we were living in the midst of a world of animal life, we were about to spend the morning hours in partaking of the ineffable festival of the re-awakening of life in the spring.

We inspected the pools at the foot of the hill with especial care.   The Stickleback had put on his nuptial finery ; the scales of his belly would have shamed the gleam of silver and his throat was touched with the brightest vermilion.   At the approach of the Aulostoma, a great black leech of sinister intentions, his stickles stood erect on his back and sides promptly as though actuated by a spring.   Before this determined attitude the bandit retreated shamefully amidst the weeds.   The placid population of molluses—Physa, Paludina, Limnæa, Planorbis—was taking the air on the surface of the water.   The Hydrophilus, a black water-beetle, the pirate of the fresh-water pond, garrotted, in passing, now one of them, now another, but to all seeming the foolish herd was not even aware of him.   But I must reluctantly pass on, to tell you of the most valuable capture of the day.   " The most valuable capture " : perhaps you will expect the equivalent of a Crocodile or Alligator ?   Don't be disappointed ; I am speaking only of a fragile worm, known to science as the Naiad.   My captive, placed in a bottle with some water and a few scraps of Duckweed, was carried off in my waistcoat pocket.   On returning home I dropped the tiny creature into a watch-glass full of water, and, magnifying-glass in hand, I drew a pen-portrait of it in the following terms :

Imagine a frail scrap of ribbon, of inappreciable width and in length about an inch, translucid as amber and divided into rings or segments by almost imperceptible transverse indentations. This structure of rings or segments, welded end to end, is common to all the worms, which for this reason are known as *Annelidae*. Each segment of the Naiad bears as weapons two fine, white, stiff silken hairs, one on the right hand and one on the left ; so that the whole worm is not unlike the backbone of a very small fish. Remove the flesh of a sardine, and what remains is an enlarged model of the animal swimming in the watch-glass. The consecutive bones of the spine, the vertebrae, are like the segments of the Naiad ; the two ribs, one on either side, stand for the silken threads. A long straight line of a darker shade is visible from end to end of the Naiad's body ; sometimes brown, sometimes greenish, sometimes red, according to the creature's food. This is the alimentary canal. But which is the head and which the tail of the tiny animal ? See—at one end, on the top of the body, are two minute reddish spots : these are the eyes. On the under surface of the same extremity is a sort of tongue or proboscis, highly extensible, which pops in and out, now extended, now retracted, waving to and fro in the water, apparently to seize as prey the tiny creatures that come within its reach. The terminal segment which bears the two eye-spots and the tongue is therefore the head ; while the terminal segment of the other extremity is the tail.

But, as you will see, there are heads and heads, tails and tails. Let us carefully scan the Naiad from end to end with the magnifying-glass. At first the successive segments, counting from the head, are all equipped with two silken hairs or spines ; one is precisely like another. Then, about one-third of the length of the body from the head, after a constriction more marked than the rest, is yet another segment with two eye-spots and a tongue. It can only be a head ; it is indeed a head ; there can be no mistake, for this segment is the replica of the first segment of the body. What are we to make of this? A head near the middle of the body in addition to that in front! It would take an animal to think of such a thing; I can assure you they are clever enough for a whole family! But this is not all. Let us look farther back. Again the segments are identical in their resemblance; there comes another constriction, and again two eye-spots and a tongue; in short, a third head. You are astonished: but let us continue. Here is a fourth head, here a fifth, and that is the last; the worm ends in a tail, this time a real tail, since there is nothing beyond it. In brief, the Naiad consists of five similar creatures, welded end to end, each holding in its mouth the tail of the one in front of it.

How does this strange chaplet of worms come into being? You will remember the Hydra: you know how it puts forth warts or buds, which blossom into little Hydras. The Naiad likewise buds, not all over its body indiscriminately, but only at the tip of its tail. It produces there a second Naiad, as a bud is grown on the tip of a twig. When the new Naiad is of sufficient size the parent proceeds to grow another, still from the tip of its tail, and the new-born worm, joined to the tail of its parent by its head, and by its tail to its predecessor, pushes the latter backwards. It is the same with the rest; they are always born between the mother and the string of sisters which have preceded them, so that in the complete family we see that the Naiads increase in length as they are farther removed from the mother, for the reason that they are in proportion older.

In this string of Naiad which one has the care of providing food? Which hunts and digests the food, and prepares the alimentary pap? The mother only. It is she who, with her proboscis, snaps up the particles of decaying vegetable matter, the animalculae gyrating in the water ; it is she who digests them, and, once the nutritive pulp is at the point of perfection, she distributes it to the community by means of the alimentary canal which runs without a break from one end of the chain to the other.

By this process of budding the original Naiad produces three, four or five more, according to her vigour. But before long, worn out by organic labours that are accomplished at the expense of nourishment, she sets a term to the production of buds. Now, do these offspring suffice to assure the conservation of the species and maintain it in a flourishing condition amidst the Duckweed and Hairweed of the pond ? I know, of course, that if the Naiads disappeared from our ponds the earth would not cease to rotate, nor would the order of things in general be perceptibly affected. After all, supposing some supreme catastrophe were to sweep away the whole human race, would the sun veil itself in token of mourning and the planets turn backwards in their courses ? Not a bit of it ; the Crickets would continue to chirp in the tussocks, and the Tadpoles to wriggle in the ponds, absolutely as though nothing of the kind had happened. Whether the race of Naiads were extinguished, or that of the Elephants, or that of the Whales, those monstrous monu- ments of flesh and bone, it would be all one ; it would be the irreparable loss of one type of animal life, of one of the medals coined in the mint of Creation. It is not therefore idle to ask whether the budding of four or five Naiads by a first one is enough to perpetuate the species. Science, in its loftiest meditations, has no other object than the search of providential harmonies that maintain the species in a just equilibrium of prosperity.

Well ! five Naiads succeed to one. This would be far too much had we not to give considerable weight to the causes of destruction. If one replaces one the population remains the same ; if five replace one the numbers of the species, in a few generations, must have increased beyond all tolerable limits. By the end of a few years the constantly quintupled offspring of one original worm would find the world too small for them. But there is Death, the great Reaper, who sets an insuperable obstacle in the way of all overcrowding, counterbalancing life, with its all-invading fecundity, and co-operating with it to keep all things perpetually young. In the most peaceful-looking pond there is at every moment of time a struggle between destruction and procreation. Here sooner, there later, all its inhabitants submit to the common law ; to-day they devour others, to-morrow are themselves devoured. But the small, the humble, the feeble creatures are the habitual pasture, the daily bread of the big eaters. To how many dangers is the Naiad exposed—a creature so small, with no defences other than its double row of silken bristles, which are an adornment rather than a weapon ! Let a Stickleback discover, with its piercing eyes, a spot frequented by the Naiads, and it will swallow hundreds of them, merely to whet its appetite. And the Aulostoma, the hideous black Leech, a far more rapacious creature, joins in the feast : the Naiad race must indeed be in peril ! But no : the Leech and the Stickleback, with many another creature of prey, devour the Naiads, yet there are always Naiads left. Is it the process of budding that balances such destruction ? Surely not ! For to contend on equal terms against all the chances of destruction, to maintain themselves in sufficient strength despite all the creatures that devour them, the Naiads must possess another means of multiplication, less costly of substance, but more rapid in respect of numerical increase.

This other method is the animal seed, the egg, the miracle of miracles, which, in a barely visible speck of matter, concentrates all the forces of life, and, by its small volume, lends itself to an inconceivably profuse production ; the egg, innumerable past counting [1] and therefore able to contend successfully with destruction, all of whose causes conspire to annihilate the race ; and it is here—in the struggle between fecundity, that restores, and the stern conflict of life, that destroys—it is here that the weak excel in setting against the chances of extinction the defence of innumerable legions.   In vain do the destroyers rush to the feast ; the victims survive by sacrificing a hundred thousand in order to preserve one.   The more they are sacrificed, the more faithful they are.   The Herring, Sardine and Codfish are so much pasture to the devourers of the sea, the earth and the air.   When they undertake long migrations, in order to spawn in propitious localities, all conspire to destroy them.   The ravenous creatures of the ocean surround the shoal, the hungry creatures of the air glide above it as it travels, and the shoal is browsed upon, nibbled away, at once from above, below, and every side.   Tarry-breeks hastens from the shore to secure his share of this ocean manna ; he equips fleets of fishing-boats and goes in

[1] The following fact, which is so obvious that it often escapes one, was first, I believe, pointed out by Carl Ewald in one of his delightful "nature stories." The majority of animal species being, over such periods as come under human observation, moderately stable, it follows that of the millions of eggs produced by a fish, or the scores of puppies brought to light by a wild dog or of baby mice produced by a mouse, precisely two survive for each female parent, the numerical strength of the sexes being about equal ; where the female greatly predominates the proportion is one and a fraction ; and in primitive hermaphroditic forms that propagate only by budding or fusion only one of the offspring survives out of an often overwhelming flood of fertility.   If *two* codfish, for example, finally survived for every fish now living, the seas would in a century or two be almost solid with cannibal codfish, which would then either perish, or breathe by coming to the surface, exposing their moist gills to the sea breezes and the oxygenated surface-water, for the depths would be irrespirable.   The fertile species are mostly defenceless, so that profusion means a gathering of the destroyers, and the balance is maintained.—*Translator*.

search of the fish with a marine army in which all the
nations are enlisted ; he dries his captures in the sun,
salts them, smokes them and packs them in boxes.   But
we can hardly speak of extermination, for along the trail
of the emigrants the sea is no longer sea ; it is almost a
solid, so closely serried are the ranks of the fish.   The
journey is pursued without deviation ; there is no question
of flight, of escape from the enemy.   The numbers of the
defenceless are indefinite.   One Codfish produces from
four to five million eggs.   Where are the creatures of
prey that will consume such a family as this ? [1]

It is true that the Naiads, in their ponds, do not have
to struggle against such tremendous odds as these in
favour of destruction ; they are not the victims of such
frightful depredations as those on the Codfish ; yet they
must have eggs, and numbers of eggs, to repair the gaps
made in their ranks.   Now where shall we find these eggs ?
The transparency of the worm makes it easy to look for
them.   The first Naiad has none at all ; from head to
tail we see only the brown thread of the alimentary canal ;
nothing more.   The last Naiad of the string, the eldest
of the budding family, is, on the other hand, full of eggs,
like a bag stuffed with fine granulations.   The next
below it in seniority, which precedes it in the series of
sister-organisms, has as many eggs, but these appear less
mature.   The others also contain eggs, but they are less
and less mature in proportion as the Naiad is younger
and therefore nearer the mother.   Thus the head of the
chain, the head of the family, is incapable of producing
eggs.   It produces, by budding, a small number of other
Naiads and feeds the whole community ; it is the only
one to seek food, to seize it, digest it and pass it on to
its buds ; but it never becomes great with eggs to sow the

[1] As already pointed out, they *do* consume the offspring of all but
two of the eggs produced by each female codfish during the whole
term of its life.—*Translator·*

race abroad and enable the latter to hold its own, by force of numbers, against the causes of destruction. True maternity, which creates more life by the egg, is the privilege of the buds.

Let us consider the eldest of the chain, the last of the series. When it feels that the seed, the hope of the race, is ripe within its flanks, it spontaneously detaches itself from the community, and, henceforth living an independent life, goes hither and thither, sowing its eggs in obedience to its instincts. When this supreme duty has been fulfilled it dies, for it is not capable of seeking food or digesting it. To feed itself is not its function, but rather to produce and scatter eggs. This done, its part is played. One after another, when the time is ripe, the remainder of the Naiads detach themselves, and wander about the pond for a few days, scattering their eggs, afterwards fading out of life as do the flowers when their fruit has " set." The great act has then been accomplished ; despite all the hungry mouths, the ponds will contain their population of Naiads in the spring.

Now these eggs hatch into worms which resemble not the mother that laid them, but the grandmother that budded. These Naiads are able to obtain food and digest it ; they are tenacious of life and their stomachs are robust, while they are cunning in the chase as their grandmother was ; and, like her, they begin, as soon as they are full-grown, to produce, by budding, other Naiads, unable to feed themselves, with no desire to eat, living an ephemeral, independent life, but swollen with eggs. And the same order of things begins anew, indefinitely ; the daughters are the grandmothers over again and the grand-daughters are like the mothers. The race of Naiads is thus composed of two castes which follow one another in an invariable order of succession : the caste of Naiads which form buds is followed by that of Naiads

which lay eggs. Their outward form is practically the
same, but their instincts and their internal organization
are absolutely different.   On the one hand, we have an
organism whose function is that of nutrition : it goes in
search of food, digests it, and transmits it to the community of buds ; on the other hand we have an organism
whose function is reproduction, which, once it is free,
wanders about sowing its eggs, but is unable to feed itself.

FIG. 110.—Medusa.

Now you must not
get it into your head
that the Naiads, with
their peculiar way of
life, their s t r a n g e
method of multiplica-
tion, are so excep-
tional, so far outside
the ordinary laws of
animal life, that one
cannot mention other
examples. As a matter
of fact, the choice of
such is so wide as to
be e m b a r r a s s i n g.

However, there is one example of the kind to which
we ourselves give harbour and nourishment : the hideous
Tape-Worm or Toenia.   The sea, the great nurse of
strange essays in life, is swarming with such creatures.
To corroborate the history of the Naiad I will confine
myself to mentioning the Medusa.

The sea contains a strange population in which life
seems to aim at the least possib'e expenditure of material,
while achieving a sufficient vo!ume and the greatest
possible elegance of form.   This population is that of
the Medusae, of which the largest, weighing from ten to
twelve pounds, contain barely a hundred and fifty grains

of animal substance. Distended with water, converted into a voluminous jelly, these scanty materials form the make-up of creatures which evaporate in the sun and are reduced almost to nothing, when the waves cast them up on the shore. The Medusae are as a general thing most exquisite in shape. The most usual form is that of a strongly convex or gibbous dome, sometimes limpid as the purest crystal, sometimes opalescent as water in which a few drops of milk have fallen. The colour is sometimes uniform, but the dome is frequently traversed by fine meridian-threads or ribbons of orange, crimson, or sapphire, radiating from the summit of the dome to the border, where the bright colour fades by imperceptible degrees. Such a dome reminds you of the cupola of some Oriental mosque or basilica, a work of the most refined and patient art. From the circumference of the living hemisphere depend filaments of opal, or floating draperies of chiffon, or fringes of a foamy white ; then, in the centre of the base, are great spirals of crystal, or snowy furbelows and flounces, in the centre of which is the mouth.

The Medusae drift at the sea's will ; suspended between two currents, they dilate and contract, pulsing somewhat as the human chest rises and falls, so that the French knew them by the popular name of *poumons marins*— lungs of the sea ; and by this palpitating movement they advance, retreat, ascend and descend. There is no more lovely sight than that of the legions of the Medusae gently travelling through the peaceful waters of some sheltered inlet.

On emerging from the egg the Medusa is the most elementary expression of animal life. It is a pear-shaped corpuscle, a nucleus of jelly, a speck dancing in the water by favour of the vibratory cilia with which it fairly bristles. The tiny thing gyrates, wanders hither and thither, and sets off on its travels through the water of

the vast ocean. It seeks a favourable site whereon to
establish itself. It cannot see or hear or know what is
about it ; at most it experiences the vague impressions
inherent in all flesh which quivers at the painful touch of
a foreign body. But is it flesh—this miserable atom,
consisting of next to nothing but the water that impreg-
nates and sustains it ? None the less does it explore
the ocean, discern, and select. What guides it ? The
universal Conscious ; instinct ; the infallible inspiration
of the Begetter of all things. In the asperities of a rock
a propitious spot offers itself. The living speck of jelly sees
it without eyes, scents it without a sense of smell, feels
the touch of it without organs of touch. Without hesitation it attaches itself to the rock by its lesser extremity ;
it takes root, so to speak ; and there it is established for
life. The tiny wanderer has taken on the fixity of the
plant ; and now it first develops and then proceeds to
bud.

At the upper end of the corpuscle a tiny buttonhole
forms, opens and becomes a mouth, destined, as in the
Hydra, not only to absorb food, but also to reject the
residue of digestion. The mouth is the entrance to a
tunnel ; on its lips are nodosities which lengthen into
tentacles, and finally the animalcule assumes the form
of a Greek urn standing on its base and crowned, at the
rim, by a circle of fine flexible lustres which wave in all
directions. The organization of the Medusa is thus
identical with that of the Hydra ; we find the same
digestive sac, fixed by its base, open at the top, the
opening serving a twofold function, and crowned by a
circular line of tentacles which seize the prey and carry
it to the mouth. Consequently the creature that issues
from the egg is known as a *Hydroid Polyp*.

Here, as far as the conservation of the individual is
concerned, the development of the Medusa ceases ; but

the conservation of the species demands more than this. At the mouth of the urn a bud forms, expanding into a disk, and then becoming a hollow goblet. Another succeeds it and thrusts it upwards. Others yet appear, so that presently the urn is surmounted by a pile of goblets, of which the eldest is at the top and the youngest at the bottom. This is budding or *gemmation*, as in the Naiad, between the parent and the chain of buds already put forth. Now the superposed goblets become more deeply hollowed and more isolated each from each, and their rims reveal a fringe of cilia ; until at length the eldest, the topmost, tears itself loose from the pile, and swims freely through the water. Turn by turn the others follow. Its family thus emancipated, the Hydroid Polyp is left alone fixed to the rock and does not live much longer. As for the cup-shaped offspring, they finally achieve the exquisite organization which I described at the outset, and one day their domes of crystal and opal are distended with eggs. These, in their wanderings, they scatter broadcast. From these eggs hatch not Medusae, but animalcules with vibratory cilia, which become Hydroid Polyps, the parent stocks of further generations of Medusae. The lowly polyp buds and gives birth to the graceful Medusa, and the Medusa, by means of its eggs, regenerates the polyp. Compare the point of departure and the final achievement—the tiny albuminous sac affixed by its base to the rock and the lovely dome of crystal floating between current and current. Who would ever suspect, without repeated observations, that the polyp, budding, gives birth to the Medusa, and that the latter produces eggs that give birth to the polyp ? Nevertheless the facts most unmistakably affirm as much ; the polyp and the Medusa belong to the same species ; they are complementary beings which partake, under different shapes, of the twofold function

21

of every animal. The polyp looks to the present, preserving the individual by nutrition ; the Medusa to the
future, propagating the species by means of the egg.

Certain Corals, certain Madrepores, present analogous
facts ; that is, they reveal two forms of the one species.
The ordinary polyps expand their tentacles, snap up any
little quarry that may pass within reach, digest it, and
nourish the community. This, with the budding of new
polyps, is their sole task. They are the providers of food.
Others, less numerous but more graceful in shape, richer
in colour, though incapable of nourishing themselves,
being fed at the expense of the community, have as
their mission the perpetuation of the species by means
of eggs, which, abandoned to the tides, become the
starting-point of fresh polyparies. Well !—this partition
of two primordial functions between two differently
organized individuals, this double form of the species,
one form appertaining to its present and one to its future
prosperity ; this strange succession of individuals, one
type of which is the food-provider and one the procreator,
as the Naiads and the Medusae have shown us, will be
found reproduced feature for feature in the world of
plants.

CHAPTER II

THE FLOWER

Seed a necessity—The flower—Its general structure—Essential organs—
Calyx—Corolla—Stamens—Pistil—Numerical laws of the flowers—
Multiplication of floral verticils—The law of alternation of the verticils
—Diagram of the flower—Monœcious and diœcious plants.

In addition to such artificial operations as budding and grafting, which are employed in the industry of horticulture, we have already examined the propagation of the vegetable organism by means of buds which isolate themselves from the parent stem and become distinct plants. The reader may recall to mind the stolons or runners of the Strawberry, the eyes of the Potato, the bulbils of Garlic, the tubercles of the Orchids. But these means of perpetuation are far from being general ; the great majority of plants do not employ them. Moreover, if they were universal they would be quite insufficient to maintain life in a prosperous and thriving condition for indefinite periods of time. Buds that isolate themselves from the parent have to be provided with a store of food, and are therefore never sufficiently numerous, by reason of their bulk. I shall not insist further on this point as it has already been discussed, but will pass on to another order of ideas.

A bud, a simple dismemberment of the whole of which it forms a part, repeats, with unvarying fidelity, the characteristics of its source of origin ; with monotonous fidelity, but does not contain within itself any new tendencies or forces. The most it can do is to retain intact the vital force of which it is the depository, without the power to rejuvenate it by a fresh vital impulse. Consequently indefinitely-continued descent by buds must inevitably have the consequence of monotony, in the first place, since the species, deprived of the faculty of varying in details, is composed of identical plants. In the second place—and this is a more serious matter—this line of offspring, which is liable to perish by the thousand accidents of long descent, but is powerless to regenerate a failing vitality, must sooner or later suffer degeneration, and finally the extinction of the species.

Plants therefore need another method of propagation, which will multiply the species in a degree sufficient to balance the risks of destruction ; which will bestow on the species a perpetually regenerated vigour and special tendencies to vary in details. This is effected by the employment of *seed*. All vegetables, withcut exception, multiply themselves by means of seed, and thereby the different species maintain themselves in prosperity and are able to look to an indefinite future. To this mode of reproduction some add that of accessory propagation by buds which cut themselves loose from the parent stem. Our cultivated plants, if too long propagated by means of buds and cuttings, finally perish ; and to revive their failing vitality we must have recourse to the sowing of their seed.

Here we have over again the double organization of the Naiads, the Medusae and certain Polyps. Two kinds of individual, differing in structure and in attributes, make up the vegetable association of the plant. The more numerous and robust species, clad in modest green, decompose carbonic acid gas when the sun is shining, compound the sap, and feed the community. These food-providers, these humble toilers, are simply the plant ;

ordinary buds developed into leaf-bearing branches. As for the other buds, which are provided with raiment as for festival, embellished with brilliant colours, steeped in perfume and endowed with the most graceful and striking form, their function is to produce the seeds of the plant. They are, to the plant, what the elegant Medusa with its crystal dome is to the Hydroid Polyp ; what the exquisite Coral animalcules which display their luxury of form and colour are to their humble fellow-members of the polypary. Unable to decompose carbon dioxide, they take no part in the preparation of sap and are fed at the cost of the community. These sumptuous buds, the propagators of the seed, are what we call *flowers*.

Despite its richness of colour and beauty of form the flower is, fundamentally, simply a branch, but a very short branch, whose leaves are metamorphosed in view of new functions. To produce this delicate, lovely thing, Life, that incomparable artist, mocking at difficulties, employs the same materials as for an ordinary, clumsy branch ; an axis, and leaves. Nothing new is created ; what already exists becomes a flower by an exquisite transformation. The branch is contracted upon itself, its foliage compacted into a rosette of metamorphosed leaves, and the miracle is accomplished. There are thus two kinds of branch found in association on the same plant. The branches of one type are devised for the purposes of nutrition—that is, the conservation of the individual, the needs of the present. The others are designed with reference to the future, to the conservation of the species—that is, to reproduction. These are the metamorphosed branches which we call flowers.

Let us now examine the general make-up of the flower, taking as our example the Lily, which, being a large flower, is easy to examine. The portion which strikes the observer's eye at the onset consists of six large pieces of a beautiful white, which, when the flowering-time is over, detach themselves separately. Each of these pieces is a *petal*, and the full arrangement of petals is known as the *corolla*. Next we find six long filaments, each of which bears at its free end, transversally suspended at the very tip, a capsule with two compartments, packed full of yellow dust. Each of these organs as a whole is known as a *stamen*. The two-celled capsule supported

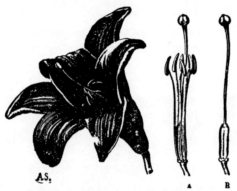

FIG. 111.—Flower of the White Lily.
A, stamens and pistil. B, the pistil separately

on the filament of the stamen is the *anther*, and the yellow dust is the *pollen*. At the centre of the flower, surrounded by the bundle of six stamens, is the *pistil*. In this we perceive, at the base, a distended portion with three convex sides ; this is the *ovary*, containing the seeds in process of formation : that is, the *ovules*. Above the ovary is a long erect filament known as the *stylus* ; and the stylus ends in a head divided into three by as many sinuses ; this is the *stigma*.

The structure of the Lily is repeated in many of the monocotyledons ; for example, in the Tulip and the Hyacinth ; but a very large number of plants, belonging above all to the dicotyledons, have, outside the corolla, a green protection envelope, which is called the *calyx*. Thus, we find on the outside of the rose five pointed green tongues, which, on the bud, are fitted exactly together, enveloping and protecting the more delicate internal portions, and which part and open out when the corolla bursts into blossom. Each of these portions of the calyx is called a *sepal*. In a complete flower, then, we find, going from the outside to the centre : 1, the calyx, composed of sepals ; 2, the corolla, composed of petals ; 3, the stamens ; 4, the pistil.

The essential parts of the flower, the only parts really necessary for the production of seeds, are the stamens and the pistil ; the calyx and the corolla are only protective envelopes and ornaments ; either or both may be lacking, and the flower none the less exists. We have already seen that the Lily has no calyx. A flower exists wherever there are the organs necessary for the formation of fertile seeds, were it only the pistil or a single stamen. Thus, a host of plants commonly regarded as flowerless do in reality possess flowers, but these are reduced to the merely necessary elements, without the beautiful accessories which habitually charm our eyes. Without any exception, every vegetable has its flowers, able to produce seed, though they are often inconspicuous enough. Let me add that in the acotyledonous vegetables —Mosses, Algae, Bracken and Ferns—the propagating organs differ so greatly from those of ordinary flowers that they will require a separate description. We will pass them over in silence, turning for the present to the flower as we knew it in the more highly developed vegetables, the dicotyledons and monocotyledons.

The external envelope of a complete flower is the calyx, composed of sepals. Its colour is usually green, and its texture is firmer and coarser than that of the inner organs, whose function is to protect and even wholly to enclose the flower in the bud. The number of sepals varies in different species. There are two in the Poppy, which are plainly to be seen on the bud, but they are ephemeral, for they detach themselves and fall away as soon as the flower expands its great red, crinkled petals. There are four in the Wallflower and five in the Rose.

Whatever their number, the sepals are in some cases distinct and plainly separated one from another, while in others they are more or less welded together at the edges and are then in appearance a single organ, but they show, at the top of the calyx, open intervals which

FIG. 112.—Polysepalous calyx   FIG. 113.—Monosepalous
        of a Flax-flower.   calyx of a Silenus.

enable us without difficulty to recognize the number of sepals thus assembled. When the sepals are perfectly distinct the calyx is qualified as *polysepalous* or *gamosepalous*; the Flax-flower has such a calyx. When they are more or less welded together the calyx is called *monosepalous*; this is the case with the Silenus. Whether distinct or assembled, the sepals are grouped about the axis of the flower and surround it as the verticillate leaves surround the stem. To recall this similarity of grouping, we say that the calyx forms the external *verticil* of the flower.

The petals form the inner verticil or corolla. They are large, thin blades or laminae, delicate and brightly coloured, whence green is almost always absent. There are four in the Poppy, four in the Wallflower, five in the wild

Rose and the blossom of the Cherry, the Apple, and our
various orchard trees. Like the sepals of the calyx, the
petals may be individually distinct, as in the wild Rose,
the Poppy and the Pink ; or welded together at the edges
for a varying proportion of their length, as in the Tobacco-
flower, the Campanula and the Convolvulus. In this
latter case the indentations, sinuosities and folds of the
corolla tell us of the number of petals thus assembled.
When the petals are separate the corolla is termed *polypetalous* or *gamopetalous* ; but *monopetalous* when they are
welded together.

Despite its size, vivid colour, and beauty of form,
which are to the superficial gaze the significant qualities
of the flower, the corolla plays only a very secondary
part, less important even than that of the calyx, which
owing to its tougher consistency is at least able to protect
the more central parts against the inclemency of the
weather. It is a luxury, a cover, a protection which is
lacking in many plants, whose flowers consequently do
not strike the eye. The majority of our forest trees, the
Oak, the Beech and the Elm, for example, have no corolla,
their only floral envelope consisting of small green scales,
the last vestiges of the calyx. When the flower has no
corolla it is called *apetalous*.

The assemblage of floral envelopes, calyx and corolla,
is termed the *perianth*. If either of the two envelopes is
lacking the flower is said to be *monoperianthous*. It is
monoperianthous by absence of the calyx in the Lily and
by lack of the corolla in our forest trees. If both envelopes are lacking, as they are more rarely, it is said to be
aperianthous or *naked*. Thus, the flower of the Duckweed
consists merely of a stamen or a pistil.

The stamens form the third circle or verticil of the
flower. The indispensable part of the stamen is the
anther, with its powdery pollen contents, whose function

is to fertilize the seeds and awaken in them the spark of
life when, as ovules, they are beginning to form in the
ovary.   An anther alone, then, is enough to make a
stamen.   The filament that carries it is of secondary
importance ; it may be longer or shorter, or may even,
though this is rather unusual, be wholly absent.   The
welding together of the stamens, more especially by their
filaments, may sometimes be observed, but it is less
frequent than the amalgamation of the sepals or petals.

The fourth and last verticil of the flower is that of the

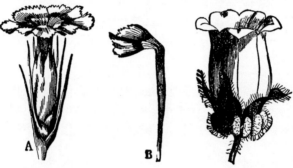

FIG. 114. Polypetalous flower of the Pink.   FIG. 115.—Monopetalous
    A, complete flower ; B, One of the   flower of the Canter-
            five petals isolated.   bury Bell.

pistil. On account of their central position, which
brings them into contact over wide surfaces, the various
parts of which the pistil is composed are very frequently
amalgamated and so form a whole of simple appearance
though in reality complex.   Let us first of all examine a
flower in which the divers pieces of the pistil are isolated
one from another—as in the Larkspur, for example.
We shall find in this flower three little membranous,
full-bellied sacs, inside which the young seeds, in the
form of ovules, are arranged along the walls.   Each sac
is surmounted by a short filament, ending in a head,
which is, though inconspicuous, of special structure.

Each of these three divisions of the pistil bears the name of *carpel*. The membranous sac containing the ovules is the *ovary* of the carpel, the thread-like prolongation is the *style*, and the terminal head is the *stigma*. The pistil of a flower is thus composed of a verticil of carpels, which, when they are not welded together, have each their individual ovary, their style and stigma. But the carpels, pressing against one another by reason of their position at the centre of the flower, are commonly amalgamated. Sometimes it is only the ovaries that are united, the styles and stigmata remaining distinct ; sometimes the ovaries and the styles are both amalgamated, leaving only the stigmata free ; sometimes the carpels are wholly united in one organ which to all seeming is a single entity. Yet even in this case it is easy to detect the complex nature of the pistil and the number of carpels of which it is composed, either by

FIG. 116.—Pistil of Larkspur.
n, ovary ; *t*, style ; *s*, stigma.

the common stigma, which is divided by grooves or indentations into as many lobes as there are carpels assembled, or by the common ovary, the exterior of which indicates, by the number of its distended nodes, its grooves or ridges, the number of simple ovaries comprised in the whole structure. Thus, in the pistil of the Lily we find a stigma with three lobes, plainly distinguishable, and an ovary with three obtuse swellings. Despite the simplicity of the whole structure this pistil is formed by the union of three carpels.

Even if neither stigmata nor ovary were to betray by their form the number of assembled carpels, there would still be one certain method of determining this number. Let us cut the ovary of the Lily in two transversely. We shall see that it consists of three compartments or

pods, in each of which ovules are packed.   Each pod is
the cavity of a carpel ; so that their number is that of
the carpels united to form the pistil.   Now let us take
an Apple, which is the ripened and enlarged
ovary of the Apple-blossom.   In cutting it
across we find five compartments, surrounded
by a tough wall and containing the seeds or
pips.   These five compartments tell us that
five carpels are here assembled.   The rule is a
general one : the number of compartments in
the common ovary is the number of the simple
ovaries that go to its make-up, and therefore
the number of the carpels comprised in the
pistil.

FIG. 117.
Pistil of
the Lily.

a, stigma ;
b, style ;
c, ovary.

We have just seen that the flower has four
verticils, namely : that of the calyx, whose
elements are sepals ; that of the corolla, composed of petals ; that of the stamens, and
that of the pistil, formed of carpels.   According
to their number and their respective position,
the parts of these four verticils follow certain rules,
although there are many exceptions.   Let us first consider
the rules and disregard the exceptions, giv-
ing our attention to them as they present
themselves.

In the dicotyledons the number of components of each floral verticil is often five ;
and in monocotyledons it is frequently
three.   The number five is thus the
characteristic, so to speak, of the floral
architecture of the plants with two seed-
leaves and the number three that of the
plants with only one seed-leaf.   This law is consequent
upon the principle in accordance with which the leaves
are arranged on the stalk or twig.   The flower, as I

FIG. 118.
Ovary of the
Lily : showing
transverse
section.

have told you, is a branch of a special structure ; its various parts are metamorphosed leaves. We ought therefore to find in the arrangement of the elements of the flower some traces of the laws that rule the arrangement of the leaves on the stem. Now in the dicotyledons the leaves are very often arranged in superposition, in sets of five, repeating, in each whorl, the co-ordination of the first group of five ; in the monocotyledons they occur in whorls of three. When the stem is excessively compressed upon its axis to form a flower the leaves of each set of five or of three are assembled in a verticil, and so the various floral whorls are whorls of five in the dicotyledons and three in the monocotyledons.

But each type of organ—and this is notably true of the petals and stamens—does not always form one single circle about the central axis, a single verticil, as the above explanation would suggest. The corolla, for example, may comprise two or more verticils of petals, one within another, and in like wise the stamens may form two or more circular series. Now it is the rule that in these repeated verticils the number of elements remains the same, which doubles or trebles the total of the petals or stamens. You will understand, then, that the number five may be replaced by one of its multiples in the dicotyledons and the number three by one of its multiples in the monocotyledons.

As examples let us take the Apple-blossom and the Lily. The first, pertaining to a dicotyledonous vegetable, comprises five sepals in the calyx, five petals in the corolla, perhaps a score of stamens, and five carpels, recognizable in the five compartments of the Apple's core. The second, belonging to a monocotyledon, comprises a double verticil of floral envelopes, each of three petals ; a double verticil of stamens, each whorl being likewise a group of three ; lastly, a pistil composed of three carpels.

We must not forget that this numerical law has many exceptions, if not always in the general make-up of the floral whorls, at least in some of the latter. Thus the Almond-blossom, built like the Apple-blossom on the quinary type, has only a single carpel in the pistil, as we perceive in the ripe ovary or almond.

The second law concerns the arrangement of the parts of the flower. We have seen that on the branch the verticillate leaves occur in alternation : that is (the axis being vertical) the leaves of any verticil are placed perpendicularly above the intervals of the verticils immediately above and below it, in order that the light shall have ready access to the leaves. There is a similar alternation in the floral organs, each whorl alternating with that preceding it. Thus the petals face the intervals between the sepals, the stamen the intervals of the petals, and the carpel those of the stamen. There are few exceptions to this rule of alternation.

To represent the shape and arrangement of a building an architect will depict the section of its walls in the horizontal plane. The design of this section is the *plan*. The botanist will give you, in the same manner, the plan of a flower, showing the various organs by a section along a plane perpendicular to the axis, which makes it possible to depict, with geometrical accuracy, the mutual arrangement of the floral parts. Such a drawing is called the *diagram* of the flower. Here, in Figs. 119 and 120, are the general diagrams which show the numerical law and the law of alternation for a dicotyledonous and a monocotyledonous flower respectively.

In the diagram of the dicotyledonous flower the five outermost lines, *s*, represent the five petals of the calyx. Opposite the intervals between them are placed the five petals, *p* ; then, still in alternate order, come the five stamens, *e*, which are represented by a doubled circle in token of the two-celled anther ; lastly, the five carpels, *c*, with their content of ovules, face the intervals of the stamens.

In the diagram of the monocotyledonous flower, *p* and *p'* represent two verticils of floral envelopes, arranged in mutual alternation, and as a rule both imbued with the coloration proper to corallae. Thus, in the Lily and the Tulip we find three inner petals, almost as richly coloured as the outer three. With reference to their position, only the three outer petals might be likened to a calyx, but they do not, during the greater part of their existence,

FIG. 119.—Diagram of a dicotyledonous flower. *s*, sepals ; *p*, petals ; *e*, stamens ; *c*, carpels.

FIG. 120.—Diagram of a monocotyledonous flower. *p* and *p'*, petals ; *e*, stamens ; *c*, carpels.

display any trace of green coloration. Nevertheless, a few monocotyledonous flowers, such as the Virginia Ephemerine, have the three outer elements green, and are thus really endowed with a calyx. A few others combine, in this outer verticil, the characteristics of the calyx with those of the corolla. Thus the Star of Bethlehem (*Ornithogallus*), so common in our cultivated fields, has the three outer petals white inside and green outside. Judging by the outside of the flower this verticil in the Star of Bethlehem is a calyx ; judging by the inside it is a corolla. Whatever hesitation we may feel in respect of the outer verticil of the perianth in the monocotyledonous plants, we find three stamens, *e*, alternating with the three inner petals. Sometimes, as in the Lily and the

Tulip, these three stamens are supplemented by three more, standing just within the whorl of the first three and alternating with them. Lastly, three carpels, *c*, are seen, facing the intervals of the inner whorl of stamens.

In a flower the absolutely indispensable organs are the pistil, whose ovary contains the ovules, and, secondly, the stamens, whose pollen vivifies the ovules and makes them develop into fertile seeds. In the great majority

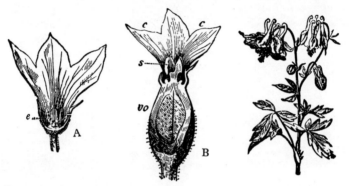

Fig. 121.—A, staminate flower of Gourd; *e*, stamens. B, pistillate flower; *vo*, ovary; *s*, stigma; *c*, corolla.

Fig. 122.—Columbine.

of plants the two kinds of organ are united in the same flower, the pistil occupying the central position, with the stamens arranged around it. But there are some plants which have two different sorts of flower, which mutually complete one another, one kind producing ovules and the other yielding pollen. Flowers destined to produce pollen only contain stamens but no pistil inside the floral envelope. They are known as *staminate flowers*. The other kind, whose sole function is to yield ovules, contain a pistil but no stamens and are known as *pistillate flowers*.

Sometimes pistillate and staminate flowers bloom together on the same plant and even on the same stalk.

To describe this community of position, this cohabitation, so to speak, we say that the plant is *monœcious*. The Pumpkin and the Melon, for example, are monœcious. Flowers with stamens and flowers with pistils are found at the same time on the same plant, the same branch. The staminate flower, after the emission of the pollen, fades and falls from the plant, leaving no trace behind ; while the pistillate flower, which may at once be recognized by its dilated lower portion, does not entirely fall when faded, but leaves in place the fertilized ovary which becomes the fruit.

Sometimes, again, staminate and pistillate flowers are found on different plants, so that for fructification two distinct plants are requisite, one furnishing pollen and the other ovules. The plant is then said to be *diœcious*. Such are Hemp and Briony. It is only the pistillate plant that yields fruits and seeds. The staminate plant never produces them, but is none the less indispensable, since, in the absence of pollen, fructification would be impossible.

CHAPTER III

THE PERIANTH

Coloration of the Calyx—Its duration—Caduceous, persistent, marcescent and accrescent calyxes—Labiate and spurred calyxes—Free and adherent calyxes—Calycle—Aigrettes—The Corolla—Polypetalous corollae, regular and irregular—Spurs—Peloria—Structure of the Pelorized Toadflax.

THE CALYX

WE have given the name of perianth to the sum of the floral envelopes, the calyx and corolla ; we will now return to these two whorls in order to examine their principal modifications. As regards its colour, which is most commonly green, and its consistency, the calyx is that one of the verticils which most reminds us of the ordinary leaves, whence the flower is derived by metamorphosis. However, this green coloration is not an invariable characteristic of the calyx, which often assumes tints that rival those of the corolla, as we see, for example, in the Pomegranate-flower, where its scarlet hue is as vivid as that of the petals. The calyx of the Fuschia may also be mentioned as possessing in the highest degree the brilliance of the corolla, and likewise that of the Glossy Sage. Sometimes, too, the sepals resemble the petals in delicacy of texture as well as in their colour, as in Aconite and the Columbine. The calyx is then said to be *petaloid*.

Generally speaking, the calyx is the most durable part of the perianth. It survives the corolla, and its protective function as regards the bud is continued in favour of the ovary while this ripens and becomes the fruit. Nevertheless, in a few plants, as in the Poppy, it falls as the corolla opens. In these conditions it is known as a *caduceous calyx*. When it survives the corolla and persists, surrounding the ovary, it sometimes retains almost its original appearance ; sometimes, on the other hand, it withers, while retaining its position and its shape ; but sometimes, too, it continues to grow, and may even become thick and fleshy. An example of this last case is furnished by the Rose, whose red fruit is composed internally of numbers of seeds mingled with short hairs, while the outer portion consists of a fleshy envelope whose wall is the calyx, expanding at the tip into five tongues, below which, by the amalgamation of the sepals, it forms a deep oval vase. In the Winter Cherry or Physalis the calyx, at first green and of no great capacity, later on becomes a voluminous bladder of a scarlet hue surrounding the ovary. Those calyxes that persist after the fall of the corolla are known as *persistent* if they retain their former aspect, *marcescent* if they become dry and hard, and *accrescent* if they continue to grow.

Whether its sepals are free or welded together, the calyx is *regular* when its divisions all resemble one another and are symmetrically arranged round a central point. Such are the calyxes of the Rose, of Borage, and of the Cherry. When this resemblance and this central arrangement are absent the calyx is *irregular*. Among the irregular calyxes one of the most remarkable is that known as the *bilabial* calyx, on account of its division into two unequal parts which have been compared to the two lips of a mouth. These lips consist of five sepals, amalgamated in their lower portion and free at the orifice, where they form five teeth divided into two unequal groups, which are separated by depressions deeper than

the others. In Sage, Thyme and the majority of the
labiate plants, the upper lip has three teeth and the lower
lip two.

An exceptional form is that of the *spurred calyx*, of which
we have examples in Monkshood and Larkspur. In
Larkspur the calyx is the more developed of the two
verticils of the perianth and has the appearance of a
showy corolla. Its uppermost sepal is prolonged at the
base into a narrow conical sac known as a *spur* ; the
other sepals are not so produced. A similar spur, but
formed by the prolongation of three pieces of the calyx,
is found in the Monkshood.

Not only may the pieces of the calyx become welded
at the edges, forming a *monosepalous* calyx : they may
also intimately adhere to the inner organs, notably to the
ovary. The calyx is *free* if it is not soldered to the
succeeding verticils ; in the other case it is *adherent*.
The flowers of the Madder, the Wild Quince, the Hawthorn
and the Pear have adherent calyxes ; the flowers of
Mulberry, the Tobacco-plant, the Pink, and the Wallflower have free calyxes.

There is one very simple way of telling to which of the
two categories a calyx belongs ; even if direct observation
is rendered impracticable by amalgamations which are
difficult of detection. Let us remember that the ovary,
being the central verticil of the flower, also occupies the
highest position on the axis, however short this may be ;
the three other verticils must therefore precede it and
must be attached to the axis beneath it. This is indeed
what we find in all those plants whose verticils do not
adhere to one another. To find the ovary, then, the
termination of the axis, we must just remove the floral
envelopes, and it will be found at their centre. But
suppose the perianth, in its lower part, is closely adherent
to the ovary, and from that level is freely expanded.

In this case the calyx and the corolla will seem to spring from a plane above the ovary although in reality they spring from underneath the latter ; further, the ovary, if surmounted by the perianth, will form at the base of the flower a swelling which nothing hides from view. Well— every flower whose ovary is concealed in the centre of the envelopes has a free calyx ; every flower whose ovary is seen externally in the shape of a swelling from above which the perianth seems to spring has an adherent calyx. On examining the flowers of the Hawthorn, the Iris, and the Narcissus, you will without difficulty perceive, at the top of the peduncle, a bare swelling. The flowers of the first category have an adherent calyx ; of the second, a free calyx.

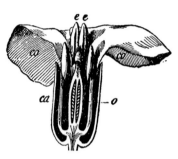

FIG. 123.—Section of Wallflower.
ca, calyx ; *co*, corolla ; *ee*, stamens; *o*, superior ovary.

When the ovary is not adherent to the calyx but is seen in its true place, occupying the extremity of the floral axis, and situated above the perianth, it is for this reason described as *superior*. By amalgamation with the preceding verticils the ovary does not in reality change its place ; it still remains the terminal verticil ; but as it then assumes the form of a swelling apparently underneath the perianth, it is then known as *inferior*. With a free calyx the ovary is superior, as in the Wallflower ; with an adherent calyx it is inferior, as in the Rose.

In some plants the bracts nearest to the flower are grouped together in a verticil having the appearance of a calyx and for this reason known as a *calycle*. We may regard these flowers as having a double calycinal verticil, first that of the calycle, then that of the calyx. In some

cases the parts of the calycle are of the same number as
the sepals, when they alternate regularly with the latter,

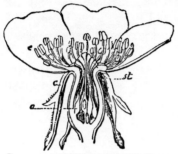

Fig. 124.—Section of Wild Rose.

c, calyx welded to ovary;
o, carpels ; st, stigmata ; e, stamens.

Fig. 125.—Strawberry-
blossom.

Alternating calycule and
calyx.

as we see in the flower of the Strawberry-plant ; in others
they are less in number, so that no alternation is possible,
as we see in the Mallows, in which the calycle consists of
three folioles.

In composite flowers the calyx is adherent and expands

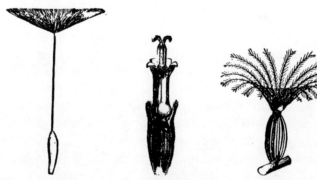

Fig. 126.—Aigrette of
the Dandelion.

Fig. 127.—Aigrette
of the Sunflower.

Fig. 128.—Aigrette of
the Centranth.

above the ovary into an *aigrette* of variable form, of
which the three appended figures (126, 127, 128) will give
you some idea. The aigrette of the Sunflower consists

of a small number of short scales ; that of the Dandelion
is elongated into a fine stem, which expands at the top
into a beautiful brush of outspread, silky filaments. In
the aigrette of the Centranth, which is one of the
Valerian family, the calyx, once more adherent, expands
into an aigrette of feathery filaments.

We call *apetalous* those flowers which possess no corolla,
the perianth consisting of the calyx alone. The form of
this sole envelope is too variable to lend itself to general
description ; we will only say that in many cases the
calycinal verticil is reduced to
its simplest expression, consisting of a few small scales, or
even of one only. Sometimes
the perianth, when it consists
of the calyx only, is so ornamental that it makes one forget
the absent corolla. Such is the
case with the Siphon Birthwort
(*Aristolochia macrophylla*), vulgarly known as the Dutchman's
Pipe, which is often grown
as an ornament of pergolas,

FIG. 129.—Dutchman's Pipe.

trellises and archways. Its perianth, of tubular form,
is streaked with yellow and a blackish red, expanding
at the orifice into three obtuse lobes, which might well be
taken for the lobes of a corolla. Let us note, in the same
flower, the inferior ovary, betrayed by the swelling which
terminates the peduncle.

THE COROLLA

The folioles of which the corolla is composed are
termed petals. Their structure is very much the same as
that of leaves ; we find in them nervures, an epidermis,
and a cellular tissue, in which, save in a few rather rare

exceptions, no green granules of chlorophyll occur ; so that these organs are not adapted to decomposing carbonic acid gas.   In the petal we distinguish an expanded area corresponding with the limb or blade of the leaf, and itself known as the *limb* ;   then a contracted portion, termed the *claw*, representing the leaf-stalk.   Very frequently the claw is very short or absent, when the petal is *sessile*. If the petals are free the corolla is said to be *polypetalous* ; if they are joined at the edges it is *monopetalous*.   In either case the corolla may be

FIG. 130.—Strawberry-blossom.   FIG. 131.—Colza.
Rosaceous corolla.   Cruciform Corolla.

composed of petals which resemble one another and are similarly disposed about the centre, or of dissimilar petals which are not arranged symmetrically round a central point.   Hence the division of corollae into *regular* and *irregular* forms.

A. REGULAR POLYPETALOUS COROLLAE

In this category we distinguish three principal forms, namely :

The *rosaceous* corolla whose type we find in the Wild or Briar Rose.   It consists of five sessile petals displayed in a rosette.   Most of our fruit-trees—Pear, Apple, Quince,

Cherry, Peach, Plum, Apricot, Almond—have flowers of this type.

The *cruciform* corolla is found in the flower of the Colza, Radish, Turnip and Cabbage—in short, in all the Crucifer family. It consists of four petals with long claws, opposed in pairs and therefore assembled in the form of a cross.

The *caryophyllous* corolla is found in its typical form in the Pink and occurs in all the Caryophyllaceae, of which

Fig. 132.—Lychnis.
Caryophyllaceous corolla.

Fig. 133.—Pea.
Butterfly corolla.

the Pink is a member.[1] It has five petals, whose blade is bent at right angles at the end of a long claw, which plunges into a deep monosepalous calyx.

B. IRREGULAR POLYPETALOUS COROLLAE

One single form bears a special name : that of *papilionaceous* or *butterfly* corolla ; the others are known by names that have no very definite meaning. Let us consider the remarkable structure of the Pea-blossom. The monosepalous calyx being removed, we perceive five unequal petals, the largest occupying the uppermost position, and expanding into a wide limb. This petal is known as the *standard*. Two other petals, of smaller

[1] *Caryophyllus aromaticus* is the shrub which bears the clove used as a spice. Carnations and Pinks are termed *caryophillaceous* because of their clove-like fragrance.—*Translator.*

dimensions and resembling one another, occupy each one side of the flower, their anterior edges in contact. These are the *wings*. Lastly, under the sort of tent formed by the wings is a petal slightly curved as to its inferior surface, shaped like the underpart of a boat, and therefore called the *keel*. It is formed by two petals which are adherent one to the other, or even united. In the cavity or shell resulting from this combination are contained the organs of fructification. The corolla thus built up is

Fig. 134. Comfrey.	Fig. 135. Convolvulus.	Fig. 136. Borage.	Fig. 137. Heather.
Tubular corolla.	Infundibuliform corolla.	Rotaceous corolla.	Urceolate corolla.

known as *papilionaceous* because of its vague appearance of a butterfly. It is characteristic of the family of Papillonaceae, to which the Pea, Bean, Clover and Lucerne belong.

The other irregular forms of the polypetalous corolla, such as those of the Pansy, Violet, Balsam-flower, Monkshood, Orchid, Aconite, Larkspur, etc., are comprised under the general heading of *anomalous* corollae.

C. REGULAR MONOPETALOUS COROLLAE

In this division are seven forms :

1. *Tubular* corolla.—This consists of a tube of varying

length, which does not notably expand. Composite flowers such as Comfrey are of this form.

2. *Campanulate* or bell-shaped corolla.—This, by its gradually expanding tube, recalls the form of a bell. Example: the Campanulae: Canterbury-bells, Harebells.

3. *Infundibuliform* or funnel-shaped corolla.—As its name tells us, this has the form of a funnel, of varying width in proportion to its length. Convolvulus, Nicotine, Stramonius.

4. *Hypocrateriform* corolla.—The limb is expanded, flattened saucer-wise at the extremity of a long, narrow tube. Jasmine, Lilac, Primrose.

5. *Rotaceous* corolla.—The limbs of the petal are flat and outspreading like the spokes of a wheel, at the end of a very short tube. Borage, Pimpernel.

6. *Stellate* corolla.—The limb has five acute points like the five points of a star, at the end of a very short tube. Madder; Cheese-rennet; most Rubiaceae.

7. *Urceolate* corolla.—This is shaped like a tiny urn and narrowed at the mouth. Various Heathers.

D. IRREGULAR MONOPETALOUS COROLLAE

In this division are the following forms:

1. *Labiate* corolla.—Five lobes, sometimes more, sometimes less distinct, compose the limb, which expands at the extremity of a long tubular portion, indicating five petals in the structure of this corolla. These are divided into two groups or *lips*, divided one from the other by two deep lateral indentations. The upper lip comprises two lobes, often, but not always, marked by a median fissure; the lower lip has three lobes, almost always clearly defined. Moreover, the two lips are wide open, revealing the entrance or *throat* of the tubular portion. The Labiate family, to which belong Thyme, Sage, Basil, Peppermint, Lavender, Rosemary and Marum, owe their

name to the labiate form of the corolla, which is general in all the plants which it comprises. The calyx is itself *labiate*, but the alternation of the petals and sepals leads to an inverse arrangement of the lips of the two consecutive verticils. The upper lip of the calyx has three sepals and that of the corolla two ; while the lower lip comprises two sepals in the calyx and, in the corolla, three.

2. *Personate* corolla.—As in the preceding case, this corolla is divided into two lips ; the upper lip has two lobes and the lower three ; but this latter is distended

Fig. 138.—Dumb   Fig. 139.—Snapdragon.   Fig. 140.—Foxglove
      Nettle.   Personate corolla.   (Digitalis).

Labiate corolla.   Digitaliform corolla.

in such a way as to close the throat of the flower. The pressure of the fingers on either side of the throat makes the two lips gape ; they close again when the pressure is removed. Hence a certain resemblance to the mouth or muzzle of an animal, so that the flower in which this form is most accentuated is called the Snapdragon or Calf's Snout. Some have seen some resemblance between the two thick lips of the Snapdragon and the exaggerated features of the mask which the actors in the old Greek theatres wore, to represent the characters which they were representing. Hence the term *personate* corolla, from the Latin *persona*, a theatrical mask.

3. *Digitaliform* corolla.—The Common Foxglove or
Digitalis has slightly irregular
flowers, in shape like the finger
of a glove. The scientific name
of the plant, like that of the
corolla, and its vulgar name,
allude to its shape.

We have seen that the base of
certain sepals is prolonged into
a deep, narrow, conical cavity,

FIG. 141.—Columbine.
Spurred petals.

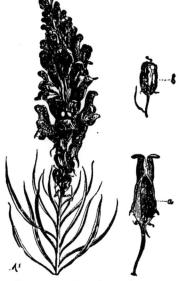

FIG. 142.—Toadflax.   Spurred
flowers.

which is called a *spur*.
The same peculiarity is
seen in the petals of some
flowers. Thus, the Col-
umbine has five petaloid
sepals, whose form is in
no wise peculiar, but al-
ternating with them are
five petals of which each
is prolonged into a long
spur, slightly crooked at
the tip. The spur is often
found in irregular flowers.
In the Snapdragon it is
reduced to a blunt swell-
ing ; in the Violet it is
a slightly curved sac ; in
the Toadflax it is a long, sharp-pointed appendage.

Under certain conditions irregular flowers accidentally
assume a regular form, as though returning to a symmetrical type from which they were but permanent devia-
tions. This transformation is known as *peloria*. While
it is always infrequent, it appears more especially in

personate flowers, notably in the Toadflaxes. As a rule the flower of the Toadflax comprises five petals distributed in two lips. The two petals whose union forms the upper lip are similar to one another, but they differ from those of the lower lip. Of these latter the two lateral petals are alike, but the central or lowest petal has a special form, being the only one that is prolonged into a spur. When the flower assumes a *pelorized* or regular form all the petals are precisely like the spurred petal described. The corolla is then perfectly regular and comprises five equal lobes, each ending in a terminal spur. This regularity is not confined to the corolla, but affects also the succeeding corolla. In its ordinary state the flower of the Toadflax contains four stamens instead of the five that would be the normal number ; the absent stamen being represented by a vestige of filament without an anther. Of the four remaining stamens two are longer and two shorter. In the pelorized form the absent stamen reappears, the four others being its equal in length, while the five, all exactly alike, form a regular verticil alternating with the five lobes of the corolla.

CHAPTER IV

THE ORGANS OF FRUCTIFICATION

The structure of the stamens—Their number—Didynamous stamens—
Vestiges of the fifth stamen—The disposition of lateral stamens—
Tetradynamous stamens—Monadelphous, diadelphous, polyadelphous
stamens—Syngenetic stamens—Structure of the anther—Pollen sacs
and connective diaphragm—Pollen : its colour and form—Pollinic
envelopes—Fovilla—Pollinic tubes—Experiments—Structure of the
pistil—Placenta—Various methods of placentation—Theories of the
carpel—Ovules—Their structure.

STAMENS

A STAMEN commonly consists of a flexible support, of
variable length, termed the *filament,* and a terminal organ,
the *anther,* containing the dust, usually yellow, known
as *pollen.* The anther, with its powdery contents, is the
truly indispensable part of the stamen ; the filament is
of quite secondary importance. It may stand quite free
of the adjacent organs or it may be joined to them for a
variable portion of its length. Thus, in the monopetalous
flowers the filaments are often welded to the corolla.

The stamens are frequently present in the same numbers
as the petals, with which they alternate ; but they are
also frequently either greater or less in number than the
petals. Their multiplicity often results in several verticils
which alternate with one another, doubling or trebling
the numbers of a single whorl. We find, for example,
two verticils of five stamens each in the Pink and the
Saxifrages, whose petals number five. Sometimes again
the stamens are so numerous that the alternation of

successive verticils is, it may be, impracticable, or at all events impossible, to verify. We find this state of affairs in the Poppy. Lastly, when the stamens are fewer in number than the petals it will often be found that the inequality comes from the defective development of some of the stamens ; and as we shall see, it is often easy to determine the position of these and even to discover their vestiges.

Irregular corollae are often affected by unequal development in the verticil of the stamens. Labiate and personate corollae are especially remarkable in this respect. Let us first of all once more define, in a few words, the structure of these corollae. They are divided into two lips which are separated by deep lateral indentations. In the middle of the upper lip, formed of the union of two petals,

FIG. 143.—Didynamous stamens.
a, the longer inferior stamens; b, the superior and shorter stamens.

we see a fissure, sometimes more and sometimes less pronounced, the index of its binary composition. The lower lip shows two fissures, the index of three assembled petals. The limb of the corolla thus has, in all, five indentations, corresponding to the lines of demarcation of the five amalgamated petals : namely, two above and three below. To each petal, according to the law of alternation, there should be a corresponding stamen. But the irregular formation of the flower leads to the following arrangement : 1, the upper stamen is lacking ; 2, the two lateral stamens are short ; 3, the two lower stamens are long. Thus in labiate and personate corollae there are but four stamens, two of which are longer than the other pair. This arrangement of unequal pairs is indicated by saying that the stamens are *didynamous*.

Of the five stamens which the flower would contain were it regular, and which are indeed found in the pelorized corolla, it is always the uppermost that is missing, but it sometimes leaves vestiges. Thus, in various personate flowers we see, opposite the superior fissure, a short filament, a rudimentary appendix, which is the base of the undeveloped stamen. If the flower is less irregular this vestige of a stamen may become a true filament, but it bears no anther. Thus the Penstemon, whose name alludes to the presence of five stamens, although the plant belongs to the Personates, has four staminal filaments provided with anthers and a fifth—the uppermost one— without an anther. Lastly, in the pelorized flowers of the Toadflax it is the upper stamen which reappears to complete the verticil.

The two lateral stamens, corresponding with the deep indentations which divide the two lips, are always shorter than the lower stamens. This diminution in length indicates a decadence which, if exaggerated, would result in the disappearance of the two lateral stamens, so that the verticil would be reduced to the two lower stamens. This is the case in some of the Labiates—for example, in Sage and Rosemary.

Habitually, in a regular flower, the stamens are equal in length, at all events in the same verticil; but if the flower has two staminal verticils it is often the case that the stamens of one verticil are longer than those of the other, as in the Pink and the Silénus. The inequality is more striking when there is only one staminal verticil. We find such a state of affairs, as a general thing, in the whole family of Cruciferae, constituting one of its most definite characteristics. Let us take, for example, the Wallflower, or the flower of the Cabbage, or of the Radish, or of Colza; we find that the four sepals of the calyx are not precisely equal in size; there are two opposing

23

sepals which are slightly swollen at the base, and as it were embossed ; the other pair show no such peculiarity. Now, opposite each embossed sepal we find a short stamen, while facing each of the other sepals we find a pair of long stamens. The verticil thus consists of six stamens, of which four are long and two short. The four longer stamens are assembled in pairs facing the ordinary sepals ; the two shorter ones are set singly opposite the embossed sepals. Referring to the greater

FIG. 144. — Tetra-dynamous stamens of a Crucifer.

FIG. 145.—Mona-delphous stamens of a Mallow.

FIG. 146.—Diadelphous stamens of a Papil-ionaceous flower.

length of the four stamens as compared with the other two, we say that the stamens of the Cruciferae are *tetradynamous*. We have to refer, to this expression, the idea of a grouping in equal pairs on the one hand and of isolated stamens on the other, as we have just seen them.

When the stamens adhere among themselves it is usually the filaments that are united. Sometimes all the filaments are welded into a hollow column traversed by the pistil, the top of which is divided into an abundant cluster of anthers. This arrangement may be observed in the flower of the Mallow, the Marsh-Mallow, and, in short, the whole family of Malvaceous plants. Sometimes the filaments are united only at the base, as in the common Lysimachus. In either case the stamens are termed *monadelphous*—that is, united in a single bundle by the adherence of the filaments.

They are *diadelphous* when the adherence of the filaments divides the staminal verticil into two groups. Thus the various flowers of the Papilionaceae, such as those of the Pea, the Bean and the Vetches, have ten stamens, of which nine are welded together by their filaments into a tube of which the upper part is split, the tenth being free, occupying the hiatus left in the group of nine. The ovary is situated in this species of sheath, and is able to grow unimpeded, thanks to the fissure occupied by the tenth stamen, by gradually pushing aside the narrow envelope formed by the staminal filaments. The same term, diadelphous, applies to the six stamens of the Fumitory, assembled by the filaments in two unequal groups.

Lastly, the stamens are said to be *polyadelphous* when they are welded by the filaments into several mutually distinct groups. This arrangement is seen in the Orange and St.-John's-wort.

FIG. 148. Syngenetic stamens of the Composites.

The five stamens of the florets and semiflorets of the composite flowers adhere by the anthers, while having the filaments free. These are known as *syngenetic* stamens.

The anther is divided by a median groove into two equal parts, each containing a cavity or sac in which the pollen is formed. The partition placed between the two lobes

is known as the *connective*.   At maturity each sac opens
along a longitudinal cleft to allow its pollinic contents to
escape. From this form, which is the most general one,
others are derived, of which the most important are :
In the Sages (1, Fig. 149) the connective is developed
into a long stem, *c*, placed transversally at the tip of the
staminal filament like the beam of a balance at the top
of the supporting standard.   The two sacs are thus
widely separated ; moreover, one of them, *b*, remains

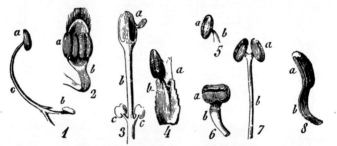

FIG. 149.—Various forms of stamen.

1. Sage : *c*, connective : *a*, fertile lobe of the anther ; *b*, sterile lobe.
  2. Periwinkle : *a*, lobes of the anther ; *b*, filament. 3. Laurel :
  a, a lobe of the anther opened ; *b*, filament ; *c, c*, sterile anthers.
  4. Borage : *a*, scale ; *b*, filament. 5. Buckthorn. 6. Lady's Mantle.
  7. Lime.   8. Water-lily.   In the last four figures *a* is the anther
  and *b* the filament.

sterile ; that is, it yields no pollen.   The staminal verticil
is here greatly reduced ; three are lacking of the five
normal stamens—the uppermost, as in all the Labiates,
and the two laterals ; moreover, the two remaining
stamens have only one fertile sac, *a*.—The stamens of the
Lime-flower (7, Fig. 149) have also the two sacs, *a*,
separated from one another, but both are fertile, and the
connective is not exaggerated in its development.   In
the Laurel (3, Fig. 149) the sacs open not through a slit,
but by means of a valve, *a*, which lifts up like a lid ;
and in addition to them the base of the filament bears
two yellowish bodies, *c*, which are sterile anthers.   In

the Potato and all other plants of the same class, such as the Nightshades, the sacs open at the top of the anther by means of a hole or pore. In the Periwinkle (2, Fig. 149) the connective is prolonged beyond the anther by a hairy blade; in the Oleander it forms a long bristly prolongation. In Borage (4, Fig. 149) the filament is expanded behind the anther into a scale. In the Lady's Mantle (6, Fig. 149) a transversal slit is common to both cells.

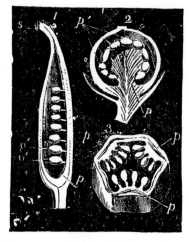

FIG. 150.—Modes of placentation. 1. Axial placentation; *p*, placenta; *p' p*, ovules; *s*, stigma. 2. Central placentation; *p*, placenta; *p'*, ovules. 3. Parietal placentation; *p, p, p,* placentae.

The pollen is generally yellow, like flowers of sulphur. In the spring, when the Pine- and Fir-woods produce their innumerable catkins, the gusty winds carry off clouds of this yellow dust, which, falling at a distance, whether by itself or accompanied with rain, causes the so-called showers of sulphur. In the Bindweeds and Mallows the pollen is white, in the Poppy violet, and in the Willow-Herbs bluish.

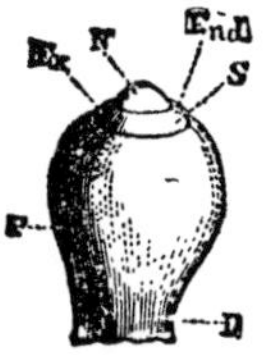

FIG. 151.—Ovule. N, nucelle; S, inner envelope; P, outer envelope; F, base, which may be protracted into a funicle.

Examined under the microscope, pollen appears as a mass of countless granules, all similar in shape and size in the same plant, but varying greatly in different vegetables. Among the different varieties of pollen the largest are those of the Lavaterae, the grains of which are $\frac{1}{123}$ inch in length; and among the smallest are those of the Elastic Fig, which are only $\frac{1}{26}$th to $\frac{1}{28}$th as long. By reason of their varied shapes and the ornate designs on their surfaces the grains of pollen are one of the most interesting subjects of microscopic observation. They may be spherical, or oval, or elongated like grains of wheat. Others are like little barrels, or balls wound with a spiral ribbon. Some are triangular with rounded corners, and others seem to result from the assemblage of three short cylinders, grouped together at their bases, while others yet are like cubes with blunted edges. Some have smooth surfaces; others are covered with delicate, uniform corrugations; some are polyhedral in form, their facets enclosed in projecting ridges, and still others are marked with grooves that run like

FIG. 152 —Grain of pollen.

a, external membrane; *b*, internal membrane; *f*, granules of fovilla.

meridian lines from pole to pole. All alike show minute circular spaces of a lighter shade, distributed with geometrical regularity, their circumference being marked by a perfectly definite line. These spaces are called *pores*.

Each grain of pollen consists of a single cell, with a double envelope; the outer one is coloured, opaque, firm, elastic, frequently embellished with ornate granulations; the inner one is thin, smooth, extensible, colourless, diaphanous. At the translucid points which we know as spores the external membrane is lacking and the wall consists of the internal membrane only. Sometimes, as in the pollen-grain of the Pumpkin, the pores are closed with a round lid, which comes away intact, leaving the opening to the internal envelope free.

The content of a grain of pollen consists of a viscous liquid, in which float numbers of very minute granulations. This content is known as the *fovilla*. Under the micro-scope, if the grains are placed in pure water, we shall observe the following facts, which are of the greatest interest. Two liquids are here separated only by the membranous walls of the grain; that inside the grain, which is the denser and more viscous, and that outside, which is less dense and more fluid. Consequently endosmosis takes place. We see the grain gradually swelling, losing its folds and wrinkles, if it has any to

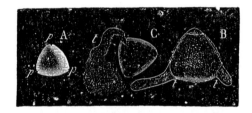

Fig. 153.

A, grain of pollen intact: *p, p, p,* pores. C, grain swelling in pure water; *t,* pollinic tube spilling the fovilla. B, grain distended in a solution of sugar or gum; *t, t,* pollinic tube.

begin with, finally becoming distended by the afflux of water to the viscous content of the pollinic cell. The inner membrane, being thus pushed outwards, protrudes through the pores of the outer membrane, appearing in the shape of diaphanous nipple-like projections, which for some time extend themselves into elongated sacs, finally bursting at the tip, spilling out the fovilla, when the rapid endosmosis increases their tension too suddenly.

Let us now repeat the experiment with water containing a little gum or sugar, which will retard the rate of endosmosis, the two liquids differing less in viscosity. The same process is seen as before, but it occurs more slowly; the inner membrane, protruding from the pores, yielding gradually, without rupture, to steady but more moderate tension, is protracted into a long tube, extremely flexible, diaphanous and full of fovilla. This long sac is known as a *pollinic tube*. A later chapter will explain the great importance of its function.

THE PISTIL

A single carpel, or it may be a verticil of carpels, whether free or more or less united, forms the pistil. A carpel results from a leaf whose two halves, to the right and left of the median nervure, are folded together, enclosing a cavity known as the *ovary*. The prolongation of the median nervure becomes the style, and the dilated terminal of the nervure constitutes the stigma. The edges of the carpellary leaf are joined toward the centre of the flower, and are welded together, either closely or by a little fold that enters inwards. The line of junction is known as the *placenta*. This is the thickest part of the ovarian wall and it is on this that the *ovules* are born : that is, the rudiments of future seeds.

If several carpels enter into the composition of the pistil they are set in a circle, the median nervure on the outside and the placenta in the centre. In some cases the carpels thus assembled remain free, but more frequently they are united by the parts of their walls in contact. The general ovary is then subdivided into as many partial cavities or lodges as there are elementary ovaries in its composition. Lastly, these lodges are divided from one another by *partitions*, resulting from the double wall formed by the contact of two contiguous carpels. The adherence may include more than the ovaries, affecting the styles and finally the stigmata, so that a pistil, apparently a simple organ, is sometimes in reality complex. By ascertaining the number of its lodges we can tell the number of the carpels assembled.

When the edges of the carpellary leaf are joined together, as we have just noted, the line of suture, the origin of the ovules, or in other words the placentae, always points toward the centre of the flower, so that the placentae of the whole verticil of carpels are grouped round the floral axis.   In such cases we say that the placentation is *axial*.   We find this arrangement in the five carpels of the Pear and Apple, in the three carpels of Aconite, and in Larkspur.

The carpellary leaves, instead of forming each its closed cavity, may also be joined together by their edges, thus containing a common cavity.   The lines of union, which are still the origin of the ovules—in a word, the placentae—are then distributed over the wall of the general cavity instead of being centred round the axis ; more, each placenta is half the property of each of two contiguous carpels.   This arrangement of the rows of ovules against the wall of a general cavity without partitions is known as *parietal placentation*.   We find it in the Violet.   The number of carpels in the make-up of such an ovary may be ascertained either from the number of rows of ovules or from that of the valves or pieces into which the ripe fruit is divided.   The pod of the Violet opens out into three valves, and the ovary contains three rows of ovules affixed to its wall ; the pistil therefore comprises three carpels.

Lastly, it may be that the carpellary leaves are assembled by the edges into a common casket, as in parietal placentation, but without bearing the ovules along the lines of union.   In this case the terminal axis of the flower expands in the centre of the single ovarian cavity into a fleshy prominence covered with ovules, which is itself the placenta.   Under these conditions the placenta is *central*. We have an example in the Primroses.   With this method of placentation, when there are no partitions or rows of ovules, we cannot tell the number of carpels except by examining the ripe fruit, unless we are given the desired information by distinct styles or stigmata. Thus, the fruit of the Primrose is a casket or capsule which opens, on maturity, in five parts or valves, so that the ovary consists of five carpels.

The seed begins its development in the form of *ovules.* These are special buds, incapable by themselves of further development until they have experienced the vivifying influence of the pollen. These buds come into being either singly or in numerous groups. They occupy sometimes the welded edges of the carpellary leaves, as in central placentation. From its first appearance the ovule forms, on the placenta, a small nipple-like prominence, known as the *nucelle,* around which we soon detect two envelopes, distinguished by two concentric fillets. These two fillets decrease in diameter, eventually covering the nucelle, and finally leave only a very minute orifice known as the *micropile.* At the same time, beneath the micropile, the nucelle acquires a cavity termed the *embryonic sac,* because it is the receptacle in which the *embryo,* or rudiment of the future seed, will come into being when called forth by the pollen. Lastly, the ovule, at first a mere nipple protruding from the placenta, becomes attached to it by a fine suspensory thread known as the *funicle.*

CHAPTER V

THE POLLEN

*Emission of pollinic tubes—Arrival of the pollinic tube in the ovule—
Appearance of the germ—Proofs of the necessity of pollen—The Carob-
tree—The Date-tree—The Pumpkin—Ablation of the stamens—
Transport of pollen to the stigma—Harmful action of water on pollen
—Falling of fruit—Flowering of aquatic plants—Frogbit—Bladder-
wort—Water-chestnut—Zostera or Sea-grass—Water Crowfoot—
Water-Lily—Villarsia—Stratiotes or Water-Soldier.*

By itself the ovule cannot become grain ; without the
help of a complementary agent it would soon wither,
unable to pass the state which I have described. This
complementary agent is the pollen, which awakens life
in the ovule and evokes the birth of a germ by a
mysterious co-operation which will always be one of the
subjects to appeal most profoundly to the scientist.

At the moment when the flower is fully blown the
stigma exudes a viscous liquor by which the grains of
pollen fallen from the anthers, or carried thither by
insects or the wind, are glued to its surface. Here
occurs the process of endosmosis already described, not
in water, the rapid absorption of which causes the
rupture of the grain, but on the surface of a layer of
viscous moisture, which penetrates the interior of the
pollen-grain slowly, enabling the inner membrane to
issue from the pores in the form of long pollinic tubes.
From the face in contact with the moist stigma each
grain emits a flexible tube like the fine radicle escaping
from a tiny seed. Like a radicle again, which always

347

extends itself in a downward direction and plunges into
the earth, the pollinic tube traverses the thickness of
the stigma, enters the tissue of the style, opens a way
for itself by slightly parting the rows of cells, always
insinuating itself farther and farther, until it has at
last travelled the whole length of the style, however

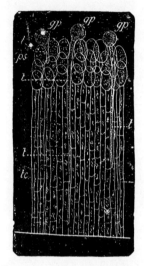

great this may be. The grain of
pollen, as though it had struck
root, remains on the surface of
the stigma ; by the contraction
of the outer membrane it expels
the contained fovilla, and, in
emptying itself, fills the tube as
this becomes longer.

The materials thus expelled
doubtless serve in some degree
to increase the growth of the
pollinic tube, for the internal
membrane, however extensible
by nature, could not of itself
suffice for the requisite elongation. In plants with a long

FIG. 154.—Portion of the
stigma at the moment
when the pollinic tubes *t*
emitted by the grains of
pollen *g p* are thrusting
through the cellular tissue
t c.

style the tube, in order to reach
the ovary, is obliged to attain
a length several hundreds and
even thousands of times as great
as the diameter of the pollen-
grain from which it proceeds. The time required for
the necessary protraction does not depend only on the
distance covered ; it depends above all on the intimate
structure of the style. In a few plants a few hours
suffice ; in others the pollinic tube takes several days
to complete its journey.

When this first activity is completed the stigma,
powdered with numerous grains of pollen, each plunging

its tube into the tissue of the style, might be likened to a long cylindrical pincushion in which a number of pins are buried to the head. Now the pollinic tubes, filled with fovilla, plunge their tips into the cavity of the ovary. They are directed by a force whose clear precision fills us with amazement. Without difficulty or confusion, despite their number, as though guided by the infallible wisdom of an inconceivable instinct, each tube turns in the direction of the neighbouring placenta and plunges its extremity into the micropyle of an ovule. The pollinic filament penetrates the embryonic sac and reaches the wall of the latter, and at the point of contact slowly organizes a new living entity, the living germ of the grain. How? No one knows. Before these mysteries of life reason bows, helpless, and abandons itself to an impulse of adoration of the Author of these ineffable miracles.

Without the help of the pollen the ovary would wither, incapable of becoming a fruit, incapable of producing seed. There are abundant proofs of this fact; I will cite the simplest; those which are produced by diœcious or monœcious vegetables. The Carob-tree is a tree found in the extreme south of France; it produces the fruit known as the Carob, or St. John's Bread; like the pods of a pea, but brown, very long and very broad. These fruits provide not only seeds but a sugary pulp. Now the Carob is diœcious; it bears, on different trees, flowers with stamens or flowers with a pistil only. Planted singly in a garden in a suitable climate the Carob-tree producing the pistil-bearing or female flower blossoms abundantly but gives no fruit, for its flowers fall without leaving a single ovary on the boughs, unless there is in the neighbourhood some Carob-tree bearing stamens, from which the wind or insects may bring the pollen. Why does it not bear fruit? Because there is no pollen to act upon its ovules. Well, plant near this pistil-bearing tree another Carob-tree bearing staminal flowers. Now fructification takes place unimpeded. The breezes, and the insects, that pillage flower after flower, carry the pollen of the staminate tree to the stigmata of the pistillate tree, and the ovaries awake to life, the fruits grow and ripen, full of grain able to germinate.

In the oases of North Africa the Arabs cultivate numbers of Date-palms which furnish them with dates, their principal alimentary resource. The Date-palms also are diœcious. Now amid the sandy plains, scorched by the sun, spots of fertile soil provided with water are rare ; it is important to make the best of them. The Arabs therefore plant only pistillate trees, as these are the only kind that yield fruit, but when the blossoming season has come they go in search of clusters of staminate flowers growing on wild Date-trees, in order to shake the pollinic dust over the flowers of the trees in their plantations. If this precaution is not taken there is no date-harvest.

The Pumpkin or Gourd is monœcious ; on the same plant pistillate and staminate flowers are found, very easy to distinguish from one another, even before they bloom. The first display a large swelling, which is the ovary, underneath the perianth ; the second have nothing of this nature. Taking an isolated vine, let us cut off the staminate flowers before they open, leaving the pistillate flowers. For greater safety we will wrap each of the latter in a gauze or muslin hood, ample enough to permit the flower to develop unimpeded. This sequestration must be effected before the flowers open in order to ensure that the pistils receive no pollen. Under these conditions, as they cannot receive the dust of the anthers, since the staminate flowers have been suppressed and a muslin envelope checks the insects that might bring the pollen of neighbouring vines, the pistillate flowers fade after languishing awhile and their ovaries wither without growing into pumpkins. But if, on the contrary, we wish this or that particular flower, in accordance with our will, to fructify despite the gauze envelope and the suppression of the staminate flowers? Let us take a little pollen on the tip of a finger and lay it on the stigma, afterwards replacing the envelope. This is enough to ensure that the ovary shall become a pumpkin and yield fertile seeds.

Although it calls for considerable care, a similar experiment may be carried out with flowers provided with both pistils and stamens. From a flower on the verge of maturity we remove the anthers before their sacs are open for the emission of pollen. The mutilated flower is then hooded with muslin to prevent any access of pollen from neighbouring flowers. This treatment is sufficient to sterilize the ovary, which withers without further development. But if some pollen is laid on the stigma of the flower with a camel-hair brush the ovary develops as usual despite the gauze envelope and the ablation of the stamens.

Since pollen is indispensable to the production of fertile seeds its transference from the anther to the pistil must be assured by means appropriate to the structure of the flower and the conditions of the plant's existence. And indeed the most ingenious resources, the most astonishing combinations sometimes, are set in motion in order that the staminal dust may reach its destination. Botany has no more interesting chapter than that devoted to the thousand little miracles which occur at the solemn moment of the emission of pollen. I will try to give the reader some faint idea of these marvels.

If the flower possesses both pistils and stamens the

arrival of pollen on the stigma is generally a simple
enough matter : the least breath of air is sufficient, or
the passage of a pilfering fly, to shake the stamens and
cause the pollen to fall. For the rest, the stamens are
so arranged that the fertilizing dust shall fall on the
stigma. If the flower is upright, as in the Tulips, the
stamens are longer than the pistil ; if it is pendant, as
in the Fuschias, the pistil is longer than the stamens ;
so that in either case the falling pollen reaches the
stigma, which is lower than the anthers. In the
Campanulas the five anthers, cohering together, form a
tube containing the style, which is at first shorter than
the stamens. When the pollen is mature the style is
rapidly elongated, the stigma rises above the tube of
anthers and with its rough hairy surface brushes off the
pollen and moves away with it.

In aquatic plants special precautions are taken on
account of the harmful effect of water on pollen. You
will remember that the grains of pollen, brought into
contact with pure water, become too rapidly distended
by endosmosis ; which results in the rupture of the
envelopes and the dispersion of the fovilla. In this
condition the pollen-grain is no longer able to fulfil its
function, which is to send to each ovule, through the
tissue of the style, a pollinic tube full of fovilla. Moist
pollen is therefore useless. We find in this fact the
explanation of the harmful effect of continued rains at
the moment of blossoming. Partly swept away by the
rain, partly burst by contact with water, the pollen no
longer acts on the ovaries and the flowers fall without
being able to fructify. This destruction of the harvest
by rain is described by gardeners and fruit-growers by
saying that the fruit has fallen off, or the blossom has
not set.

Because of this fact no aquatic plant, in the absence

of special arrangements which we shall presently examine, can open its flowers under water, or the fruit would be spoiled ; it is absolutely necessary that the flowering should take place in the open air. Let us look into some of the means by which the immerged flowers are brought up into the air. Vallisneria or Frogbit lives at the bottom of the water ; it is excessively abundant in the Canal du Midi, where it would impede navigation if numbers of men were not employed every year to remove it. Its leaves are narrow green ribbons and its flowers are dioecious. The pistillate flowers are borne on long, thin, flexible stalks, which are coiled like a corkscrew. When the moment of flowering has come the spiral stalk gradually uncoils and the flower, owing to its light specific gravity, floats to the surface, where it blooms. The staminate flowers, on the other hand, are carried on very short stems, which keep them right at the bottom. Here the difficulty would appear insuperable ; yet it is removed in a most remarkable manner. While still in the bud, while the stamens are as yet protected by the closely shut perianth, the flowers of themselves break their connection with the plant, spontaneously detaching themselves and rising to the surface, where they float among the pistillate flowers. They then open their perianth and yield their pollen to the wind and the insects, which bear it to the pistillate flowers. Finally these retract their spirals and return to the bottom of the water, where their ovaries quietly ripen.

The mechanism for lifting the flowers above the water is no less remarkable in the Bladderworts, plants which live submerged in our ditches and ponds. Their leaves, which consist of very fine branching thongs, bear numbers of globular capsules, like tiny delicate leathern bottles, which have given their name to the plant. These capsules or bladderlets—*utricles* as they are called—

24

have the orifice furnished with a sort of valve or movable
lid. At first they contain a mucosity heavier than
water. Retained by their weight the plant keeps to
the bottom, but when the flowering season draws near
a bubble of air is breathed into the bottom of the utricles,
expelling the mucosity, which flows out through the
orifice, forcing the lid. Thus, lightened by a host of
little floats the plant slowly rises and comes to the surface
that its flowers may open in the air. Then, when the
fruits are nearly mature, the utricles replace their contained air by mucosity, which weighs the plant down,
making it sink once more to
the bottom, where the seeds
mature, scatter themselves,
and germinate.

FIG. 155—A, fragment of
Bladderwort ; B, one of the
utricles, enlarged.

The floating Water - Cal-
throp, so called because of
the spines on its angular sides,
or Water Chestnut, because of
its large, starchy, edible seed,
which recalls the chestnut—
inhabits the quiet waters of our ponds. The submerged leaves are divided into fine filaments ; the
aerial leaves, with four-sided blades, are upborne by
hollowed petioles, full of air, like so many tiny swimming
bladders ; and thus sustained by this system of floats,
the upper portion of the plant lies outspread on the
surface of the water in a broad, unsinkable rosette, a
sort of raft, whence the flowers spring. After flowering
the floats fill with water and the plant sinks to the bottom
to ripen its fruit.

To preserve the pollen from harmful contact with the
water every aquatic plant has its resources. We have
just been considering plants which make themselves
light by means of a system of utricles filled with air or

petioles turned into hollow floats; and now we will examine others which, although they have no means of rising through the water, are yet able to surround their flowers with an artificial atmosphere which enables them to blossom even beneath the surface. Zostera, Eel-grass or Grass Wrack, whose foliage forms a bundle of long narrow ribbons of a sombre green, lives rooted to the bottom of the sea, at great depths. The flowers are enclosed in a sort of sheath which is filled with air breathed out by the plant and prevents the water from gaining access to them. Thanks to this air-chamber flowering takes place unhindered under water. The Water Crowfoot habitually expands its flowers at the surface of the water, but if a sudden flood submerges it, reaching a level unattainable by the flower-stalks, the flowers cease to open their envelopes, remaining in the state of globular, tightly shut buds, in which a bubble of air collects. It is in this confined atmosphere, breathed forth by the flower, that the emission of pollen takes place.

Of the various means which enable aquatic flowers to reach the air the simplest, and that most frequently employed, consists in the elongation of the flower-stalks until they attain to the surface. Thus the Water-Lily has for its stem a rhizome which creeps through the mud without the power of rising; but its sturdy flower-stalks go vertically upwards, growing longer and longer, until their great blossoms are within a few inches only of the surface, however deep the water. In some cases, the peduncles being unable to grow to such lengths as the depth of the water requires, the whole plant forsakes the floor of the pond or river, tearing itself away from the mud and rising toward the air in order to flower. This migration to the surface results from the small number and the weakness of the roots, the small resistance of the muddy bottom, and the pressure of the water, which, acting on a plant specifically lighter than water,[1] finally tears it from is hold. Thus the Frogbit or False Water-Lily, the *Stratiotis Haloides*, and other denizens of stagnant waters, leave the soil from which they sprang and float half out of water when the flowering season has come.

[1] It must be remembered that although the pressure of water on the top of a submerged object may be very great, this pressure increases by nearly half a pound to the square inch for every foot of depth. Actually, the upward pressure on the bottom of a cube of twelve inches a side is 62·5 lbs.; on the bottom of an inch cube, nearly three-fifths of an ounce.—*Translator*

CHAPTER VI

FLOWERS AND INSECTS

Wind-borne pollen—An observation of Bernard de Jussieu's—Conditions favourable to the transportation of pollen—The pollen of the Conifers —Stamens and pistils of the Graminaceae—Transportation of pollen by insects—The value of fertilization by the pollen from another flower— Nectar—Signal-points—The Snapdragon—The Iris—The Dutchman's Pipe—Eupomatia laurina—Spontaneous movements of the stamens— Rue, Spiny Briony, Parietary, Barbary Fig—Maintenance of the Species—Hybrids—Return to primitive forms.

THE transportation of the pollen is not effected only from the anthers to the pistil of one and the same flower ; it also occurs from one flower to another, from one plant to another, and sometimes over great distances. In monœcious and diœcious vegetables alike the grains of pollen that vivify the ovary always come from another flower than that to which the ovary belongs ; in the other vegetables the action of pollen coming from elsewhere is quite as frequent as that of the pollen of the flower itself. The agents of transportation are the winds and insects.

Of the innumerable facts that might be cited in proof of the arrival of pollen from a distance we will mention only this : The Botanical Garden of Paris had for a long time two pistillate Pistachio-trees, which were covered with flowers each year but never produced fruit ; they needed, in order to fructify, the assistance of pollen. Great was the astonishment when one year, without any known cause, their ovaries turned into nuts and ripened in a normal fashion. Bernard de Jussieu

357

thought there must be some Pistachio-tree in the neighbourhood. Search was made and it was found that
there was indeed a staminate Pistachio-tree in a nursery-
garden on the outskirts of Paris, which was flowering
for the first time. Borne by the wind over the houses
of part of Paris, its pollen had come to fertilize the two
trees that had until then been
sterile.

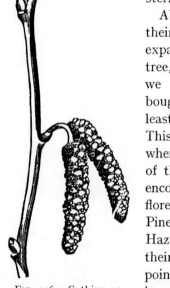

About the end of winter, when
their innumerable catkins have
expanded, let us shake a Pine-
tree, a Cypress or a Hazel-bush ;
we shall see, flying from the
boughs, a sort of smoke, which the
least current of air carries away.
This smoke, their pollinic dust,
when abandoned to the chances
of the atmosphere, may perhaps
encounter, in its fall, the inflorescences of the pistils of other
Pines, other Cypresses, other
Hazel-bushes, and awaken life in
their ovules miles away from its
point of departure. In a meadow,
in a field of corn in flower, every
breath of air that shakes the

FIG. 156.—Catkins or
Staminate flowers of Hazel.

grasses or the standing corn raises, in the same way, a
fine cloud of pollen, which, alighting as it drifts on the
stigmata, fertilizes those flowers of the same species that
receive it.

Certain conditions are indispensable if the wind is to
be efficacious. The pollen must be extremely abundant,
on account of its enormous wastage over the areas across
which hazard leads it. Of an eddy of staminal dust
swept off by a gust of wind, how many grains will reach

J. Boyer.

MALE FLOWERS OF THE HAZEL.

To face p. 358.

their destination ? Very few, of a certainty ; possibly none. Quantity has thus to make up for innumerable chances of misfortune. The grains of pollen must also be very minute and very dry, in order that they may be readily dispersed by the first breath of wind. These conditions of abundance, minuteness and aridity are realized in the pollen of trees producing catkins, especially

FIG 157.—Catkins and Pistillate flowers of the Spanish Chestnut.

the Conifers, which loose clouds of pollen upon the air. These clouds of yellow dust, like so much flower of sulphur, are often swept away to great distances by gales of wind, and on falling to earth, whether accompanied by rain or not, they give rise to childish terrors in the minds of ignorant folk, who imagine that they are witnessing a hail of sulphur descending from the heavens. The Gramineous plants likewise, with their thin pendant anthers hanging from the flower, being easily shaken, suspended loosely at the end of long filaments, lend themselves readily to the dispersion of pollen by the wind. These unprotected anthers, which are violently shaken by the slightest movement of the air, surrender their pollinic dust to the caprices of the atmosphere as soon as their cells open. In order to stop the pollen-grains that are blown by the wind among the ears of standing corn, or the heads of grass-seed in the pastures, the stigmata branch into long plumy tassels, whose downy filaments wave in the air. In short, the assistance of the wind is necessary to the majority of those vegetables that produce flowers having for perianth only scales without brilliance or colour or perfume or nectar, and have therefore no means of attracting insects and securing their visits.

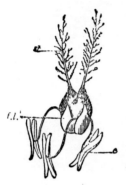

FIG. 158.—Flower of Wheat. *e*, stamens ; *st*, stigmata; *f.l.*, floral envelopes.

Insects are above all the auxiliaries of the flower. Flies, wasps, bees, beetles, moths, butterflies—all hasten in eager rivalry to assist in transporting the pollen of the stamens to the stigma. They plunge into the flower, their senses attracted by a drop of honeyed liquid expressly prepared in the depths of the corolla. In their efforts to reach this they shake the stamens and bedaub themselves with pollen, which they carry from one flower to another. We have all seen hive-bees and bumble-bees emerge all floury from the heart of the flowers. Their velvety bodies, powdered with pollen, have only to touch a stigma in order to communicate life to it.

The flowers to which insects are necessary possess, at the bottom of the corolla, a drop of sugary liquid known as *nectar*. This nectar enters into the composition of honey. In order to drink it from those corollae which are in form like deep long-necked funnels, moths and butterflies have a long proboscis, which is rolled up in a flat spiral when not in use ; they unroll it and thrust it into the flower like a sounding-tube when the delicious brew is ready for them. But insects which do not possess such a suction-tube must themselves, at the cost of some effort, descend to the bottom of the corolla, shaking the anthers in their struggles and making the pollen fall on them as they pass ; so that when they emerge, struggling backwards, they are covered with staminal dust. These hasty visits effect as their inevitable result the fertilization of the ovary, whether the insect, on emerging, grazes the head of the pistil with its powdery fleece, or whether the stamens, on being shaken, let their pollen fall directly on the stigmata.

More frequently still, perhaps, there is an exchange of pollen between flower and flower, either on the same plant or on other plants of the same species. All yellow with pollen, the insect emerges from the first flower and proceeds to pillage a second, which thus receives the pollinic dust from an extraneous source, itself providing the pollen to fertilize a third flower ; in this way all the flowers that have opened in a single cluster, or on a single plant, are fertilized by one another. This exchange of pollen, a matter of complex distribution which only the insects could accomplish by their numbers and their activity, is of great importance, as it forestalls certain causes of decadence in the successive generations, in which the least vital defect would become progressively aggravated by a process of heredity which no extraneous aid would intervene to check. It is in fact recognized that a flower fertilized by its own pollen will yield seed which is generally less robust than when the vivifying dust comes from another flower. By means of this aid the plant that provides the pollen associates its own energies with those of the plant that furnishes the ovule, so that the vitality of the offspring is maintained indefinitely in full vigour. From this point of view it is

FIG. 159.—Cowslip.

the insect that is the great and most essential distributor of pollen.

If you cut or tear in two the blossom of the Narcissus, the Cowslip, or Clover, or any of a host of other plants, you will be able to detect, by the eye or the tongue, at the base of the corolla, a sugary fluid known as *nectar*. This is the bait that lures the insect to the flower. Sometimes the nectar consists of a slight exudation which merely moistens the base of the ovary ; sometimes it collects in a little tear like a dewdrop. This fluid exudes from different organs in different families, orders and species. In Monkshood it oozes from the calyx; in the Ranunculae from the claws of the petals; in the Plumbagoes from the base of the stamens; in the Hyacinths from the circumference of the ovary. In the Fritillary, commonly known from the arrangement of its flowers as the Crown Imperial, the six pieces of the perianth are hollowed at the base, forming a glandular dimple which secretes the nectar. Sometimes reservoirs are contrived for storing the sweet liquid: these usually take the shape of bosses, spurs, capsules, and pits or dimples, to be found at the base of either the sepals or the petals. Thus, the nectar-yielding organs of the Cruci-ferae are the glandular sup-ports of the two short stamens, while the liquid is received by the recesses or bosses of the two sepals facing

FIG. 160.—Crown Imperial Fritillary.

these stamens. Monkshood stores up its nectar at the bottom of the single spur of the calyx; Columbine in the five spurs of its corolla. The secretion of this liquor rarely begins before the flower has bloomed; it is pro-duced in greater abundance at the period when the emission of pollen is taking place, just when the plant has the greatest need of the assistance of insects; it ceases as soon as the fruit begins to develop, drying up the moment it is no longer of service.

A drop of nectar, distilled expressly for this purpose, lures the insects to the depths of the corolla; and a *signal point* shows them the path to follow in order to reach the sugared liquid by brushing past the stamens. This signal-point is a patch of vivid colour, very often orange or yellow, the tint endowed with the greatest luminous power. This patch is at the entrance to the corolla, in the immediate neighbourhood of the anthers ; it catches the eye by its brilliancy and is a sure guide to the insects in their quest. This guide-point which leads the hive-bee or bumble-bee to the precise spot where its activities are necessary : that is, to the site of the anthers, is especially remarkable in the closed flowers. Let me cite a couple of examples.

The corolla of the Snap-dragon is closed by the tight-fitting lips, which leave no thoroughfare. Its colour is a uniform crimson-purple, but precisely in the centre of the lower lip is a spot of very bright yellow. Now, let

Fig. 161.—The Snapdragon. Flower and fruit.

us watch a bumble-bee pillaging a Snapdragon. We shall see that she always charges down on the yellow spot, never elsewhere. Forced down by the insect's weight, the lips open and the throat of the corolla gapes ; the insect enters, brushing the anthers with her shaggy back in passing, powdering herself with pollen, and laps the nectar, then proceeding to other flowers, to distribute, all unwittingly, the staminal dust adhering to her fleece.

DUMB NETTLE (RED).

To face p. 364.

The flower of the Iris is even more remarkable. Its perianth is composed of six pieces, three bending outwards, each curved into the arc of a circle, and three standing upright, in contact, forming at their tips a sort of dome. These latter are of a uniform blue-violet ; the others have, down the centre, a wide band set thickly with papillae, like a coarse yellow velvet. These yellow bands, whose saffron tint makes a vivid contrast with the violet background of the flower as a whole, are the signals that lead to the stamens, invisible from without and, to an inexperienced eye, difficult to locate. At the centre of the flower are three broad violet blades having all the appearance of petals ; but appearance is deceptive, for these blades are in reality the styles of the pistil. Each blade is curved like a Norman arch and the free end rests against the yellow band of a petal, so that the two parts form together a closed chamber. In each chamber is a stamen, whose anther

FIG. 162.—Iris.

lies close against the concavity of the arched roof, and whose two sacs, by a somewhat rare exception which is here a necessity, open on their outer side instead of on the inner side as is usual. Lastly, at the very entrance to the chamber the petaloid blade of the style is edged with a narrow membranous border. This border is the stigma, the part to which the pollen must be applied.

Complete your acquaintance with the flower by the actual sight of it, for words are really powerless to describe it, and you will see that without assistance the pollen cannot possibly reach the stigma. The anther is at the bottom of a chamber sheltered from the movements of the air ; the stigma is outside the chamber, at its entrance. If the pollen falls it will drop on the floor of the cavity, not on the stigmatic border outside. But let an insect arrive and the difficulty disappears, and the most wonderful things occur. The signal, the band of yellow velvet, is the path that leads to the door of the chamber ; here it is that the flies and hive- and bumble-bees in search of nectar invariably alight ; none of them ever makes a mistake as to the way about the flower, which, with its hidden stamens and its petaloid styles, deceives our own eyes. The insect raises the blade of the style and enters, its furry back brushing the roof against which lies the anther, the two sacs opening on the outer surface ; it makes its way to the very end of the narrow gallery, drinks the nectar, and emerges dusty with pollen. Let us follow it to another flower. Now the stigmatic border of the entrance acts as a scraper on the back of the insect entering the chamber, removing the pollen from its hairy body. We can but perceive in these wonderful correspondences between the flower and its auxiliary the insect devices contrived by the eternal Intelligence !

A few words more of this interesting examination of the relation between the insect and the flower. I have already spoken of the Dutchman's Pipe, whose flower, streaked with yellow and a reddish black, has the shape of a crooked pipe-bowl. The stamens are so placed that it would be very difficult for them to convey their pollen to the stigma. Now a slender-bodied insect, a Crane-fly, enters the tube of the flower, which is furnished with hairs pointing downwards, giving readily before the entering fly. But when it wants to emerge from the flower the insect is held up by these very hairs, which now present their points, making an insuperable palisade ; it struggles and strives to regain its liberty, scattering the pollen, which falls on the stigma. Presently the floral tube withers and the hairs, becoming limp, lie against the wall, and the prisoner escapes unhindered.

According to one of the most exact and profound observers of our time—Robert Brown—the flowers of a certain exotic tree, *Eupomatia laurina,* are so constructed that without the help of insects the pollen could never reach the stigmata. In these flowers the inner rows of stamens are sterile and transformed into petals closely packed against one another and covering the stigmata with an impenetrable envelope. Thus separated from the outer stamens, which alone are fertile, the pistil would never receive any pollen were the flower left to itself. But insects visit it, nibbling through the inner petals and destroying the tent covering the pistils without touching either these or the fertile stamens. Thenceforth the pollen has unimpeded access to the stigmata.

To assure the arrival of the pollen on the stigmata many plants, at the moment of flowering, resort to spontaneous movements of their stamens, like those which we have already considered in the case of various leaves. Rue, an evil-smelling plant that grows on arid hillsides, has flowers with four and sometimes five petals, and eight or ten stamens, half of which face the petals and half the intervals between them. In the newly opened flower all the stamens are seen to be outspread in a horizontal plane, half of them lying in the cavity of the corresponding petal and half in the intervals. Presently, with a slow insensible movement, a stamen erects itself, bends its filament inwards and presses its anther against the stigma. During this contact, which is prolonged for some time, the sacs of the anthers open and give up their pollen. This done, the stamen slowly retires and lies down again in its first horizontal position ; but simultaneously with its return the stamen succeeding it in the spiral order of the verticil erects itself and replaces it against the stigma. A third follows, and so on, one rising after another, until all the stamens have laid their tribute of pollen on the pistil. The flower then fades ; the function of its floral envelopes and its stamens has been fulfilled. Owing to the slowness of these movements only prolonged observation, maintained over a period of several days, will verify these curious facts in their entirety ; but a mere glance is enough to show the erection of the stamens one by one, for we always see, in the flowers of Rue, a single stamen applying its anther to the stigma while the others lie flat.

In other instances the movement is a sudden one. In the Spiny Clematis, for example, each staminal filament is held at the base between two minute glands situated on the claw of the opposing petal. This, when the petals open, drags the stamen with it, captive and fettered. But presently, under the rays of the sun, the filament grows thinner by evaporation, and the glands that retain it become slightly diminished in size. Then the stamen, by virtue of its own elasticity, returns to its first position as suddenly as a spring released, striking against the pistil and throwing upon it a tiny cloud of pollen. This release may be artificially provoked : it is enough to scratch the filament with the point of a pin or to shake the bough. The least shock, the slightest touch, and the delicate equilibrium is broken ; the stamens escape from their glandular stocks and cast themselves upon the pistil.

The Nettle and the Parietary have the staminal filaments coiled up in the folioles of the perianth. If we touch these filaments ever so lightly with the point of a needle we shall see them suddenly uncoil themselves, spring erect and shake their anthers, whence escapes a jet of pollinic dust. In the large yellow flowers of the fleshy plant known as the Barbary Fig there are hundreds of stamens. When the flowers have opened these are outspread almost at right angles to the axis of the flower. If a passing insect grazes them, if a slight shock reaches them, if a cloud intercepts the sunlight, they at once tumultuously spring erect, and the pollen flies from their colliding anthers, as they bend inwards and form a close-walled tent over the pistil. When all is quiet again they once more spread themselves out and lie prone, crowding together once more again if touched or shaken. On each occasion a cloud of pollen falls on the stigma.

The winds that sweep the meadows where all sorts of plants are growing, the insects, pillaging flower after flower without distinction of species, of necessity bear to the stigmata all kinds of pollen. Sainfoin receives the pollen of Clover ; Clover receives the pollen of Wheat. What results from these exchanges between such dissimilar vegetables ? Absolutely nothing ; the pollen of one vegetable species has no effect on the flowers of another species. In vain, for example, shall we place on the stigma of the Lily the pollinic dust of the Rose, or on the stigma of the Rose that of the Lily ; unless each flower receives its own pollen or that of another flower of its own species the ovaries wither without producing fertile seed.

Each species requires the pollen of its own species ; all other pollen remains as inactive as would so much dust from the roads. The most conclusive experimental researches have emphasized the inflexibility of this great law, which safeguards the species against any profound alteration and maintains them as they were in the beginning and will be for undefined future ages. The action of the pollen is not confined to awakening life in

25

the ovules ; it also impresses on the seeds the characteristics of the plant that furnished the anther. The
pistil and the stamen, each in its own way, communicate
to the seed the characteristics which will be revealed in
the resulting vegetable ; each helps to determine in the
plant born of the seed a resemblance to the plants which
provided the ovule and the pollen. What would happen
were the stigma affected by the pollen from any anther
indiscriminately ?   The seeds issuing from such a mixture
would not reproduce the original plants, but would give
rise to new forms recalling by some of their characteristics
the plant which provided the pollen and by others the
plant producing the ovules ; the species would possess
no fixity ; the vegetation of the present would not
resemble that of the past ; each year would see the
appearance of strange, unknown and unprecedented
forms, which would again be unlike their successors ;
finally, growing ever more mixed, more fantastic, more
distorted, the vegetable world would lose the harmonious
order that now rules over its distribution and would die
out in a sterile chaos. As it is the whole is maintained
in immutable uniformity and like succeeds always to
like, seeing that each species is affected only by its
own pollen.

Nevertheless, when two species are very closely akin
in their organization the pollen of one may act on the
ovules of the other. The seeds resulting from this
association yield plants whose characteristics are not
precisely those of either parent. Intermediate between
the two, they both differ from and resemble the latter.
These plants of twofold origin are known as *hybrids*.

Hybridization is the artificial deposition of an alien
pollen on the stigma of a flower and is frequently
employed in horticulture in order to obtain fresh varieties
of colour, plant formation, foliage, or fruit ; it is one of

the most potent resources for the improvement of plants
with a view to our own use of them. Apart from the
devices of man it is sometimes produced by the agency
of the insects and the winds between two plants growing
near one another and of closely similar organization.
Hybrids are generally sterile ; their flowers, although
provided with pistils and stamens, cannot produce seeds
able to germinate. Nature thus abruptly puts an end,
by an insuperable barrier, to the alteration of the species
shaped by a first association. To preserve these hybrid
forms when they have any value we have the resources
of grafting, planting cuttings, and layering ; but the
seeds absolutely refuse to germinate. More rarely
hybrids are fertile, when their offspring are so likewise ;
their seeds germinate and yield plants which are also
able to produce fertile seed. Nevertheless, the new
form is far from stable ; from one generation to another
the mingled characteristics disappear while the original
characteristics are more strongly affirmed ; finally, sooner
or later, the seed produces, in varying proportions, on
the one hand the species that produced the ovule and
on the other that which gave the pollen, without any
intermediate forms. Separating that which hybridization brought together, the plant returns of itself to its
first origins, and thereby gives us the most striking
example of the inflexible power appointed by the Creator
to maintain the species unchanged.

CHAPTER VII

THE FRUIT

Pericarp—Its structure—Epicarp, mesocarp, endocarp—Pericarp composed of several carpels—Fleshy fruit and hard fruit ; apocarpous and syncarpous ; dehiscent and indehiscent—Sutures—Valves—Classification of fruit—Characteristics of the different classes of fruit—Anthccarpous fruit—Aggregated fruit—Comestible parts of fruits.

WHEN the pollinic tubes have reached the ovules and caused in them the appearance of the germ or embryo, the final end of the flower, the floral envelopes, whose function is then performed, soon fade and fall. The stamens too detach themselves, the styles wither and nothing is left on the flower-stalk save the ovary. Animated by the pollen with new life the ovary grows and matures in its chambers its ovules, that have become fertile seeds. The fully developed ovary with its content of seed is called the *fruit.*

The fruit is formed for the sake of the seeds intended to perpetuate the species ; all that accompanies the seeds, whatever importance it may possess for us, is of secondary importance in the economy of the plant, being merely an envelope whose function is to protect the seeds until they are mature. This envelope is known as the *pericarp.* It is formed by the carpellary leaves, which, sometimes isolated, one by one, sometimes grouped together, free or amalgamated, compose the pistil.

A carpel, like any other leaf, comprises in its structure a sheet of epidermis on each face, and between the two a cellular layer or parenchyma. The pericarp, whether resulting from one carpellary leaf or several, reproduces their structure, but often with modifications which completely transform the original characteristics. Let us consider, for example, a Peach, a Cherry, a Plum, an Apricot. Each of these four fruits comes of a single carpel, containing a single seed in its chamber. The hard, strong "stone" which protects the seed until

FIG. 163.—The Walnut.

the period of germination, the succulent pulp which for us is a valuable alimentary resource, the fine skin that covers the pulp, all taken together form the pericarp and are developed from a metamorphosed leaf. The inner epidermis of the carpellary leaf has become the stone or pit ; its parenchyma has become the pulp ; and its outer epidermis the skin of the fruit.

Three analogous layers, varying greatly as to the nature, aspect, consistency and thickness of their tissue, are found in every pericarp. The outer layer is called the *epicarp*, the middle one the *mesocarp* and the inner layer the *endocarp*. The first represents the outer epidermis of the carpellary leaf, the second the parenchyma and the third the inner epidermis. In the four fruits above mentioned the epicarp is the skin that covers the pulp, the mesocarp the pulp itself and the endocarp the stone or pit.

The Walnut and the Almond are similarly organized, with the difference that the mesocarp is without value for us and the edible portion is reduced to the seed.

FIG. 164.—Pod of the Bladdernut.
l, l, l, carpillary leaf forming the pericarp ; *n*, suture of its edges ; *t*, style ; *s*, stigma.

The woody shell of the Walnut and the Almond is the endocarp ; the husk, so bitter in the walnut and barely eatable in the unripe Almond, is the mesocarp, which falls off when the fruit is c o m p l e t e l y matured, leaving the naked shell ; lastly, the epidermis of the husk is the epicarp, smooth in the Walnut, downy in the Almond.

In other species the foliaceous nature of the carpellary leaf transformed into the pericarp is still recognizable. Thus, the pod of the Bean and the Pea bears a fairly close resemblance to a leaf folded into a long sac. Its endocarp and epicarp are sheets of epidermis differing but little from the epidermis of leaves ; its mesocarp, somewhat thickened, is almost the ordinary parenchyma. In the pod of the Bladdernut-tree or Bastard Senna the foliaceous nature of the pericarp is even more evident.

If several carpels welded together concur in the formation of the fruit each of them likewise results from three layers which are known by the same names. Thus,

the Apple is formed from five carpellary leaves assembled
into a whole, apparently unique, but whose make-up
may be recognized from the number of its divisions.
The tough skin of these divisions, that is, the cartilaginous
sheath enclosing the pips, is the endocarp of the corresponding carpel; the pulp of the Apple is the mesocarp
of the five carpels united and its skin is the epicarp.   In
the Medlar, which also has five amalgamated carpels,
the endocarp has become five stones not unlike those
of the Cherry; the edible pulpy portion is still the
mesocarp enveloped in its epidermis or epicarp.

In the Orange and the Lemon, composed of numerous
carpels of which each forms a segment of the fruit, the
epicarp is the outer layer, yellow and thickly sown with
small glands which secrete a fragrant essential oil; the
mesocarp is the white layer, savourless and rather
spongy in texture; lastly, the endocarp is the fine pellicle
which lines the segments and contains within it the
edible portion of the fruit and its seeds.   Now what does
this edible portion represent ?   We see at once, especially
in a rather dry Orange, that the comestible part is
composed of a mass of small elongated capsules, little bags
full of juice and assembled side by side.   The endocarp
is the inner epidermis of the carpellary leaf; now we
know that in a leaf the epidermis is frequently covered
with the cellular prolongations which we know as hairs.
Well, in the Orange and the Lemon the hairs of the
carpellary envelope, the hairs, in fact, of the endocarp,
assume an excessive development and become long
capsules full of juice.   The flesh of these fruits is thus
a mass of hairs dilated into juicy cells.

These few examples show us what a variety of aspects
the same organ may assume in different fruits.   The
inner epidermis of the carpel remains ordinary epidermis
in the pods of the Pea; it becomes an extremely hard

"stone" in the Peach and Apricot, a solid shell in the Walnut and Almond, a leathery sheath in the Apple, and a delicate membrane bristling with succulent vesicles in the Orange and the Lemon. Despite these differences of organization the part we are considering is always the endocarp. Lastly, the endocarp may disappear and leave not a trace. This has happened in most of the fruits of the Cucurbitaceae—the Rock-melon, the Water-melon, the Pumpkin, the Cucumber, the Gourd, the Gherkin. The Rock-melon, for example, presents on the outside strips of a thin epicarp, split by the rough crevices of the rind ; all the rest of it is the mesocarp, green and inedible as to its exterior, but within sweet and melting in the mouth. But there is no endocarp inside the mesocarp ; the ovary, in its growth, has not developed the inner epidermis of the carpellary leaves.

When the pericarp is transformed into an abundant parenchyma the fruit is said to be fleshy or *pulpy* ; if it is hard, with thin walls, it is said to be *dry*, on account of its aridity when ripe. Apples, Plums, Pumpkins, Oranges, Gooseberries, are pulpy fruits ; the shells of the Tobacco-plant, the Snapdragon, the Poppy and the Violet are dry fruits.

The fruit may result from a single carpel or from several, either individually free or amalgamated. In the case of a single carpel or of several free carpels the fruit is said to be *apocarpous* ; but if the several carpels are united it is known as *syncarpous*. The Plum, the Peach, the Cherry, and the Almond are apocarpous fruits, derived from a single carpel ; the fruits of the Peony, Larkspur and Clematis are likewise apocarpous, but they comprise, in respect of the whole flower, several indi-vidually separate carpels. The Apple, the Orange, and the shells of the Snapdragon and the Poppy are on the contrary syncarpous fruits. The first result from five

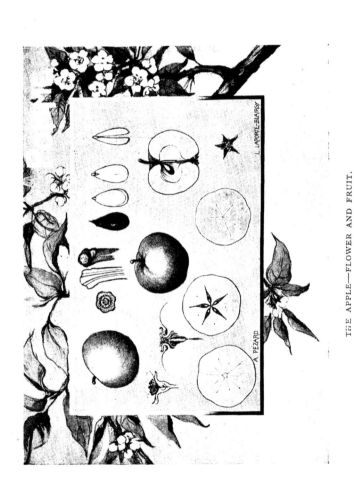

THE APPLE—FLOWER AND FRUIT.

The ripe fruit—Stalk and section of stalk—Pip and embryo plant—Flower (section)
—Rosette (section)—Longitudinal and lateral sections of apple—Rosette.

(From Pézard and Laporte-Blairsy's *L'Histoire naturelle par l'Observation directe.* Delagrave.)

To face p. 376.

united carpels; the second comprises as many carpels as segments; the pod of the Snapdragon is composed of two carpels, while the head of the Poppy comprises a large number.

You know that a carpel comes of the metamorphosis of a leaf, which, folded along its median nervure, has joined its edges together facing the axis of the flower; thus forming a closed cavity or chamber in which the seeds are developed. The line of junction of the two edges of the carpellary leaf is known as the *ventral suture*. It is this line which in the Peach, Apricot, Cherry and Plum is marked by a furrow running from one end of the fruit to the other over half its circumference. Lastly, the median nervure of the carpel, which always faces the axis of the flower, is sometimes indistinct, as in the fruits I have just mentioned, while it sometimes appears in the form of a fold, of a special cord, like a second suture. It is then known as a *false* or *dorsal suture*, on account of its position on the back of the carpel. We see excellent examples in the pods of the Pea and the Bean.

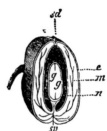

Fig. 165.—Section of Bean pod.
sv, ventral suture; *sd*, dorsal suture; *e*, epicarp; *m*, mesocarp; *n*, endocarp.

On maturity many dry fruits, but not all, open spontaneously to liberate and scatter the seeds. In each species of plant the rupture of the pericarp is effected in an invariable manner, following the lines of least resistance, that is, following one or another of the sutures, or even both at once. The walls of the fruit thus divide into separate pieces or *valves*, of which the number is equal to that of the carpels if only one suture opens, or twice that of the carpels if the two sutures open simultaneously. Thus the three-carpelled fruit of the Violet

divides into three valves by splitting along the dorsal
sutures, while the monocarpelous fruit of the Pea divides
into two valves by the simultaneous rupture of both
sutures. More rarely the fruit liberates the seeds by
splitting at points which do not correspond to the sutures.
Thus the capsule of the Snapdragon becomes perforated
at the summit by three large pores or holes of which
one corresponds to the upper and the other two to the
lower chambers.

The spontaneous opening of the pericarp, in whatever
manner it is effected, is known as *dehiscence,* and fruits
endowed with this property are known as *dehiscent*
fruits. Those which do not open of themselves are
known as *indehiscent.* Among the dry fruits some belong
to one category and some to the other, but the pulpy
fruits are all indehiscent ; their pericarp decomposes in
order to liberate the seed.

By collating the characteristics of separation or union
of the carpels, of the dry or fleshy nature of the pericarp,
of dehiscence or indehiscence, we arrive at the following
classification of fruits :

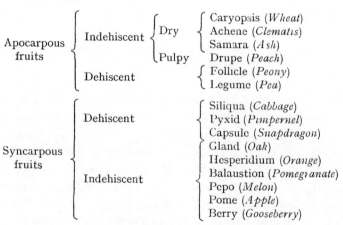

The *caryopsis* is the fruit of Wheat and the Gramineous

plants in general. It is characterized by the intimate adherence of the pericarp to the envelope of the grain. The bran, which in the grinding becomes detached from the berry, contains, combined in a thin pellicle, the wall of the pericarp and the integuments of the only seed contained by it. In this species of fruit the carpellary leaf is so reduced that the caryopsis was at first supposed to be without a pericarp, whence it was given the name of *naked seed*.

The *achene* differs from the caryopsis in that the pericarp is distinct and separable from the integuments proper of the only seed which it encloses. The fruits of the Sunflower, Dandelion, Chicory, Lettuce and Thistle—in short, of the whole family of composite flowers—are achenes. The triangular fruits of Buckwheat, of the Clematis, which are prolonged by a long feathery style, and of the Ranunculi, which are grouped together in a rounded head, belong likewise to this division. It is the same with the fruits of the Rose

Fig. 166.
Achene of
Ranunculus.

and the Strawberry-blossom, which deserve a special mention.

Considered as a whole the fruit of the Rose-tree is an ovoid body, crimson in colour when mature. It is open at the summit, and around its orifice the sepals and stamens are outspread ; lastly, it is hollowed out into a deep urn-shaped cavity full of seeds with short stiff hairs, which cause persistent itching if they come in contact with the skin. Now these seeds are in reality distinct fruits, each being composed of a pericarp bristling with hairs, and of the seed enclosed in this pericarp ; in a word, they are so many achenes. As for the common envelope, red and pulpy, it proceeds from the calyx ; it is therefore not really a pericarp, since no carpellary leaves go to its formation. Neither does the edible portion of the Strawberry derive from the carpels. Over

the surface of the pulpy mass are scattered small, dark, hard bodies, of which each is an achene with pericarp and seed enclosed. As for the pulpy swelling in which they are embedded, this is merely the extremity of the peduncle, the receptacle of the flower.

The *samara* is easily recognized by the membranous wing formed by the pericarp. This wing sometimes encloses the fruit, as in the Elm ; sometimes it is prolonged into a single tip, as in the Ash ; sometimes it projects sideways, as in the Sycamore, whose samarae are assembled in pairs.

FIG. 167.—Strawberry.

The *drupe* comprises all the apocarpous indehiscent fruits, and has a single seed, whose mesocarp is pulpy, while the endocarp takes the form of a woody " stone." Such are the Peach, Apricot, Plum, Cherry, Olive and Almond.

The *follicle* has a thin pericarp foliaceous in aspect.

FIG. 168.—Samarae of the Elm.

FIG. 169.—Samarae of the Sycamore.

It has the peculiarity of opening when ripe by its ventral suture, each side of which bears a more or less numerous row of seeds. As a rule several follicles succeed to each flower : two, three, or more. The Peony, Larkspur and Hellebore offer us examples of this fruit.

The *legume,* to which we also give the name of *pod,* is the fruit of the Bean, the Pea and the leguminous family in general. By the rupture of both sutures at once its carpellary leaf divides into two valves, each of which bears seeds along its ventral suture only.

FIG. 170. Follicle of Larkspur.

The *siliqua* or two-valved pod of the Cabbage, Wallflower, and Colza, is formed of two carpels forming two cavities separated by a median partition. On maturity this opens from stalk to tip into two valves, while the partition remains in place, with a row of seeds along either edge, and on both sides. This type of fruit retains the name of siliqua when it is much longer than its breadth, as in Colza ; it is called a *silicule* when the length is not very different from the breadth, as in the Thlaspis. The siliqua and the silicule pertain to the family of Cruciferæ.

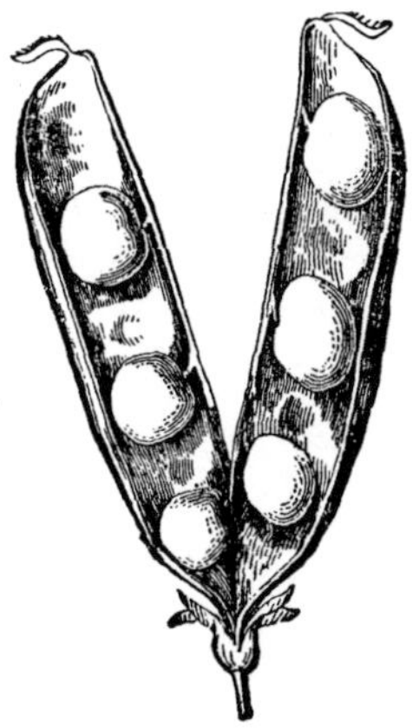

FIG. 171. Pod of Pea.

FIG. 172.—Siliqua of Colza.
v, v, valves ; *s,* partition.

The *pyxid* is a dry fruit which opens when mature along a transversal circular fissure, thus dividing into two hemispheres, the lower of which remains in place with the seeds contained in it while the upper one comes away like the lid of a soap-box. Such are the fruits of the Pimpernel and of Henbane.

The *capsule* comprises all the dehiscent syncarpous fruits which do not fall within the two above-mentioned divisions ; their form and their mode of dehiscence are widely variable. Among them are the capsule of the Poppy, which opens by means of a row of orifices situated beneath the projecting border of a broad terminal disc ; that of the Snapdragon, pierced at the summit with three holes ; that of the Pinks and Sileni, whose extremity yawns and displays a certain number of denticulations, and that of the Violet, which splits up into three valves.

Fig. 173.—Pyxid of Pimpernel.

The *gland*, of which the fruit of the Oak is the type, appears to be the result of a single carpel, since the cavity is simple and entirely filled with a single seed ; however, if we study this fruit at the time of its first appearance we recognize in it three or four carpels welded together. Later these carpels, with one exception, die, and the fruit, in reality complex in its origin, is, in maturity, simple. We place it among the syncarpous fruits to recall its original structure, although when ripe it has all the appearance of an apocarpous fruit. The Acorn is easy to recognize, with its base encrusted in a receptacle or goblet known as the *cup* or *cupule*. The fruits of the Hazel-bush and the Spanish Chestnut belong to the same division. The cupule is scaly in the case of the Acorn, foliaceous in the Hazel-nut or Filbert, and spiny in the Chestnut ; moreover, before maturity it envelopes the fruit like a pericarp.

The *hesperidium* is the fruit of the Orange-tree and the Lemon-tree. I have already described its structure

and the formation of its juicy pulp from the basis of
the endocarp.

The *balaustion* or fruit of the Pomegranate is crowned

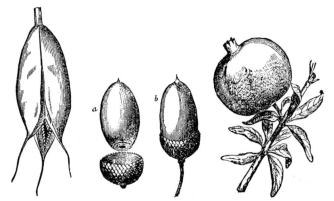

FIG. 174.—Capsule   FIG. 175.—Acorn.   FIG. 176.—Pomegranate.
of Colchicum.

by the calyx.   Its pericarp is leathery and divides the
cavity into two stories of irregular seeds, each surrounded
by a thick succulent envelope.

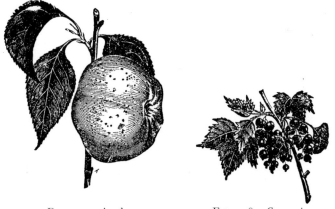

FIG. 177.—Apple.   FIG. 178.—Currants.

The *pepo* is typified by the Melon and the Gourd ; it
is the fruit of the Cucurbitaceae.   It usually derives from

an ovary with three chambers. Its essential characteristic is that it diminishes in consistency from without
inwards and has in the centre a large cavity, to the wall
of which the seeds are attached.

The *pomaceous* fruits comprise not only the fruit of
Apple-trees, but also Pears, Quinces, Service-berries, and
the various trees producing hips and haws. The pomaceous fruit, thus generally considered, presents at the
summit a depres-
sion or *eye* sur-
rounded by the
withered calyx ; it
is divided com-
monly into five
segments, whose
endocarp is car-
tilaginous, or
more rarely

Fig. 179.—A, anthocarpous fruit of Yew.
B. The same, cut open to show
envelope, C.

hardened into stones, as in the Medlar.

We group under the name of *berry* the pulpy or syncarpous fruits whose endocarp is not distinct from the
mesocarp. In this category fall Grapes, Gooseberries
and Tomatoes.

Besides the envelope formed by the pericarp some
fruits present a second envelope derived from some part
of the flower other than the ovary. Thus the fruit of
the Peruvian Marvel is included in the base of the
perianth, hardened into a solid ball, and that of the
Yew is contained in a red pulpy capsule representing
the calyx. To recall this presence of floral organs which
do not enter into the composition of the ovary itself we
call such fruits *anthocarpous*.

Since the fruit is the matured ovary, a fruit, in the
strict sense of the term, must be the product of a single
flower. However, it is usual to employ the same term

to denote the production of certain inflorescences which, by the close assemblage, or adherence, or even the union of their ovaries, seem to produce a single fruit when in reality there are as many fruits as there were flowers in the bloom. These agglomerations are known as *aggregate* fruits. The three following classes are distinguished :

The *sorosis* results from fruits which are welded together by their highly developed pericarps and have become pulpy. Such are the Pineapple and the Mulberry.

FIG. 180.—Sorosis of   FIG. 181.—Cone   FIG. 182.—Fig.
Pineapple.   of Hop.

The first is like a great Pine-cone transformed into a succulent mass ; it is crowned with a bundle of leaves. The second fruit recalls by its form that of the Bramble or Raspberry ; but its origin is very different. The fruit of the Bramble and that of the Raspberry-canes each comes of a single flower, whose numerous carpels, changed into tiny drupes, are united by their fleshy pericarp ; while that of the Mulberry is derived from a very short spike of pistillate flowers and has, for its false pericarp, the perianth of these flowers distended into a pulpy nipple.

The *cone* is an assemblage of dry fruits, achenes or samarae, situated in the axil of closely packed scales,

26

sometimes thick and woody ; sometimes thin and leaf-like ; sometimes even fleshy, as in the Juniper. The cone belongs to the family of Conifers—Pine, Fir, Cedar, Cypress, Larch ; it is also found in the Alder, the Birch, and the Hop.

The *Fig* is a branch hollowed into a deep receptacle which, on its fleshy wall, bears the true fruits, consisting of a great number of tiny drupes.

To assist the memory with examples which are familiar to us, and therefore recall the chief features of the organization of the fruits, let us now review the comestible parts of the fruits which appear on our tables. The Peach, the Plum, the Apricot and the Cherry are drupes ; one eats the mesocarp. The Almond and the Walnut belong to the same family of fruits, but we reject the pericarp entirely, eating only the seed. The ordinary Apple, the Pear, the Quince and the Service belong to the Apple family (pomaceous fruits). It is again the mesocarp that we eat in the Medlar, whose endocarp, instead of being cartilaginous, forms a group of woody pits. The Olive, a drupe, offers us its mesocarp. The Rock-Melon, the Water-Melon (pepous) have an edible mesocarp ; their endocarp is almost non-existent. In the Orange and the Lemon (*hesperidia*) it is the endocarp that furnishes the pulp in the form of hairs become plump cells full of juice. The Pomegranate, a balaustion, gives us the integuments of the seeds, transformed into succulent pulp. The Grape and Gooseberry, berries, proffer us their mesocarp, not distinguished from the endocarp. The Raspberry is a mass of tiny drupes whose mesocarp is the edible portion. Of the Chestnut and the Hazel-nut, which are glands, we use the seed. In the Strawberry the edible part is the receptacle of the flower ; the very extremity of the floral branch swollen into a succulent mass ; the true fruits, achenes, are the small, hard, brownish bodies encrusted in the pulpy flesh. The sugary pulp of the Fig is likewise furnished by the floral branch, hollowed into a deep receptacle. To this flesh is added the pulp of the innumerable small drupes contained in the cavity of the Fig.

CHAPTER VIII

THE SEED

*Structure of the Seed—Testa and tegmen—Hilum, funicle and micropyle—
Embryo—Cotyledons, radicle, gemmule, tigellus—Perisperm or
albumen—Analogy between the egg and the seed—Nature of the peris-
perm—Presence or absence of the perisperm—Dissemination—The
Elastic Ecbalium, the Sand-Box-tree, the Balsamin—Wings and
Aigrettes—The Dandelion and the Erodium—Samarae—The Yellow
Wallflower—The Elm—Dissemination by Animals—The Burdock and
Goose-grass—Dissemination by man—Germination—Necessity of water,
warmth and air—Chemical phenomena of germination—Time necessary
for germination—Duration of capacity for germination.*

LET us consider the fruit of the Almond-tree in the
ripe and in the unripe state. Having cracked the woody
shell constituting the endocarp we obtain the grain,
vulgarly known as the Almond. On this we easily
recognize two envelopes, readily detachable if the Almond
is unripe : the outer skin is rough and in colour a russet-
brown ; the inner skin is fine and white. These two
envelopes together are termed the *integuments* of the
seed. The outer one is known as the *testa* because of
its consistency, which, in certain seeds other than that
of the Almond-tree, is comparable to a nutshell in
hardness ; the second is known as the *tegmen*.

For a second example let us take the Pea and the
Kidney-Bean. We shall recognize in these the two
envelopes found in the Almond ; a tegmen, in the form
of a fine membrane, a testa, more robust, greenish in
the Pea, and white or splashed with red and brown in
the Kidney-Bean. On either seed a white oval patch

388

is plainly discernible ; this is the *hile* or *hilum* ; to this adheres the nourishing cord or *funicle*, which holds the seed suspended from the wall of the carpel and distributes to it the sap necessary for its growth.   Lastly, in the Pea we can with a little attention detect near the hile a very small orifice like the puncture of a fine needle-point : this is the *micropyle,* through which the pollinic tube made its way into the embryonic sac of the ovule.

Such are the most salient features of the exterior of any seed, but with an ex-treme variety of modifica-tions.   Thus the hile, so distinct in the Pea and Kidney-Bean, cannot be plainly seen in the Almond, and the micropyle cannot be readily recognized save in a small number of seeds, the pea in particular.   As for the testae, some are soft and flexible, some fleshy as in the Passion-fruit ; some are hard and brittle, thickened i n t o

Fig. 183.—Pod of Cotton.

robust shells.   Some are polished, glistening as though varnished ; others are dull, rough, furrowed with grooves, armed with ridges, papillae or ribs.   Some are vividly coloured, as we see in certain Kidney-Beans ; but others, and these are the more numerous, are dull in colour, fre-quently black or brown.   Lastly, the testae of some seeds are bristling with stiff hairs, or covered with long silky hairs, which form a padded envelope for the seeds.   Such is the origin of the white down which protrudes in the spring of the little capsules of the Poplar and the Willow ;

such is the origin of the cotton contained in the capsules
of the Cotton-plant.

If we divest of their integuments the Almond, the Pea
or the Kidney-Bean, there remains the *embryo*, that is,
the plant in its nascent state. The embryo consists
almost entirely of two fleshy bodies equal in size, placed
side by side. These are the *cotyledons* or first leaves
(seed-leaves) of the little plant. In their dispropor-
tionate thickness are amassed the stores of nutriment
which are to serve for future development. At the

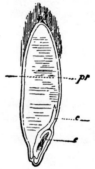

FIG. 184—Embryo of Almond.
  c, cotyledon; *c'*, point of
  attachment of the second
  cotyledon; *g*, gemmule;
  t, tigellus; *r*, radicle.

FIG. 185.—Seed of Wheat.
  c, cotyledon; *e*, gemmule;
  pr, perisperm.

base of the cotyledons a small conical process makes a
slight prominence; this is the *radicle*, representing the
rudiments of the root. Above this, between the two
cotyledons, is the *gemmule*, consisting of a bundle of very
small leaves packed one against another. The gemmule
is the initial bud of the plant; it is this which, unfolding
and developing, yields its first foliage. Lastly, the
narrow line of demarcation between the radicle and the
gemmule bears the name of *tigellus*; from this the first
sprout of the stem develops. Such a structure is found
in all seeds belonging to the dicotyledonous vegetables.

Wheat, the Tulip, the Iris—the monocotyledons, in short—commonly have a cylindrical embryo. In the side of this germ there is visible a narrow slit by which the gemmule will emerge ; what lies above this aperture constitutes the single cotyledon ; what lies beneath it represents the tigellus and the radicle. These various parts are not plainly visible until after germination has commenced.

You will see from the illustration that the embryo of Wheat forms only a fraction of the seed. There is also, beneath the integuments of the seed, an abundant starchy mass which does not exist in the seeds of the Pea, the Kidney-Bean and the Almond. This is known as the *perisperm*. This is an alimentary reserve which, at the moment of germination, becomes fluid and with its juices imbibes and nourishes the young plant. We may liken the perisperm to the white of an egg, or albumen, which surrounds the germ with a layer of food and whose materials serve to form the nascent organs of the bird. The comparison is all the more just in that the egg is the seed of the animal as the seed is the egg of the plant. This close analogy has not escaped the general observation, which gives the eggs of the Bombyx of the Mulberry-tree the name of " silkworm-seed." Eggs and seed are similarly organized : under cover of a defensive wall, shell or testa, there is a germ with a mass of foodstuff, perisperm or albumen. Incubation and germination call the new being to life ; the nutritive store provides the first material for its organs. On account of the similarity of its functions the perisperm of the seed is given the same name as the white of the egg—that is, the name *albumen*.

The albumen does not adhere to the germ of the plant ; it forms a distinct mass, cleanly separable from the embryo, which is encrusted in its thickness or laid against its surface. Its colour is frequently white. Its substance is sometimes floury and rich in starch, as in the cereals ; sometimes impregnated with oil, as in the Euphorbiae ; sometimes tough and cartilaginous, as in the Ombelliferae ; sometimes horny of texture, as in the seeds of Coffee. The perisperm of Wheat gives us the best flour ; that of the Castor-oil seed gives us a medicine ; that of the Coffee-shrub, roasted and powdered, gives us the material of our familiar beverages.

Two stores of nourishment are laid up for the germ in the seed : that of the cotyledons and that of the

Chickweed. Ivy.

FIG. 186. — Seeds whose embryo is surrounded by a perisperm or albumen.

albumen. The cotyledons always exist, but the albumen is not found in all seeds. There is none in the Almond, the Acorn, the Chestnut, the Apricot, the Kidney-Bean, the Pea, the Broad Bean, etc. ; in compensation, the cotyledons in these seeds are of considerable size. Buckwheat, on the other hand, like Wheat, is provided with it ; but in the first the two cotyledons are small and the second has only one cotyledon, too little developed to constitute an efficient means of nourishing the germ. This observation holds good as a general rule. The cotyledons and the albumen have similar functions ; they supplement one another in feeding the young plant during its early stage. But the excess of one organ leads to the diminishment or even the absence of the other, so that bulky seed-leaves correspond with little or no albumen ; and inversely, an abundance of albumen means small cotyledons. In general it is the seeds with large cotyledons that have no perisperm : for examples, the Acorn, the Almond and the Bean ; but the seed with small cotyledons is provided with a perisperm : as Buckwheat. Lastly, monocotyledonous vegetables, whose seed has only one seed-leaf, almost always of small bulk, are more frequently provided with albumen than the dicotyledonous vegetables.

Once ripe inside their fruits, the seeds must be scattered over the surface of the soil, to germinate at points as yet unoccupied, and populate areas where the conditions are favourable. We will here examine some of the precautions, often wonderful in their nature, which ensure the dispersion of the seeds, or *dissemination*. On the rubbish by the roadside grows a cucurbitaceous plant, the Elastic Ecbalium, commonly called the Ass's Cucumber, whose fruits, small, rough-skinned Cucumbers of extreme bitterness, are about the size of a date. On maturity the central pulp resolves itself into a liquid in which float the seeds. Compressed by the elastic wall of the fruit, this liquid presses on the base of the peduncle, which, gradually thrust outwards, like a cork, becomes disarticulated, freeing an orifice through which a vigorous jet of liquid pulp and seeds is immediately expelled. If, with an experienced hand, one shakes the plant laden with fruit turned yellow by a burning sun, one is always a little startled to hear a sort of little explosion amidst the leaves, and to receive the projectiles of the Cucumber in his face.

The fruit of a Euphorbia found in the Antilles, the Sand-Box-tree, is composed of twelve to eighteen woody shells assembled in a crown, like the carpels of our mallows. On maturity these shells unfasten themselves, opening in two valves, and casting forth their seed so suddenly and with such violence that a sort of explosion occurs. To prevent these fruits from bursting and maintain them intact for botanical collections they have to be bound round with wire.

The fruits of the Balsam of our gardens, if ever so

lightly touched when ripe, suddenly split into five fleshy valves which roll themselves up and hurl forth the seeds. The botanical name of Impatient Balsam alludes to this sudden dehiscence of the capsules, which cannot suffer the least touch without exploding. In moist and shady spots of the forests there grows a plant of the same family, which, for similar reasons, bears the still more expressive name of Impatient Touch-me-not. The capsule of the Pansy opens into three valves which are hollowed out like a boat and laden down the middle with a double row of seeds. Through dessication the edges of these valves curl inwards, pressing on the seeds and expelling them.

The buoyant seeds, especially those of the composite flowers, have aerostatic appliances, aigrettes, plumes and streamers, which sustain them in the air and enable them to make long voyages. Thus, at the least breath the seeds of the Dandelion, surmounted by a feathery aigrette, fly from their desiccated receptacle and float gently on the air. One condition is necessary to these travelling seeds ; the delicate aeronautical apparatus must be incapable of capsizing, for if on its descent the aigrette were to be the first to touch the soil, it would hold the seed above the ground so that germination could not take place. But the seed, always heavier, serves as ballast to its parachute ; it therefore always reatins the lower place during the voyage, and touches the earth first. Blow on the head of a matured Dandelion and you will see that the fruits always float with the seed undermost.

The aigrette of the Erodiums and the Geraniums is still more remarkable. The fruit, which by its form recalls the bill of a crane, splits from top to bottom into five achenes, which surmount a long prolongation covered on one side with silky hairs. This appendix is extremely

hygrometric ; in dry weather it coils itself up tight like
a corkscrew ; in damp weather it uncoils itself. Its free
extremity moves now in this direction, now in that,
like a pointer moving over a dial, backwards and forwards
according to the humidity of the atmosphere. The fruit
leaves the plant in the shape of a somewhat compressed
corkscrew ; its outspread hairs give the wind a purchase,
sustaining it in the air and serving as a parachute for
the seed. Finally it falls, the seed undermost. The
latter, sharply pointed at the tip, enters a very little
way into the loose earth ; but
presently, under the alternate in-
fluences of drought and moisture,
the aigrette rolls and unrolls itself,
and by the thrust of this species of
auger in perpetual movement the
grain buries itself deeply enough for
germination.

After the aigrette the wing is the
apparatus best adapted to dissemination by the wind. Thanks to their
membranous border, which makes

FIG. 187.—Samarae of Ash.

them resemble thin scales, the seeds of the yellow
Wallflower reach the high walls of houses, the crevices
of inaccessible rocks, or chinks in ruined buildings,
where they germinate in the small supply of earth
resulting from the previous arrival of the mosses. The
samarae of the Elm, consisting of one long, broad wing,
in the centre of which the seed is embedded, those of
the Sycamores, associated in pairs, like the outspread
wings of a bird, and those of the Ash, shaped like
the pallet of an anchor, accomplish the most distant
journeys by riding the tempest. Other seeds travel by
water, the germ being protected by an impermeable
swimming apparatus. The Walnut has its seed anchored

between two hulls shaped like coracles, welded together to form a shell, while the Hazel-nut protects its seed by a little cask made in one piece. The Coconut, which populates all the islands of the Equatorial seas, confides its dissemination to the waves. Its enormous seeds, packed in oakum and protected by a strong, hard shell, brave the violence of the waves for long periods, travelling from one archipelago to another, landing and germinating on fresh soil.

Many seeds are disseminated by animals, and for this reason are armed with hooks that catch in the fleece of passing flocks or the pelt of wild beasts following a trail. The Burdock, growing by the wayside, and the Goose-grass in the hedges fasten their fruits to the wool of the passing sheep, or even to our clothes, with a security that defies the longest journeys. The drupes, berries and other fruits which seem intended, by their weight, to remain at the foot of the tree from which they fall, are often those whose seeds travel furthest. Birds and mammals make a meal of them ; but the seeds, covered with an indigestible shell, resist the action of the stomach and are rejected whole, ready to ger-minate, at points far removed from the point of departure. Such a seed, travelling in the crop of a bird, may cross ranges of mountains and arms of the sea. Finally, certain rodent animals—Field-mice, Dor-mice, etc.—store up provision for the winter under-ground. If the owner of the granary dies, if the hiding-place is forgotten, if the provisions are too abundant, the untouched seeds germinate when the spring returns. Thus, by an exchange of services, each species of animal assists in the dissemination of the plant that feeds it.

It is man, however, who contributes most to propagate the vegetable species, whether he sows them for his pleasure or for food, or whether he transports their seeds without intending it with the objects of his commercial activity. Thanks to his assistance the alimentary or industrial plants are to-day profusely multiplied in all countries where it is possible for them to thrive. In our gardens we have growing side by side, pell-mell, vegetables coming from every quarter of the globe : from the Cape, from India, from Australia, from Siberia. Others, despite all we can do, keep our cultivated plants company. When sowing Wheat we also unwittingly sow the Poppy, the Cornflower, the Corncockle, which, like it, came from the East. With our merchandise and our packing materials a host of plants pass from one hemisphere to the other. Since the beginning of the nineteenth century the Canadian Groundsel, introduced into France with bales of merchandise, has become the commonest pest of our cultivated lands. The port of Juvénal near Montpellier owes its botanical fame to the numerous plants of all origins which grow there yearly, brought thither in the foreign wools which are washed there. Conversely, many European species have sailed with us across the ocean. The common wildflowers and weeds—the Nettle, Chickweed, Borage, Mallow—imported by our vessels, are growing in America as in their native country.

To the somnolence of the germ as we see it in the seed succeeds, under the stimulus of certain conditions, an active awakening to life, during which the embryo frees itself from its wrappings, fortifies itself with its alimentary ration, develops its earliest organs, and appears in the light of day. This hatching of the vegetable egg is known as *germination*. Humidity, warmth, and the oxygen of the air are the determining causes ; without their assistance the seeds would persist a certain time in their state of torpor and finally lose their power of germination.

In the absence of moisture no seed can germinate. Water fulfils a multiplicity of functions. First, it soaks into the albumen and the embryo, which, swelling more than does the envelope, bursts the latter, however hard the shell. Through the rents in the burst integuments the gemmule issues on the one side and the radicle on the other, and the young plant is henceforth under the influence of external agencies. The embryo takes a longer or shorter time to liberate itself in accordance with the degree of resistance to be overcome in the walls of the seed. If the seed is imprisoned in a hard " stone " it is a very long business to imbibe moisture and finally to burst its prison. Thus, to shorten the period of germination we may crack the too robust integuments on a rock. This mechanical function of water, destined to force the seeds to open, is followed by another, more concerned with the feeding of the plant. The chemical activities by which the foodstuffs of the perisperm and the cotyledons are liquefied, and transformed into substances that can be absorbed, can only take place in the presence of water. On the other hand, this liquid is indispensable to the solution of nutritive principles and their circulation in the tissues of the young plant. It will be understood that in a dry environment no seed could possibly germinate, and that in order to conserve the seeds the first condition is to guarantee them plenty of moisture.

Together with water they must also have warmth. Germination usually takes place most favourably in a temperature of 50° to 68° Fahrenheit ; however, some tropical plants germinate most rapidly in a rather higher temperature. Beyond these limits, whether above them or below, germination tales place more slowly and ceases altogether if the discrepancy is too great.

The assistance of the air, or rather of oxygen, is no

less essential. Expose the seeds to the proper degrees of temperature and moisture under glass bell-jars full of some other gas; for example, hydrogen, nitrogen, carbonic acid gas, etc. ; if the experiment is a long one germination will not take place. But if this atmosphere is replaced by air or by oxygen only the seeds begin to germinate and follow the usual phases of their development. We have already seen that in water deprived of air by boiling germination is impossible, and that it does not take place even under ordinary water except in the case of the seeds of aquatic plants. It has been discovered, in short, that during germination the seeds consume oxygen and give off carbonic acid gas. The embryo, from the time of its first awakening, is therefore subject to the laws of vital combustion, the characteristic of all living things, of the plant as well as the animal ; it breathes ; that is, it lives by consuming itself, for which reason the presence of oxygen is indispensable.

This need of the combustible principle of air explains why seeds too deeply buried do not succeed in germinating; why germination is easier in a loose soil permeable to the air than in a close-packed soil ; why delicate seeds must be covered to a very slight depth or simply laid on the surface of the moist earth ; why land that is broken up sometimes becomes covered with fresh vegetation owing to the presence of seeds which have slumbered inactive for many years, but which at the contact of the air proceed to germinate when our spades or ploughs bring them from the depth of the soil to the surface.

The substance most widely distributed and most abundant in the perisperm and the cotyledons, the alimentary reservoirs of the germ, is fecula, which cannot directly serve for the nutrition of the young plant as it is insoluble in water. In order that it may soak the tissues and distribute to them the materials necessary to growth it must become a soluble substance. For this reason the embryo is accompanied by a special compound, *diastase*, the mere presence of which, without taking anything from the starch or fecula, or yielding up anything, transforms it into a saccharine substance known as *glucose*, which is soluble in water in any proportions. To cause this wonderful transformation warmth and water are necessary. As long as the seed cannot germinate the provision of starch remains intact, but as soon as germination commences, with the aid of warmth, air and moisture, the diastase acts on the starch and turns it into grape-sugar. It is this liquid, formed at the expense either of the perisperm or the cotyledons, which is imbibed into the tissues, feeding them until the root and the first leaves are sufficient for nutrition. The metamorphosis of the starch into glucose, by the action of diastase; the absorption of oxygen from the process of vital combustion and the liberation of carbon dioxide : these are the most salient facts accomplished in a germinating seed.

With the same conditions of temperature, moisture and aeration, all seeds are far from requiring the same period of time for germination. The seeds of Mangroves and some other trees which, in tropical regions, people the muddy shores of the sea, germinate even in the heart of the fruit still hanging from its branch. When the fruit falls the embryo, already developed, implants itself in the mud and continues its evolution unchecked. Garden Cress germinates, on an average, in about two days ; Spinach, the Turnip and the Kidney-Beans require three days ; the Lettuce, four ; the Rock-Melon and Water-Melon five ; and most of the gramens about a week. The Rose, the Hawthorn and the seeds of stone fruits require two years and sometimes longer. In general seeds with hard, thick integuments are the slowest to germinate, on account of the obstacle which they oppose to the entrance of moisture. Lastly, if sown when fresh—that is, directly they have become mature— seeds germinate more rapidly than if they are old, because in the latter case they must recover by a prolonged sojourn underground the moisture which they have lost by long dessication.

The seeds, according to their species, retain the capacity to germinate for a longer or shorter period ; but as yet we know nothing of the determining causes of this persistence of life. Neither bulk, nor the highly variable nature of the envelope, nor the presence or absence of an albumen, appears to be decisive as to longevity. One seed will remain alive for years, even for centuries, while another loses its power to germinate after a few months, without any reasons that we can detect. The seeds of some Rubiaceous plants, notably the Coffee-bean, and those of certain Ombelliferae, in particular Angelica, do not germinate unless the seed is sown directly after maturity. But seeds of the Sensitive Mimosa have grown after sixty years of storage, Kidney-Beans after more than a hundred years and Barley after forty years. Protected from the air, some seeds will live for centuries, still able to germinate if the favouring conditions present themselves. Thus, seeds of the Raspberry, the Cornflower, Rosemary, Camomile and Mercurialis, found in Gallo-Roman or even Keltic sepulchres, have germinated as though they had been seeds of the previous year. Lastly, seeds of Rushes found deep in the earth in the Île de la Seine, the primitive site of Paris, have sprouted. These seeds doubtless dated from the time when Paris, known in those days as Lutetia, consisted of a few huts of mud and wattled reeds on the marshy banks of the river.

INDEX

Numerals in italics indicate entire chapters devoted to the subject in question.

Connective 340–1
Conservation of species *291–306* ;
  307–8
Convolvulus 125
Copse-wood 143–4
Coral, compared with tree *3–13* ;
  21, 306
  ,, islands 10–12
  ,, polyps 6–13, 306
Cork 76–8 ; false 79 ; 274 ; *see*
  Suber, Suberose
Cork-Oak 77
Corn 167
Corncockle 52, 53, 54
Corolla 310 ; forms of 327–34
Cotton 389
Cotyledons 56, 179, 390
Couch-grass 128, 129
Cow-tree 82
Cowslip 362
Creepers 105–6
Cross-fertilization 357–62
Crowfoot 216
Cruciferae 329, 337
Cucumber 123 ; the Ass's 393
Cucurbitaceae 376
Currant 138
Cutting back growth 143
Cuttings, propagation by 19,
  109–10
Cypress 27–8
Cytinus 283

Dahlia 158–9
Dandelion 379
Date-Palm 185, 350
Decandolle 211–12, 264
Decay of wood 70
Deciduous Buds *see* Migratory
  Buds
Dehiscent fruits 378
Descending sap *see* Sap
Diastase 400
Dicotyledonous plants 57–8
Dicotyledonous stem 51–2 ; struc-
  ture of *59–68*
Diœcious plants 321, 350
Dionœa 199–200
Directional impulse of root and
  skin 97–100
Dodder 271

Dog-Rose 165–6, 171
Dragon-tree 29
Drugs, vegetable 80–1, 83
Drupe 380, 386
Duckweed 3, 4
Dumb Nettle 332
Dunes, anchoring of 130–2
Dutchman's Pipe 323, 327, 366

Earthing of vegetables 112–13
Ebony 328
Eel-grass 355
Elastic Ecbalium 393
  ,, Fig 342
  ,, Gum 82
Elements, the 247–8, 251
Elm 74, 90, 100, 184, 380
Embryo 390
Endocarp 374
Endosmosis 234–6, 238–9 ; in
  pollen 343–4
Epicarp 374
Epidermis 59, 61, 76, 214–18
Etiolation 268
Euphorbiae 82
Eupomatia 367
Evaporation from leaves 229,
  226, 243
Exchanges, gaseous, of plants 279
Exhalation from leaves 224–7 ;
  volume of 243
Explosive fruits 393–4

Fasciculated root 100
Fecula 41–2, 44
Fennel 178
Ferns 57, 58, 92–4
Fertilization *see* Pollen, Ovules ;
  artificial 351–2
  ,, , cross 357–62, 367–8
Fibres, types of 34–5 ; function
  of 39, 83–4 ; industrial 84–6 ;
  arrangement of 114–15
Fig 108, 109, 123, 186, 385, 386,
  387
Fig-plant 148
Filament 314, 335
Fir 130
Fireflies 285–6
Flax 84–5
Flesh, animal 249, 252–3